THE *Winter* GARDEN

THE Winter GARDEN

PLANNING AND PLANTING FOR THE SOUTHEAST

PETER LOEWER & LARRY MELLICHAMP

STACKPOLE
BOOKS

Published by
STACKPOLE BOOKS
5067 Ritter Road
Mechanicsburg, PA 17055

Printed in the United States of America

10 9 8 7 6 5 4 3 2 1

FIRST EDITION

Cover design by Tracy Patterson
Cover photographs by Larry Mellichamp

All photographs within the book are by Larry Mellichamp except as follows:
Ann Armstrong: 12, 31, 48, 50–52, 58, 63, 77–78, 117, 134, 141, 148, 152, 165, 171–172, 174–175, 177
Peter Loewer: 5, 6 (left), 7, 65, 76, 105, 109, 113, 178, 180, 183–184

Jacket photo of Peter Loewer by Lynne Baldwin
Jacket photo of Larry Mellichamp by Audrey D. Mellichamp

Photo on p. x: *Erythronium americanum*, trout lily or adder's tongue, is a charming American wildflower found in rich deciduous woods in various forms throughout most of eastern North America. In the woodland garden, it is one of the earliest of our native plants to bloom in late winter, but the attractive, spotted, 6-inch leaves usually disappear within a few weeks, as the plants die back to small, deep bulbs. They slowly form clumps. Not all leafy individuals bloom every year.

Library of Congress Cataloging-in-Publication Data

Loewer, H. Peter
    The winter garden : planning and planting for the Southeast / Peter Loewer and Larry Mellichamp. —1st ed.
        p.   cm.
    Includes bibliographical references (p. 187) and index.
    ISBN 0-8117-1925-1
    1. Winter gardening—Southern States.   2. Winter garden plants—Southern States.   I. Mellichamp, Larry.   II. Title.
SB439.5.L64   1997
635.9'53—dc21   97-8311
                                                                          CIP

To the memory of

Elizabeth Lawrence

and

J. C. Raulston

CONTENTS

ACKNOWLEDGMENTS

A NUMBER OF GARDENERS AND HORTICULTURISTS, BOTH amateur and professional, helped gather the information necessary to produce this book, especially because it covers such a large area of our country. Larry and I could not have finished the task this book represents without their help. But for performance above and beyond that of friendship in the garden, we wish to thank not only our wives, Jean Loewer and Audrey Mellichamp, but Ann Armstrong of Charlotte (for her knowledge of plants as well as for her peerless photography) and Peter Gentling of Asheville.

The following people also helped Larry with much of the photography, not only by providing marvelous winter gardens but also by assisting in locating various plants: Rob Gardner, Betty Wilson, and Mary Jane Baker in Chapel Hill, North Carolina; Sally Cooper and Paul Pawlowski in Charlotte, North Carolina; Donald Rose in Alamo, California; and Dr. Don Jacobs of Eco-Gardens in Decatur, Georgia.

The following people and nurseries provided plants featured in various photographs: Kim Hawks of Niche Gardens, Tony Avent of Plant Delights Nursery, Kay Kincaid of Farmhouse Gardeners, all in North Carolina; Robert Mackintosh and Bob McCartney of Wood-landers Nursery in South Carolina; and Heronswood Nursery near Seattle, Washington.

Larry would especially like to thank Dr. Herbert Hechenbleikner of Charlotte for: being his horticultural mentor, taking him on field trips to see native plants of the Carolinas, introducing him to Elizabeth Lawrence, and starting the Botanical Gardens at the University of North Carolina at Charlotte in 1966.

Finally, the following southern botanical gardens have good displays of winter plants: The J. C. Raulston Arboretum at North Carolina State University; The University of North Carolina at Charlotte Botanical Gardens; Brookgreen Gardens, Murrells Inlet, South Carolina; The Atlanta Botanical Garden; Callaway Gardens, Pine Mountain, Georgia; Riverbanks Zoo and Botanical Garden, Columbia, South Carolina; Norfolk Botanical Garden, Virginia; The State Botanical Garden of Georgia in Athens; Brookside Gardens, Wheaton, Maryland; Wing Haven Gardens in Charlotte, North Carolina; Kalmia Gardens, Hartsville, South Carolina; South Carolina Botanical Garden in Clemson; The Sarah P. Duke Gardens in Durham, North Carolina; Lewis Ginter Botanical Garden in Richmond, Virginia; Birmingham Botanical Gardens; and U.S. National Arboretum in Washington, DC.

INTRODUCTION

And since to look at things in bloom
Fifty springs are little room,
About the woodlands I will go
To see the cherry hung with snow.
—Alfred E. Housman, *A Shropshire Lad*

IT'S A CHILLY DAY JUST ONE WEEK BEFORE CHRISTMAS. A mizzly rain floats through the air, not falling but just drifting through the rhododendron leaves on the pathway that connects the various garden spots on our 9/10-acre garden on the shores of Kenilworth Lake.

For most of the Southeast, winter is a time of reduced heat rather than harsh cold (although many people who live in the colder parts of the South would disagree with that viewpoint). If snow does fall or if temperatures do plummet, such weather is usually limited to the mountain regions and rarely in the Piedmont or the coastal parts of the southern states.

Yet there is a definite time of winter here. Shadows lengthen, and suddenly it seems we are more aware of the physical sun because it floats lower in the sky. On clear days the sky is bluer, the result of the disappearance of summer humidity, and the air has a shiny glow rather than a misty haze. Leaves change colors from green to an almost infinite range of colors, chiefly purples, maroons, and yellows. Except for the tropical parts of the country, trees shed their leaves and go into dormancy for a few months, temperatures fall, and the days get shorter until December 22, when they begin their lengthy climb to the long days of summer.

Which leads to an interesting question: Just what limits are we using to define winter? Well, we decided to begin our garden at the Thanksgiving holiday and extend it through April Fool's Day. So our winter garden in the Southeast covers about 120 days in the year, more or less. But temperature has to be another limitation, so in this book we have chosen the warmer parts of USDA Zone 6, where the lowest winter temperature is usually about –5°F. Our area extends from the Mississippi River on the west; the warm waters of the Gulf and the Atlantic on the south; and Kentucky, a small part of West Virginia, and (regardless of the Mason-Dixon line) a bit of Pennsylvania to New Jersey on the north. This book was written with the Southeast in mind; however, it will also be useful to gardeners living along the East Coast, as far up as Staten Island and the New Jersey shore; the southern section of the Midwest, including parts of Oklahoma, Arkansas, Texas, New Mexico, Arizona, and Nevada; and the West Coast of California, up to Oregon and Washington, and even British Columbia.

We have classified the plants in five different categories:

1. Texture: trees, shrubs, and bushes with interesting or beautiful bark, buds, and twigs.
2. Pods, fruits, and berries: plants whose fruits exhibit winter interest from the viewpoint of color, texture, or form.
3. Blossoms: plants that bloom during the winter months. This is subdivided into flowering herbaceous plants and bulbs, and trees and shrubs.
4. Fragrance: plants that perfume the winter garden.
5. Evergreen foliage: a broad category that we have used to include conifers, broad-leaved evergreens, and other plants that continue to have interesting foliage well into the winter.

This book is not a primer on making a garden from scratch. It is assumed that readers all have some

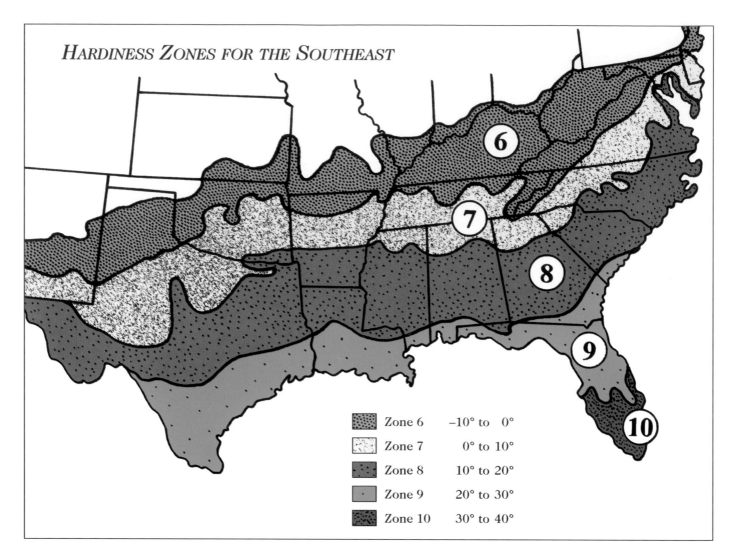

HARDINESS ZONES FOR THE SOUTHEAST

	Zone 6	–10° to 0°
	Zone 7	0° to 10°
	Zone 8	10° to 20°
	Zone 9	20° to 30°
	Zone 10	30° to 40°

basic horticultural knowledge. For those who are just starting out, there are selected references listed in the Bibliography.

There is a trend in publishing—especially popular magazines—to "glitz it up and dumb it down." Many editors and publishers now believe that the public is too ignorant to deal with scientific names for plants, especially because they are in Latin, and therefore, only popular names should be used. That's fine as long as you are dealing with dahlias and delphiniums (those two common names, by the by, are also the Latin names). But as soon as you branch out into more unusual plants, you will find that common names not only change from region to region, but also from country to country.

All the plants known to man have been given scientific names, and each name is unique. Even when names change, for what often seem like whimsical reasons, they remain one of a kind. There is a fascinating

history behind many of those scientific names, and in this book we give these histories whenever we can. These names are easily understood throughout the world; whether in China, Japan, Saudi Arabia, Russia, or Chicago—and regardless of the language spoken by the native gardener—*Cynara scolymus* is the artichoke and *Taraxacum officinale* is the common dandelion. And don't worry about pronunciation; very few people can speak these names with impunity, and you will generally be using them in the written sense alone.

Five terms are in general use: genus, species, variety, cultivar, and hybrid. All reference books, most good gardening books and magazines, nearly all catalogs and nurseries, and today even most seed packets list the scientific name under the common.

In print, the *genus* and *species* are set off from the accompanying text by the use of italic type (if the text is in italics, the scientific name is set in regular, or roman, type). *Genus* refers to a group of plants that are closely related; the *species* suggests an individual plant's unique quality or color, or perhaps honors the individual who discovered it. Usually the Genus has an initial capital and the species is lowercased, but when the species is derived from a former generic name, a person's name, or a common name, it too can begin with a capital letter. This is the pattern in the American standard, *Hortus III*. In this book, however, as in many others, all the species names are lowercased.

The *variety* is also italicized and is usually preceded by the abbreviation "var." set in roman type. A *variety* is a plant that develops a noticeable change in characteristics that breeds true from generation to generation; it may be found in the wild.

A *cultivar* is a variation—either by chance or design—that appears while a plant is in cultivation. Thus cultivars are created by men and women and are propagated in cultivation. The word is derived from *cultivated variety*, and the cultivar name is set in roman type inside single quotation marks. And though it would seem to violate a well-known rule of copy editing, any other punctuation marks follow the single quote at the end of a cultivar name.

A *hybrid* is a horticultural cross between two plants, each with enough individual characteristics to set them apart. Hybrids are noted by the use of a multiplication sign or the letter "x" between the parents.

Thus the beautiful shrub known as the winter-fragrant honeysuckle has the scientific name of *Lonicera fragrantissima*. The genus of this plant is named in honor of the German botanist Adam Lonicer (1528–86), and the species refers to the unusual fragrance of the flower. There is a hybrid between *Lonicera fragrantissima* and *Lonicera standishii* that is known as *L.* × *purpusii*. It is somewhat more floriferous than the parents, producing exceedingly fragrant flowers over four months, usually beginning in January. And if there is ever a cultivar of this honeysuckle bearing variegated leaves, it might be known as *L.* × *purpusii* 'Variegata'.

While we were working on this book, our list of plants that have a place in the winter garden just kept growing and growing. We cover some 450 different kinds of plants, but we are sure there are many we have missed. So if you find us lacking in any way whatsoever, please drop us a line at Stackpole Books. We will answer all our mail.

1
PLANNING YOUR WINTER GARDEN

Winter as well as summer gave us many happy garden hours . . . [a]nd the delights
of making a snow man, or a snow fort, even of rolling great globes of snow, were
infinite and varied. More subtle was the charm of shaping certain things from dried
twigs and evergreen sprigs, and pouring water over them to freeze into a beautiful
resemblance of the original form. These might be the ornate initials or name of a
dear girl friend, or a tiny tower or pagoda. I once had a real winter garden in miniature set in twigs of cedar and spruce, and frozen into a fairy garden.

—Alice Morse Earle, *Old Time Gardens*

IN OUR WORLD, THE MOST BEAUTIFUL GARDEN IS ONE THAT charms the gardener throughout the year. Such a garden should revive the senses in the spring, stun them in the summer, calm them in the autumn, but still offer some opportunity for exciting the eye and the mind preparing to float through the winter doldrums.

We've seen some magnificent gardens in winter. Edith Edelmann's long border at the J. C. Raulston Arboretum at Raleigh, though not as flamboyant in the winter as the summer, still maintains a grand sense of color, only now the tones are muted. The garden also exhibits a grand sense of the massing of textures. Larry's selection of winter plants in the Botanical Gardens at the University of North Carolina at Charlotte is always a treat to wander past, but it is particularly choice in the winter—especially since the weather in that part of North Carolina is never really as potent as the winters farther up in the western mountains of the state. But those mountains often excel. Take Peter Gentling's garden in Asheville, where again, a calculated and careful selection of plants delights the summer visitor yet fills the months from December to March with burnished leaf tones, patterned bark, and interesting masses of color. Peter's garden on Lake Kenilworth was originally designed many years ago to enable a winter walker to wander along pathways lined with rhododendrons and yews, leading to clipped boxwoods, and framed overhead by massive oaks, many clothed from top to bottom with mature ivies.

Winter gardens around the world also may be seen in books and magazines, described in charming text and illustrated with glowing photographs. Rosemary Verey's garden at Barnsley House in Gloucestershire is well represented in her book, *The Garden in Winter* (Boston: Little, Brown and Company, 1988). Here we are offered a view of the brick path at Barnsley, where the summer's herbaceous plants have been cut low, but interest is still heightened by the marvelous rows of perfectly shaped box balls that in summer are almost drowned in foliage from other plants.

The English magazine *Gardens Illustrated* (December/January 1995/1996) features The Grove, the Oxfordshire home of David Hicks. The garden reflects the grandiose elegance that often surrounds a great French chateau, but in addition it includes a garden room with walls of horse chestnuts (*Aesculus hippocastanum*) that surround a swimming pool, which is painted black so that it resembles a canal. Hicks also cleared a rectangular area about 8 by 12 feet, and set within it eight plastic terracotta-style pots planted with globe artichokes (*Cynara scolymus*), all bordered with small hawthorns—but these could easily be replaced by a box hedge of Korean boxwood (*Buxus microphylla* 'Koreana'), a line of mugo pines (*Pinus mugo*), or even Japanese holly (*Ilex crenata* 'Tiny Tim').

All of these lovely winter gardens began with a plan. Someone sat down and mapped out the territory before anything else was done.

Planning the Winter Garden
Nothing helps in planning like making a map. Amy Lowell thought so when, in her poem "Planning the

Aesculus pavia, the Red Buckeye, is a refined shrub or small tree for a prime spot in the garden. In late winter, the large terminal buds open slowly over several weeks to reveal large, palmately compound leaves and, eventually, bright red spring flowers, especially enjoyed by hummingbirds.

Garden," she advised taking "pencils, fine pointed, for our writing must be infinitesimal; and bring sheets of paper to spread before us." But before you actually draft the plan, you must reconnoiter your territory.

Make a List

The first thing to do when planning a winter garden is to take a walk around your property, preferably in late autumn, winter, or very early spring; you do not want to be influenced by the exuberant growth of spring and summer. Jot down every tree, bush, and shrub—in fact, anything both living and artificial that would be part of your winter landscape.

Ask yourself the following questions:

1. Where do you spend the most time in the house? Consider the windows you would most likely use during the winter months for looking out on the world. And think beyond the living room. Few people spend a lot of time in the living room, and often when they do, it's dark outside. In many homes, the center of winter activity is in the kitchen or family room.

2. How much of your property do you wish to take over for a winter garden? There is no reason to conquer unclaimed territory for the winter garden. The area you choose should be immediately lim-

ited by the amount of work you wish to do. After all, almost everybody in today's society suffers from a lack of time, so why take on additional responsibilities if the results do not warrant them? To quote Stanley Schuler in his incisive book, *The Winter Garden* (The Macmillan Company: New York, 1972), "If you limited your winter landscaping and planting to the immediate vicinity of your front walk, you would be doing more than enough for the majority of people who come knocking at your door."

3. What is your landscape's exposure? This is a very important factor, because it predetermines many of your plant choices and often the very layout of your garden. You might find that a certain protected spot in your garden will allow you to grow a Zone 7 plant in a Zone 6 garden. There is a Japanese laurel or gold-dust tree (*Aucuba japonica* 'Variegata') in Peter's garden that, because of the protection offered by a high wall behind it and its placement on a slope that leads cold air away, continues to survive Asheville winters.

4. What are the natural and man-made elements in the landscape? Include the presence of natural windbreaks, existing trees, and most important, the direction of the worst winter winds. Also, remember to include those infamous structures that only show up in the winter, things that for most of the year are hidden from the eye by foliage, such as enclosures that hold propane tanks or a heat pump, electric poles, or garbage cans. None of these are attractive in their own right, and they can detract from your enjoyment of choice trees, shrubs, and plants.

5. Are there additional uses for your winter garden? For example, will you be using your garden as a source for winter flowers or fruits? Will you be feeding birds or wild animals? There are few things in the garden more fascinating than birds at a winter feed, chipmunks foraging for acorns, and squirrels battling it out for territory.

Ilex crenata 'Dwarf Pagoda', small leaves, with ice crystals

Some Comments on Design

We are not disciples of design. You won't find a long essay on the principles of color in the garden or combining textures to the best effect. Many such choices are too personal to be preached about. But we do have a few comments to offer to first-timers in the winter garden.

Color

1. Don't be a slave to the color green. Remember that during the warm months, most gardens have many shades of green, but these are balanced by the blue sky and flowers of various colors.

Pansies are especially valuable for southern gardens, although they occasionally achieve the status of cliches. All varieties reward the gardener with glorious color, ranging from the large-flowered 'Majestic Giants' strain to the petite 'Sorbet' cultivars. The unique orange cultivar 'Padparadja' is shown here with another mid-sized strain called 'Accord Clear Blue'. Pansies should be planted in September, then well watered and fertilized to get them established. They will display flowers all winter, except possibly for the very coldest periods, with the flower production being rapid as winter warms into spring. When hot weather forces the pansies to become leggy, replace them with summer annuals. Pansies may also be interplanted among winter-dormant perennials, but the perennials will take over by late spring.

For winter color, consider the effects of ornamental grasses after their green has been bleached by the cold, the bright reds of berries against the darker background of a creeping juniper such as the dwarf Japanese juniper (*Juniperus procumbens* 'Nana'), a tree with fascinating bark such as the Chinese elm (*Ulmus parvifolia*), and winter-flowering plants such as the Japanese flowering cherry (*Prunus serrulata*). Also remember that the greens of winter are not as flashy as those of summer.

Visual Structures

2. During the summer, rocks, walls, and pathways slice their way through all sorts of colors, but in winter, they themselves are often the dominant visual structures in the garden, so be creative when it comes to paving and path design.

Molinia caerulea 'Variegata', purple moor grass, is a medium-sized ornamental grass that provides fascinating textures well into winter. Not as robust as many of the larger grasses, purple moor can be used in small spaces to provide contrast to broad-leaved foliage. As with virtually all ornamental grasses, it requires good sun and well-drained soil.

In the winter garden, more so than at any other time of year, the textures of materials used to create pathways, edgings, or walls become especially apparent. Brick, concrete blocks, stone, slate, gravel, and even mulch can be effectively used to define space and provide aesthetic settings for plants.

The beauty of walls can be enhanced by the wandering branches of a special cultivar of juniper, with its winter-tinged needles, or some attractive ivy cultivars sweeping down over the edge. And don't forget the decorative value of rocks, especially those in a rock garden.

Garden Ornaments

3. Think about the use of garden ornaments and sculpture. Many concrete pieces today are far better than those offered just twenty years ago. Sundials, latticework, fences, outdoor benches, even a birdbath with the water saucer turned upside down all have a place as decoration.

Trough gardens are becoming more popular. They can be made of concrete, hypertufa (a mixture of Portland cement, peatmoss, and perlite), and clay, or they can be carved from featherstone rock. Very hardy dwarf garden plants may be effectively grown therein. Be sure to allow for drainage as water buildup can freeze and break weaker structures. Also remember that root damage of typical plants can occur at only 15°F.

Statuary and other garden ornaments can add a spiritual lift to most any winter garden. Whether a sundial, an armillary sphere, or a small concrete Buddha, such ornaments treat the garden as an extension of the home and will brighten your mood as you wander the garden during the peaceful winter months.

Living Sculpture

4. There is such a thing as living sculpture, too. A tree with gnarled branches or an interesting shape, such as a weeping birch (*Betula pendula* 'Tristis') or Harry Lauder's walking stick (*Corylus avellana* 'Contorta'), becomes far more interesting when its leaves have fallen than it is when clothed in green, and it will become an incredible natural chandelier when coated with ice. A tree with ivy intertwined among its trunk and branches is yet another example of a living sculpture. Add some electric fairy lights to these trees at holiday time, and your garden will come alive.

Night Lighting

5. Never overlook the beauty of night lighting in the winter garden. Except for grand gardens, landscaped malls, and office buildings, most gardeners continue to ignore the startling effects of night lighting in the garden. Such lighting is delightful in the summer, but in winter, especially when reflected on fresh snow, it's magic. Use the lighting strategically. For example, light the twisted stems of a corkscrew hazel, a tree's patterned bark, or the dry plumes of ornamental grasses.

Water

6. Also consider the decorative use of water in the winter garden, in the form of small streams or ponds. While a trickling stream of water can be a charmer in the summer garden, it can be enchanting in the winter. Electric birdbath heaters can be used to keep ornamental ponds free from ice in colder parts of the Southeast.

Bittersweet and ivy are vines that, while considered by most to be a nuisance in gardens, can be useful in the winter setting. The colorful, persistent red-orange fruits of bittersweet offer subtle color while the greens of various ivies offer backdrops and living sculpture patterns. The Oriental bittersweet, *Celastrus orbiculatus*, however, with three to four fruits in a cluster at each leaf base, is a vicious and fast-growing tree-strangling vine that has no place in the garden. It is often sold as the American bittersweet. The much more sedate, and rare, native American bittersweet, *Celastrus scandens*, with elongated spikes of six to twenty fruits at the tips of delicate branches, is desirable and should be sought out. Both require a male pollinator plant along with the fruit-bearing female.

Choosing Plants for the Winter Garden

When dealing with a spring, summer, or fall garden, most people plan around the flower colors. But in a winter garden, flowers, if present, are definitely in the minority. Even so, there are a few tips to follow when buying plants:

1. Pay close attention to the eventual size of a plant, shrub, or tree. Try to visualize what it may become five years from now. It's amazing just how fast things grow in the Southeast.

2. Match the plant to the available conditions. Avoid selecting a bush that requires perfect drainage for a wet spot in clay soil. You can probably rectify any mismatch, but it is often more trouble than the effort is worth.

3. Unless you have a large area to work with, try to avoid long, straight lines. They are never found in nature and are often boring without awesome architecture to support them. Straight lines are also difficult to maintain. A gentle, sweeping curve looks much better and is easier to install and to keep up.

4. When buying plants, trust your own aesthetic judgment. After all, it's your garden and should reflect your likes and dislikes, not those of someone else.

The Definition of Hardy

When you buy plants, make sure you understand just what the word *hardy* means. Horticulturally, hardy is best used to describe the ability of a plant to withstand cold temperatures. It's the first thing you should know about any plant you bring to your garden, and it's the basis for the establishment of the hardiness zones. These zones are based on average minimum winter temperatures in a given area and represent the lowest temperature your plant can take before there is significant damage, thus indicating what can grow in any given region over time. But the word average can be misleading. You really don't want the average, but you want the absolute lowest temperature that your chosen plant can withstand. On the other hand, sometimes it's worth growing a plant for a few years, even if there is a distinct possibility it might fail during a very cold winter.

Climate Zones and Windchill

In the book you will find no hardiness map depicting zones for annual high and low temperatures of the local areas of the Southeast. To illustrate these zones with sufficient clarity would require a chart some 2 by 4 feet, and even then those local variations created by natural and artificial barriers such as hills, buildings,

APPROXIMATE RANGE OF AVERAGE ANNUAL MINIMUM TEMPERATURE FOR EACH ZONE			
USDA		Arnold Arboretum	
Zone 1	Below –50°F	Zone 1	Below –50°F
Zone 2	–50° to –40°	Zone 2	–35° to –50°
Zone 3	–40° to –30°	Zone 3	–20° to –35°
Zone 4	–30° to –20°	Zone 4	–10° to –20°
Zone 5	–20° to –10°	Zone 5	–5° to –10°
Zone 6	–10° to 0°	Zone 6	–5° to 5°
Zone 7	0° to 10°	Zone 7	5° to 10°
Zone 8	10° to 20°	Zone 8	10° to 20°
Zone 9	20° to 30°	Zone 9	20° to 30°
Zone 10	30° to 40°	Zone 10	30° to 40°

and even ponds would not be visible, nor would the effects these objects have on the course of a wind that is whipping winter's chill.

This combination of wind and cold, known as the windchill factor, will have the same effect on your plants as it would on your nose and ears. So when checking the zones listed in this book against your home zone (if in doubt, call your local county extension agent), be sure also to check on the average winter winds in your area. Then, by looking at the following windchill chart, you will see just how cold your garden can get.

Getting Ready for Winter

Karel Capek summed up the need for winter chores beautifully when he wrote in *The Gardener's Year* (New York: G. P. Putnam's Sons, 1931), "In February the gardener carries on with the jobs of January, especially in cultivating the weather. For you ought to know that February is a dangerous time, which threatens the gardener with black frosts, sun, damp, drought, and winds; this shortest month, this addle-egg among the months, this aborted, leap, and altogether unreliable month, excels them all with its wily tricks; therefore beware of it."

Dormancy

It's important to realize that virtually all of our native plants, as well as many from other temperate countries, require a cold winter dormancy in order to leaf out and grow the following year. That's why wild ferns and wildflowers make poor houseplants; once inside they lack the cold needed to break dormancy and leaf out in spring. Some species, like apples, lilacs, and other northern shrubs, need a long period of deep chill in order to wake up at winter's end. At the other end of the scale, winter honeysuckles, witch hazels, alders, forsythia, and many exotics from milder climates do not.

Plants get the signal for winter dormancy from a number of natural events. First, they detect the shorter days in late summer and early fall. The weakening sunlight triggers a number of responses: Chlorophyll breaks down, leaves turn color as they die, then drop from the tree in order to reduce water loss during the winter.

At the same time, plants begin to manufacture gelatinous substances called colloids in their cells. This thickened cell sap acts like antifreeze to keep the cells from freezing. This action determines the hardiness of a plant, or what degree of cold it can tolerate. Only healthy plants can manufacture the proper colloids at the proper time, so don't let late-summer droughts weaken your plants.

The buds on the twigs are actually the new growth for the next spring, but the tiny leaves are hidden deep within overlapping layers of bud scales that act like packing material, protecting living cells from the cold.

Many plants have separate leaf buds and flower buds, including camellias, azaleas, rhododendrons, Japanese apricots, flowering cherries, honeysuckles, witch hazels, banana shrubs, pussy willows, and alders. Sometimes the flower buds are less hardy than the leaf buds and may be killed by a period of cold. The magic number seems to be 15°F. Below that temperature, roots and flower buds may be killed on certain plants if unprotected. That's why one tree left outside in an unprotected pot will die, while another of the same species survives because it was set in the ground.

Cooler temperatures and freezes can instantly halt the growth of some plants, including subtropicals like mimosas. One touch of chill and they will go dormant on the spot. A sudden cold snap often injures plants that are following the natural process to dormancy. For example, if the temperature drops from 60°F to 20°F on a late October day, some plants can be injured. Severe temperature drops at any time can be danger-

WINDCHILL FACTOR

Temperature	Wind Speed								
	Calm	5	10	15	20	25	30	35	40
+50	50	48	40	36	32	30	28	27	26
+40	40	37	28	22	18	16	13	11	10
+30	30	27	16	9	4	0	−2	−4	−6
+20	20	16	4	−5	−10	−15	−18	−20	−21
+10	10	6	−9	−18	−25	−29	−33	−35	−37
0	0	−5	−21	−36	−39	−44	−48	−50	−53
−10	−10	−15	−33	−45	−53	−59	−63	−67	−69
−20	−20	−26	−46	−58	−67	−74	−79	−82	−85
−30	−30	−36	−58	−72	−82	−88	−94	−98	−100
−40	−40	−47	−70	−88	−96	−104	−109	−113	−116

Calm: Chimney smoke rises vertically.

1–12 mph: Leaves stir; you feel a breeze on your face.

13–24 mph: Branches stir; loose paper is blown about.

25–30 mph: Large branches move; wires whistle.

30–40 mph: Whole trees in motion; hard to walk against the wind.

ous to plants, and in colder areas of the country, tree bark can be heard snapping apart during sudden temperature changes.

When there are severe fluctuations in temperature, it is usually the introduced exotics from milder climates that suffer the most damage. These plants never quite adjust to the cold. In 1985, when Charlotte had truly cold temperatures of –6°F, the native hollies, azaleas, and rhododendrons were not harmed, but many camellias, sasanquas, banana shrubs, and 'Nellie Stevens' and 'Burford' hollies were killed to the ground.

But while the air is cold, the ground can still be warm. And here the magic number is 40°F. As long as the soil maintains that temperature, even though the tops of the plants may be dormant, the roots may continue to grow and actively absorb water. That's why fall is such a great time both to plant and to transplant. In most areas of the Southeast, tops are dormant by November 1, but new roots can continue to grow until well into December, sometimes even January. But don't prune after September 1, because new growth might not be able to harden before the frosts of October.

Neatness Counts

Never is the neatness of garden pathways more important than in the winter garden. During the days of high summer, the look of luxuriant growth sweeping over the edge of the path is just another manifestation of nature's exuberance. And what gardener can remove every weed or seedling in every crack of the paving? But in the winter garden, everything shows. This includes any litter on top of garden walls, broken branches, or piles of leaves left over from autumn cleanup. So wherever you go, carry a broom, or at least a little pocket brush. You won't be sorry.

Clean up dead or fallen vegetation, and at winter's end (when you can spot branches killed during the cold), prune for the best effect.

Also, avoid white plant labels, which will make the winter garden look untidy. Choose a darker color like green, or use metal plant tags made of copper or zinc.

Protecting the Garden from Winter Damage

There are a number of things you can do to protect your garden from winter damage when unexpected cold spells hit.

1. Mulch to protect roots from the heaving actions of freezing and thawing. Mulching also keeps the ground cold, preventing many plants from coming up too early during warm spells and then suffering frost damage. This works especially well for the hardy orchid (*Bletilla* spp.), so prone to damage from late-spring freezes.

2. Watch for any exposed roots of plants that have been forced up above the ground by the freezing and thawing of the soil. Tuck them back in before they are damaged.

3. Wrap trunks with paper and surround evergreen shrubs with burlap screens to prevent drying from severe winter winds. These winds often kill stems during a particularly bad winter. Be especially careful to protect plants on the north side of the house or a wall.

4. Winter burn—or the browning of evergreen leaves—is likely the result of sun-warmed leaves trying to evaporate water, even in subfreezing air, while the roots are frozen and unable to absorb enough water to replenish the leaves. Morning sun is the worst offender, but you can give some protection by covering the plants with larger pine branches (Christmas trees are excellent for this purpose) or by stretching a piece of burlap or aluminum screening above the plant.

5. Cold air drainage can also be a factor. If cold air accumulates in hollows or against the side of a building, damage to plants can occur. When planting, remember that cold air will drain downhill. Use hardier evergreens as windbreaks.

6. Unless you have specially fired clay pots (that are very, very expensive), you must protect them from the action of freezing water. Either move such pots indoors during freezing weather or put the pots in an insulated container where they will not get wet.

2
WALKS IN WINTER GARDENS

A winter corner should be a place, however small, where you can be sure of finding those special flowers that brave the weather, those leaves that keep their color and those berries that hang on through winter days. And it should be tucked away so that you have a positive inducement to walk out of the house to enjoy your choice of winter flowers.

—Rosemary Verey, *The Garden in Winter*

Ann Armstrong: Contrasts in the Winter Garden

On a wet afternoon in late January, Peter and Ann walked through Ann's garden in Charlotte, North Carolina. The temperature was a chilly 38°F, under a bright Carolina blue sky with just a few clouds to cut the brilliance overhead. She wore a light all-weather jacket with a sharp pair of scissors in the pocket, and a jaunty canvas hat on her short gray hair.

Ann's garden, on a small city lot that measures 1/5 acre, is just a few blocks from Winghaven, a marvelous city garden dedicated to the birds of all seasons. It's truly amazing how many plants Ann has managed to collect on such a small piece of property.

"Winter," said Ann, as she polished her glasses, "is the bridge that joins autumn and spring in our southern gardens, and there are literally hundreds of trees and shrubs that can add not only great interest, but color and texture to the winter garden. This is the time to wander along our borders and think about adding plants and new color combinations to increase our enjoyment of winter.

"Take berries, for example. Everybody's familiar with the bright red berries of hollies, nandinas, and pyracanthas, but here's a nandina with cream-colored berries (*Nandina domestica* 'Alba'), a variety with foliage of a lighter green than its red-berried brethren. Its new growth, without red pigmentation, keeps its fresh green leaves all winter, providing an airy and ferny texture without the reddish winter foliage tints of the species. And, of course, it has those beautiful almost-white berries. The ultimate height of this cultivar is between 4 and 6 feet, but it can easily be maintained at a lower height by pruning the older stalks to the ground. I have never had any disease or insect problems with any of my nandinas."

"Size is always important," Peter remarked, "especially in a small city garden. Do you do a lot of cutting and pruning?"

"I cut a great deal. Take this yellow variegated elaeagnus (*Elaeagnus pungens* 'Maculata' or 'Aureovariegata'). It keeps its lovely limy green-yellow variegation throughout the winter, but unfortunately this sun- to light-shade-loving shrub can become quite tall, sometimes up to 10 feet. I've had this plant for a number of years, though, and keep it about 3½ feet tall. The prunings make excellent foliage for floral arrangements. Besides its beautiful foliage, its blooms offer a wonderful fall fragrance, and the resulting little fruits provide food for the birds. There is one caveat, however: Gardeners must watch this plant and swiftly cut out any branch that might revert to the unvariegated state."

Ann is especially adept at combining colors and textures in her garden, and she has used the variegated elaeagnus in a number of places. When planted in full sun, she surrounds it with a ground-hugging juniper (*Juniperus horizontalis* 'Mother Lode'), which has gold-variegatied needles that echo the tones of the larger shrub and looks especially fine when creeping around the elaeagnus's skirt.

Erythsimum × *allionii* is a group of garden hybrid wallflowers that act as biennials. The name is sometimes found listed under *Cheiranthus* in seed catalogs. One may find variously colored selections that can be grown from seed and which may bloom from early winter into summer. They are very satisfactory in mild climates and brighten up the winter display with not only their cheerful colors but their delightful scent as well.

She uses the chartreuse foliage of the perennial yellow-leafed feverfew (*Tanacetum parthenium* var. *aureum* [*Chrysanthemum*]) for just a touch of solid color. "This sun-loving plant might not be perennial in our area, but it does seed true for me so I have little plants that I can add to this composition in the fall. It flowers in the summer but keeps a low mound of limy green foliage all winter and seems to be pest and disease free."

Nearby is the dark green foliage of a wallflower that Ann grew from seed many years ago. "I don't know whether it's a perennial or just comes back from self-sown seed, but I wouldn't be without it. It's a low-growing plant with deliciously fragrant yellow flowers that bloom all winter, undaunted by frigid temperatures or ice. I wish I could give you the scientific name so you could get exactly the same kind, but the little pack I bought just said wallflower."

We all agreed that this is a perfect example of the importance of using scientific names. Ann suspected that the plant was an *Erysimum* but knew it wasn't *Cheiranthus* 'Cloth of Gold'. "These two species are both known as wallflowers and are apt to be interchanged," she said, " but they are really quite different. All of these plants need good drainage and take our hot, humid summers without complaint."

We continued to walk along, the clouds above the city beginning to lighten just a bit and the air warming slightly.

In the shade garden, Ann planted a *Viburnum tinus* 'Spring Bouquet'—a variety with dark pink buds that open to white flowers in the winter, followed by metallic blue fruits that mature to black—under a deciduous river birch (*Betula nigra*). The viburnum's lustrous dark green foliage is handsome all year, and the shrub eventually reaches a height between 3 and 5 feet. It tolerates considerable shade and is insect and disease resistant, but southern gardeners are advised to plant this shrub in early spring so it's well hardened off before winter.

"I plant the glossy evergreen wild ginger [*Asarum europaeum*] under the viburnum's cover. The leaves of the ginger turn a mottled burgundy in the winter, echoing the burgundy buds of the shrub. This ginger needs moisture and good organic soil, and the viburnum likes the same conditions. Avoid the wild American ginger [*A. canadense*], because its leaves are deciduous and not glossy.

"If your garden has very light shade, it might be interesting to add a penstemon as well. Two years ago, I bought the perennial penstemon 'Husker's Red' [*Penstemon digitalis* 'Husker's Red']. The blooms have a lovely white foxglove shape, flowering in late spring, but I was unprepared for the exquisite winter foliage of burgundy red. How lovely to play this foliage against the maroon buds of the *Viburnum tinus* at this time of year. Another plant that puts on a wonderful winter display is *Ajuga* 'Burgundy Glow'. During the summer there was very little burgundy in its soft cream and green foliage, but when winter comes around, the burgundy kicks in. Wouldn't that be a great winter composition with the penstemon?

"This is what gardening is all about. The plants should be on roller skates so they can be moved around to create pleasing compositions at any time of the year. Unfortunately, what's pleasing at one time of year is disastrous at another, so gardeners must think ahead as well as remembering back. That's why it's a good reason to keep a garden journal so that you'll know what did what and when—to record those thoughts and ideas you think you'll remember but rarely do."

We've walked through Ann's garden at all times of the year. In late spring when the city air is as fresh as

air from the mountains, or days when the air is very hot, it feels as though her street has become a small Mississippi River. We've looked at plants by the light of streetlights and flashlights, in drizzle and in rain, and it's always beautiful. Ann's shade garden is especially so.

"But as lovely as such a garden can be," she said, "if we had filled our shady areas with hostas, impatiens, begonias, and the lovely deciduous ferns that disappear with the first few hard freezes, during winter we'd be left with nothing except bare ground. Since I find myself with more and more shade, I've found that there are a number of plants we can put in a shady area that keep their foliage, and even some that bloom during the winter months."

Among Ann's prized plants are the native Christmas fern (*Polystichum acrostichoides*). It abounds in her garden, providing dark evergreen 15-inch fronds all year round. If the gardener works in a considerable amount of organic matter when planting and provides sufficient moisture, this fern will increase into a sizable clump in a few years and soon can be divided to expand the garden or be given away to friends.

"After a number of hard freezes," said Ann, "Christmas ferns tend to lie down, but I've found two others that remain quite upright despite the weather. Both the tassel fern (*Polystichum polyblepharum*) and the autumn fern (*Dryopteris erythrosora*) are great additions."

Ann assumes the tassel fern derives its name from its hairy stems, and it's one of the handsomest ferns we've ever seen. The dark green fronds arch out from a central stem, eventually forming a 2-foot-wide clump about 14 inches high. The common name of the autumn fern refers to its color: The shiny, 2-foot-long leaves have a decided bronze tint on new fronds.

"If protected," Ann advised, "the holly fern (*Polystichum falcatum*) makes a wonderful stately display with its large, long, waxy fronds. But it can look tatty if we have severe weather or the sun shines on the leaves before they thaw. A well-established plant comes back full force, so plant this fern in spring so that the roots are well established before winter sets in."

The delicate blue-green scalloped leaves of the spring-flowering columbines add color, interest, and texture to the winter shade garden. Another perennial, the low-growing foamflower (*Tiarella cordifolia*), maintains its heart-shaped, 3- to 5-lobed leaves all winter. Foamflowers are stoloniferous plants, meaning that their roots run underground to form a mass of plants. If gardeners object to its ramblings, there is also a clump-forming foamflower (*T. wherryi*). Both bloom in the spring with a lovely froth of creamy, pinkish white 3- to 4-inch flowers.

Other plants that Ann suggested for the winter shade garden include *Arum italicum*, a shade-loving perennial native of Italy and the Mediterranean region that comes into its own during the winter months. The arrowhead-shaped leaves emerge in the fall, conspicuously blotched with cream. The foliage is impervious to ice, snow, and cold and remains fresh looking throughout the season. The leaves disappear from view in early summer, but not before the plants throw up a spathe-like bloom, followed by a spike of bright orange berries beloved by the mockingbirds.

Corydalis lutea is a little, low perennial with finely divided fernlike blue-green foliage. "These plants," said Ann, "love a shady, moist area that has good drainage. New plants freely seed from little yellow flowers that resemble our fringed bleeding heart, *Dicentra eximia*. For me it flowers off and on all winter, and it is always a joy to come upon its golden yellow spurred flowers. The resulting seedlings are easily removed or transplanted.

"And to my mind, no shade garden should be without some of the large family of hellebores. These are some of the finest low-growing and winter-flowering perennials we have in the South. The easiest species to grow is the Lenten rose (*Helleborus orientalis*), but I'm also fond of the so-called stinking hellebore (*H.*

Erythsimum linifolium 'Bowle's Mauve' is a shrubby wallflower that grows to about 2½ feet. It has 2-inch gray-green leaves and produces lavendar-pink flowers during the winter, which become quite showy in early spring. It is best grown as a biennial, so root cuttings from nonflowering shoots in early summer, as the plant does not produce seed and is likely to die in summer after flowering.

foetidus). Its evergreen foliage is a much darker green and more deeply divided, making it a very handsome addition to the shade garden."

Finally Ann stopped at a shrub called the sweet box (*Sarcococca hookerana* var. *digyna*). This plant adds interest to a winter shade garden. It's more compact than the species, slowly growing into a 3-by-3-foot shrub of lustrous dark green narrow leaves, followed by nondescript flowers that emit the most delicious fragrance in January and February. The plant appreciates loose, well-drained, acid soil with lots of organic matter worked into it.

"It requires shade," Ann said, "as it tends toward leaf scorch if exposed to much sun. And there's another sweet box (*Sarcococca hookerana* var. *humilis*), a ground cover only 18 inches high. It has the same bloom, fragrance, and cultural requirements as *digyna* and looks just like its little brother.

"With the exception of the arum, come spring and summer all of these plants will be in the garden, adding interest and contrast to hostas, deciduous ferns, and other seasonal shade plantings; then with winter, you'll still have an interesting garden—not just bare ground."

Lucinda Mays: A Winter Walk in Callaway Gardens
Callaway Gardens is located on 14,000 acres that are visited by more than a million people a year. The land occupied by the garden was discovered by Cason and Virginia Callaway on a summer day in 1930, when they spied the bright orange flowers of the wild azalea (*Rhododendron prunifolium*), native only to the areas surrounding Pine Mountain. Today there are 2,500 acres of cultivated garden, including greenhouse complexes, walking trails, the world's largest display of hollies, more than 700 varieties of azaleas, the Day Butterfly Center (the largest glass-enclosed butterfly conservatory in North America), and unbridled wildflowers.

Late last January, Peter attended the Southern Garden Conference at Callaway Gardens. He happened to have a bit of free time between lectures and was lucky enough to cajole Lucinda Mays, the tall, attractive director of Victory Garden South, to lead him on a guided tour of the rhododendron and broadleaf evergreen collections.

So around 11:30 A.M. on Saturday, January 27, they headed out to the gardens for a sunny but frosty late-morning stroll. It might have been Georgia, but it was still winter, for the wind blew cold, and puddles of rainwater left from the monsoons of the afternoon before were still skinned with ice.

After stopping in the hotel courtyard to look at a tree stump that Lucinda had turned into a concrete birdbath ("I used lots of Thompson's water seal on the wood," she said), they climbed into her car. As they drove past the championship golf course, Lucinda remarked that Mark Twain had once said, "Golf is a good walk spoiled."

"This was all cotton land," she said, "and it was only with vision—and money—that it's become this great garden. There are eleven interconnected lakes, and it's difficult to realize that you're not somewhere far, far away from civilization."

She parked the car and handed Peter one of two barn jackets that she kept for winter walking tours. He put it on over his wool sportcoat, as the wind had picked up and the temperature hovered just above freezing.

Walking through Callaway is not like walking through a backyard collection. Scale is at work here. One can, without realizing it, walk miles while the eye is enchanted by a garden in winter and the ear is entertained by a charming garden companion who knows her stuff.

As Peter and Lucinda started to walk down the well-kept pathway, with trees and bushes on either side, they noticed that the daffodils were already 8 inches high. Pine needles hung from the branches of the Japanese maples like ornaments, and the moss on the ground and the trees was glistening in the sparse sunlight.

"Paperwhites are hardy in the garden," Lucinda said. "These are the cultivars 'James Swan' and 'Emily Brunner,' and *Iris reticulata* blooms in late February."

Just ahead were nodding heads of white and pink Lenten roses (*Helleborus orientalis*), all with waxy petals nodding in the cold of the morning but ready to rise up and greet the sun. And just behind them the *Rhodea japonica*, an evergreen member of the lily family, was in full leaf.

"Elizabeth Lawrence," Peter said, "described their leaves as being more elegant, more polished, and just plain greener than those of the aspidistra. She said that the Japanese cultivate hundreds of varieties, the rarer cultivars valued at hundreds of dollars. The flowers aren't that much to look at, but the berries, green in late fall and turning red by November, will last until spring."

Ahead of them next was a clump of cast-iron plants (*Aspidistra elatior*), their long, waving 20-inch dark green leaves having thus far survived the Georgia frosts.

"Cast-iron plants," said Lucinda, "also are hardy, and their leaves lend a tropical touch to a pine-wooded walk."

"They're especially interesting when you know they're pollinated by slugs," Peter said.

"Slugs?"

"Slugs. In Japan, those inconspicuous, dark purple, star-shaped blossoms that hug the ground are trod upon by slugs and an occasional beetle, which then spread the pollen around."

"Maybe that's why another popular name is the barroom plant," said Lucinda.

Ahead of them they saw a number of camellias in bloom, some pink, some white, some red, and all a delight to see. A number of blossoms were wide open and magnificent; others had succumbed to the rain of the night before, and their petals lay upon the ground.

"In 1936," Peter said, "when MGM filmed *Camille*, the beautiful Greta Garbo walked into a Parisian floral shop for a nosegay of camellias and held the flowers to her nose to inhale their sumptuous fragrance. But the producers made a major mistake, because they didn't know that camellias lack fragrance."

"If it was a fragrant flower," said Lucinda, "its popularity would probably increase by leaps and bounds." She picked up a fallen flower from the ground and looked at it with the eye of a gardener and a connoisseur. "Most people don't know that the history of the camellia began more than two thousand years ago with the discovery of tea. I think that drinking tea began about 500 B.C. with steeping the leaves of *Camellia sinensis*, the common tea plant. But according to legend, the discovery of tea as a beverage is credited to a Chinese emperor sometime back in 2500 to 3000 B.C."

Beyond the grove of camellias, they came upon a number of wintersweets (*Chimonanthus praecox*) in bloom, their upright branches dotted with the very fragrant, 1-inch-wide flowers of a creamy yellow striped with brownish purple. The blossoms last for weeks when cut, if the gardener splits the stems and places them in water in a warm room. These plants are hardy in Zones 6 to 9.

The mondo grass (*Ophiopogon japonicus*), planted in circles under a canopy of skeletal trees, looked like puddles of green. As the two gardeners walked along and their angle of sight continued to shift, the sun was reflected by the many drops of rain still clinging to the leaves.

The grove of winter-blooming honeysuckles (*Lonicera fragrantissima*) was bent over by the heavy rains of the night before. These shrubs were full of bell-shaped white blossoms, and their sweet fragrance filled the air. This is an easily transplanted bush originally brought from China. In *Winter Blossoms from the Outdoor Garden* (London: L. Reeve & Co., Ltd., 1926), A. W. Darnell writes, "After a night of hoar-frost, in the early morning when the sun, shining on the frozen blossoms with which the little plant was thickly beset, thawing them, they emitted a deliciously fragrant odour which was perceptible in the still morning air for a distance of 25 yards or more."

The 6-foot Japanese paperbush, or mitsumata (*Edgeworthia papyrifera* [*E. chrysantha*]), was also in bud, with tubelike flower buds nodding from the tips of the branches. This shrub from East Asia is known for its rich yellow flowers clothed in white silky hairs, with forty to fifty packed together in a close terminal head.

"We're fortunate," said Lucinda, "that the paperbush is hardy in our area. It's a very tender shrub, and even most English gardeners never get the chance to grow it. Those tubelike flower buds will open in early spring to reveal 2- to 3-inch balls of yellowish white flowers with a subtle fragrance."

A 10-foot-high purple anisetree (*Illicium floridanum*) appeared on the side of the trail, just asking for one of its evergreen leaves to be crushed and held up to a spring-starved nose. "On cold days," wrote Elizabeth Lawrence in *Gardens in Winter* (Baton Rouge, LA: Claitor's Publishing Division, 1961), "I like to pick an aromatic leaf, for the scent is so strong that it is apparent even in the frosty air."

Soon they reached a stream that rippled alongside the road and boasted one of the most beautiful sights in the garden that day—a very large witch-hazel cultivar (*Hamamelis mollis* 'Tingle') in full bloom, its branches entirely festooned with big, bright yellow flowers.

"This is the Chinese witch hazel," said Lucinda, "a small tree that can reach a height of 20 feet if in the right place. There are a number of attractive cultivars, such as 'Diana', a hybrid between *H. mollis* and *H. japonica*, and 'Pallida', a stunning sight with its bright lemon yellow flowers. But this cultivar is one of the most beautiful I've seen, especially because of its location."

The Harry Lauder's walking stick (*Corylus avellana* 'Contorta') was named for the Scottish baritone who sang "Roamin' in the Gloamin'" and walked on stage with a contorted branch from the bush.

The winter daphne (*Daphne odora*) was covered with flowers, and the gardeners could smell its sweet fragrance as they walked by.

"We can grow this plant in Asheville gardens," Peter said, "but many years it needs a very protected spot or it can lose both leaves and buds."

"Elizabeth Lawrence says that the flower's perfume is carried for 20 feet when the air is still and cold," said Lucinda.

The thick, sculptured leaves of a leatherleaf mahonia (*Mahonia bealei*) glowed in the winter sunlight and changed from bronzy green to a deeper, darker color as the vantage point of the two walkers changed. The bright yellow flowers were in bud and gave promise to open soon.

"This is a very valuable landscape plant for the South," said Lucinda, "But you'll see how much more beautiful it is in this forest setting than in the glare of the hot southern sun."

As they walked along, they passed patches of moss glowing green in the sunlight, but here a winter shade of green that bore highlights of burnished bronze, bejeweled with prismatic gleams of color from the tiny drops of rain still sparkling in the sunlight.

"To think," Peter said, "there are people—"

"And even some gardeners," said Lucinda, who knew what he was going to say.

"—who go to great lengths to murder moss and give psychic grants to grass. I'll never understand their moss resentments."

"Nor I," said Lucinda.

They continued to walk along, passing the modern outlines of the Day Butterfly Center. Although most of the trees were bare, they still looked like Giacometti sculptures. Along the way were large areas of centipede, caterpillar, and zoysia grasses on the right side around the pavilion and annual rye to the left, the fresh greens making very attractive combinations.

"This is," said Peter, "a beautiful garden and a marvelous place to walk on a winter's day."

"I love it here," said Lucinda. "Although it's supposed to be a time of year when things slow down and we work on our garden plans for the spring, it's amazing just how much is going on if we have taken advantage of the southern climate."

There was a quickened breeze and a chill passed through the trees, but the yellow twigs of the red-osier dogwood (*Cornus sericea* [*C. stolonifera*] 'Flaviramea') began to glow in the sun, now higher in the sky, and

ahead was a Japanese quince (*Chaenomeles japonica*) in full bloom.

"There's a certain Slant of light/Winter Afternoons—/That oppresses, like the Heft/Of Cathedral Tunes—" Peter quoted from Emily Dickinson.

"Oh well," said Lucinda, "nothing's perfect."

A Walk in Peter's Garden

It's easy to write about violets, asters, and daylilies when the weather is warm and the sun is hot, but when snow falls and winter storms rage, the garden writer must call forth his imagination.

On the wall over Peter's desk is a map of the United States published by the U.S. Department of Agriculture. The map shows the ten climatic zones that ribbon across our country. Zone 5 (where the minimum winter temperatures average −20° to −10°F) is green and extends from Newfoundland through most of New England and New York; splits Pennsylvania, Ohio, and Illinois; takes a third of Missouri, half of Kansas and New Mexico, and one quarter of Arizona; then blots out most of Nevada, a smidgen of California, half of Oregon, and a third of Washington before shooting back up to Canada—where most gardeners say it all belongs in the first place.

South of this, only fourteen of the forty-eight contiguous states do not include at least some area rated Zone 5; even Texas has a dot of green in the upper northeast corner. North of Zone 5, except for a few areas around large bodies of water, is a gigantic area that includes four zones that are even colder, down to −50°F.

In Peter's garden, the protection afforded by snow cover cannot be counted on, because the base of the mountains in western North Carolina never gets a guaranteed snowfall. In one out of five years, the snow accumulations total less than 1 inch. Instead, we get sleet and downpours of rain.

Today, for example, it is inseasonably warm. Let's take advantage of this January thaw to stroll through our garden.

First we pass a large multiflora rosebush that has been growing in the same spot for more than forty years. Although its blooming period in late spring is brief, we keep the bush because of the orange rose hips that cover the bare branches well into late January, when they are finally consumed by the birds.

Now *Rosa multiflora* has had bad press for being weedy. During the 1960s it was touted as the "living fence," keeping intruders and cattle out, yet easy to install and practically carefree. Peter's was planted sometime in the 1950s, and yes, it does seed about. But if the seedlings turn up in unwanted places, they are quickly removed. No, it's not a sophisticated rose, but when it blooms in May, the blossoms are sweet. It also works as a specimen plant. And of course, the rose hips are fine.

Behind the rose is a mass of American bittersweet (*Celastrus scandens*), disliked by some gardeners for being overly rampant—and they are right. Do not plant bittersweet in the formal garden or around the backyard. And never plant it if you hate pruning and yearly pilgrimages to the brush pile. But if you confine it to the wild part of the garden and keep it cut back, you will be rewarded by first the golden yellow of the autumn leaves and then the beautiful bright orange and scarlet berries that cover the twining vines.

Next on the right, as we walk down the browned grass path that extends between the borders, is a giant clump of eulalia grass (*Miscanthus sinensis*). Its 12-foot-high stems now sport waving brown leaves topped by silver plumes of the seed heads, blooms that will persist until the following spring.

Falling over the edge of a stone scree bed are the clambering branches of a rock cotoneaster (*Cotoneaster horizontalis*), covered from base to tip with glowing red berries, a color almost ready to clash with the pink-magenta blossoms of the heath (*Erica carnea* 'King George'). Above them both are the spiraling branches of Harry Lauder's walking stick (*Corylus avellana* 'Contorta'), bare now but in early spring festooned with yellow catkins that will hang like ornaments from the stems.

Opposite the scree bed is a low stone wall that in summer marks the edge of a bed full of lamb's ear (*Stachys byzantina*), whose woolly leaves even now are still in evidence. Along the bottom edge of the wall is a line of ebony spleenwort (*Asplenium platyneuron*), green and glossy, as they will remain well into winter. A Christmas rose (*Helleborus niger*), which seldom blooms but still produces marvelous foliage, shares the space with the spleenwort. And nearby, Lenten roses (*H. orientalis*), are full of burgeoning buds.

Near them is a mound of *Sedum* 'Autumn Joy', whose flowerheads will stay the color of burnt mahogany until spring. Behind this is a clump of the eye-catching red-stemmed Siberian dogwood (*Cornus alba* 'Siberica'), generally nondescript in the spring and summer, but making up for it when the leaves fall.

At the edge of one of the wooded pathways, clumps of pearly everlasting (*Anaphalis margaritacea*), its papery white blossoms waving in a quickening wind, stand out against the darkness of the gathering night. Only a few short weeks ago, the winter winds rustled the yellow blossoms of the witch hazel (*Hamamelis virginiana*), and just a few tattered remnants are still there, hanging on for dear life.

Back near the formal garden, stone steps go down a slight slope to an area shaded by a very old white pine (*Pinus strobus*). In between the crevices of those steps are bergenias (*Bergenia cordifolia*), plants from Siberia and Mongolia. As such, they are perfectly happy at temperatures as low as –10°F, but when exposed to winds at this point, their leaves will turn brown and burn at the edges until they look like toast points. Above 0°F, the plants are evergreen and turn a reddish bronze. They prefer partial shade in the summer and a soil that is well drained but moist, with humus or leaf mold. In such a spot they make an excellent ground cover. Every spring they flower with rose pink, waxy blossoms that look like tiny ruffle-edged bells.

Above and beyond those steps are many ornamental grasses. In winter their colors are never blatant or bold. Tones here are mellow: Shades of brown or buff mingle with warm, burnished yellow ochers, highlighted by the worn silver-white of the seed plumes that wave above, a beautiful welcome sight against the snows, glowing when held within a sheath of ice.

The various cultivars of the eulalia grasses (*Miscanthus* spp.) grow, on the average, over 7 feet in one summer season and usually show their plumes as fall approaches. When the days grow shorter and colder, growth stops. Then, with the first killing frost, the leaves turn a rich golden yellow.

Right now many fields in our area are awash with the warm, rusty tones of little bluestem (*Schizachyrium scoparium* [*Andropogon scoparius*]), their tops glistening in the winter sun. Their silvery white blossoms open in mid-October and remain until the winds of March blow them out of the picture. When a grouping of individual plants is planted in a semicultivated area, this grass thrives; even fifteen plants make a wonderful show.

At the base of the bank grow lichens and mosses. Winter has no effect on them. Curling about the grays, greens, and browns of their elfin cups is a colony of poverty grass (*Dathonia spicata*). In summer the 6-inch leaves of poverty grass are at best nondescript, but by November the leaves will have curled and look like wood shavings left by a tiny carpenter.

Next to the birdbath sits a clump of another American native, northern sea oats (*Chasmanthium latifolium*), which sports oatlike seed heads that turn golden brown in the winter sun. By December each will have a frosting of ice. Pick their blossoms earlier in the garden year, and they will retain their color forever. But now, thanks to the killing cold, every hint of green is gone.

Our garden has many dwarf conifers whose steely blue and green foliage will be bright against the snow. A weeping birch that in winter becomes an abstract pattern of wavy lines vies for attention with mahogany sedums. But when winter descends from leaden skies, it's the ornamental grasses that bring warmth and beauty to the garden until spring returns to the mountains.

It's getting colder now, and the weakening rays of the setting sun have made a band of orange along the horizon. Now it is time to go back inside to the fire and think about the quiet beauty of winter and the spring that's sure to come.

3
THE BEAUTIES OF TEXTURE

Then as I walked on a little way, I came suddenly upon an enchanted forest, where the boles of the trees were columns of jade encrusted with emerald and malachite, cinnabar and chalcedony, mosses as softly colored as polished stones, and with rocks of oxblood and cinnamon, garnet and carnelian; overhead the petrified branches of the oak trees laced the low, metallic clouds that closed in on a mineral world. Nothing moved, no animal, no bird. The air was still.

—Elizabeth Lawrence, *Gardens in Winter*

In 1914 *THE TREE BOOK*, BY JULIA ELLEN ROGERS, WAS published as part of Doubleday's New Nature Library. The last chapter of the book was entitled "How Trees Spend the Winter." Miss Rogers made the claims that "nine out of every ten intelligent people will see nothing of interest in a row of bare trees" and "all trees look alike to them in winter." We hope she was wrong in her assessment, because the most stalwart members of the winter garden are the trees.

Whether they were planted with an eye to winter design or were there before you began your garden, trees are some of the most valuable members of your plant collection. The bark of many trees, especially when it supports a vast array of lichens, is more than just the outer layer of a tree's defense—it's an esthetic statement that can display an astounding number of colors, designs, and textures. The following trees and bushes not only are attractive when dressed for summer, but still add beauty to the garden when their leaves have fallen away.

Acer spp., the maples, have been farm and garden favorites for years, but it's amazing how many gardeners overlook the winter qualities of these trees. In fact, there isn't a single one of the more decorative maples that won't add beauty and interest to the winter garden. A well-grown tree, especially with lichen-encrusted bark and ivy twining around its base, is a delightful thing to see when the sky above is sullen and your fingers are cramped with cold. *Acer* is the ancient Latin name for the maple.

Acer davidii, snakebark maple

Acer buergeranum, the trident maple, reaches a height of 25 to 35 feet, with an average spread of 25 feet. It's an upright tree with a rounded top and is a suitable shade tree for the small garden. Of great winter interest are the rather smooth bark and the sturdy gray limbs with stubby, aborted branches that look like sharp spikes, a unique feature among cultivated maples. This species has excellent summer foliage and good fall color, and it does not seed around and become weedy like some maples.

Acer davidii, the gray to green snakebark maple, is adorned with white cracks, especially the cultivar 'Serpentine'. Spring leaves are red, quickly turning to dark green as the spring progresses, and finally blazing out in the fall in colors of red, yellow, and purple. This tree is native to China. It is best suited to partial shade in the South and needs rich, moisture-retentive soil and protection from excessive wind and full sun.

Acer griseum, the paperbark maple, grows about 30 feet high, with an average 20-foot spread. Because of its fascinating bark, it's grown as an accent tree throughout the country. The cinnamon-brown bark is paper thin and peels away in curling strips, revealing new bright orange-red bark underneath. The leaves are covered with fine hairs as they unfold in spring. In summer they are green on top and silvery beneath, turning bright red in the fall. Without the bark this tree would still have a dedicated following, but with this lovely bark it's a showstopper.

Acer palmatum, the Japanese maple, is grown far and wide for the form and color of its leaves in spring, summer, and fall. But there is one cultivar that is an outstanding addition to the winter garden: 'Sango Kaku', the Japanese coral-bark maple. It is difficult to describe the dramatic effect in a garden wrought by the ascending branches of this tree, all painted with a brush dipped in a brilliant shade of coral red. In *The Year in Trees* (Portland, OR: Timber Press, 1995), Kim Tripp and J. C. Raulston write that "during cold weather, the color intensifies to an almost fluorescent salmon." It takes ten to fifteen years for this tree to reach its maximum height of twenty feet, with a 12-foot spread, so here's a specimen for the small garden. When emerging in spring, the refined leaves are tinged with bright red, turning jade green for the summer and golden yellow in the fall. Purple-red flowers appear in in March. In the South, give these trees light overhead shade and good soil with decent drainage. They can be pruned to shape, but like many of the available Japanese maple cultivars, they will take on a characteristic shape without pruning. *Acer palmatum* 'Shishigashir', the lion's head, is a very unusual and distinctive Japanese maple cultivar with a deformed appearance, much like a bonsai specimen. Trees have green bark and gnarled, stunted twigs that bear dark green leaves, often curled and shaggy. It is very slow growing and expensive to acquire, but worth it in the long run for the interesting winter appearance. *Acer palmatum* 'Dissectum', lovely in the spring and summer, in winter becomes the close equivalent of a living piece of wire sculpture.

Acer tegmentosum, the Manchurian striped maple, is another tree for all seasons, but it is at its best in the

Acer griseum, paperbark maple

Acer palmatum 'Palmatifidum'

winter, when the gray-green bark incised with long, vertical white stripes is revealed. The lower branches should be removed in order to show as much of the bark textures as possible. The tree's maximum height is about 30 feet with a 25-foot spread. Again, partial shade is the rule, and well-drained soil a necessity. *Acer pensylvanicum* originates in the rich forests of the eastern United States and is the only snake-barked maple outside of Asia. It's a dead ringer for *A. tegmentosum*, and for added drama there is a cultivar 'Erythrocladum' whose striped bark is highlighted by a fluorescent glow of reddish pink on the new twigs.

Albizia julibrissin, the silk tree or mimosa, is a deciduous tree that can reach a height of 40 feet in the garden but usually stays much shorter. Some peo-

ple describe the silk tree as a noxious weed, and it's true that the tree does spread. After all, André Michaux (1746–1803) brought this tree over from Iran and planted seeds at his nursery 10 miles north of Charleston—and now look. The feathery leaves and pink powder-puff blossoms are welcome in the summer garden. But in winter, the tall straight trunks, shorn of any side branches, angle up from a center point like a bunch of tall lances slightly askew, making a flat top, much like a giant beach umbrella without the canvas cover. The sight of it is quite striking in the winter landscape. The genus is named in honor of Filippo del Albizzi, who introduced the tree into Italy in 1749. Provide full sun or partial shade in good garden soil.

Amelanchier spp., the serviceberries or shad-bushes, range from large shrubs to small trees, usually less than 25 feet high. The five-petaled flowers, pure white or sometimes with a tinge of pink, bloom in very early spring, usually when shad begin to spawn. They are over 1 inch across, on long slender pedicels, in spreading or drooping bunches. Round, crimson to dark purple fruits ripen from June to August and are soon consumed by birds. Sometimes fermenting berries cause the birds to fly in a blind stupor, often to the point of drunkenness.

In many parts of the country, the blooming time of the shadbush is too early for wild or domestic honey-bees, so the flowers are generally pollinated by little dark brown or black female bees of the andrena tribe. These bees live in burrows rather than hives, some digging numerous branched tunnels and some content to dwell in a simple straight tunnel.

Dick Bir in his book *Growing & Propagating Showy Native Woody Plants* (Chapel Hill: The University of North Carolina Press, 1992), wrote about hearing that the origin of the word "service," or "sarvice," relates to the winter ground's freezing solid. He noted that anyone who died at that time had to wait for the thawing of the earth for burial, an event often connected with the blooming of the shadbush.

Azara microphylla, the box-leaf azara, is an evergreen shrub or small tree that reaches a height of some 20 feet, but it can be pruned for a shorter stature. The stems bear small, glossy, dark green leaves that are less than an inch long and provide textural interest year-round. In late winter or very early spring, small yellowish green blossoms, described as a few yellow stamens bristling among the leaves, open and release a smell of vanilla that hangs in the air many feet from the plant. After the flowers, the orange berries appear. This is the hardiest member of this genus, which hails from Chile, and has long been a favorite of West Coast gardens. It should have a bit of shade and be positioned, in colder gardens, where it has some protection from bitter winds.

Betula spp., the birches, represent some sixty species of deciduous trees and shrubs that have been cultivated for commercial and esthetic purposes for hundreds of years. In its native China *Betula albosinensis*, the Chinese paper birch, can reach a height of 100 feet. In a garden or park setting, its height stays at about 75 feet. It is not grown for its late-winter or

(Left) *Acer palmatum* 'Sango Kaku', coral bark maple

Betula albo-sinensis, Chinese white bark birch, with *Picea orientalis*

early-spring catkins, but for its white bark, which, coupled with the rounded crown of the tree, makes it a startling addition to the winter garden. A variety called *septentrionalis* has pink, satin-smooth bark with silver bands wandering over the trunk and branches. These trees are hardy from Zone 6 south and have proven to be a reliable white-barked birch less prone to borers and root rot than the northern and European white birches.

Betula jacquemonti is a paper birch that comes from the Himalayas, specifically Nepal. It is described by Hillier's Nursery as "one of the loveliest birches, with dazzling white stems." In addition, it boasts attractively peeling bark. Garden height is between 45 and 50 feet.

Betula platyphylla var. *japonica*, the Japanese white birch, grows to a height of 30 feet, with a 15-foot spread. The tree assumes a pyramidal shape, and the white bark is very attractive. *B. platyphylla* var. *szechuanica* has silvery white bark that peels in thin strips, along with reddish brown stems and blue-green leaves. It is hardy in Zones 6 to 8.

Betula nigra, the river birch, reaches a height of 30 to 40 feet, with a 20-foot spread. The form is upright with slightly drooping twigs, bearing simple double-toothed leaves up to 3 inches long. The flowers

Betula nigra, river birch

are inconspicuous catkins. The beautiful papery bark is reddish brown to orange and peels more than any of the other birches, sometimes becoming downright shaggy. 'Heritage' is a cultivar with dark green leaves and a whitish bark. It is interesting to note that a beautiful specimen of this tree is planted in downtown Asheville and survives the fumes of both cars and buses, not to mention the summer heat.

Betula papyrifera, the paper or canoe birch, is a time-honored tree that must be mentioned for its winter beauty, but it will do well only in the relative coolness of Zone 6.

Betula pendula, the European white birch, grows up to 40 feet in cultivation, with a 15-foot spread. It is difficult to transplant and is short-lived, falling ill to a number of diseases, including the infamous bronze birch borer and a number of fungal diseases. It's recommended only in Zones 6 and 7, since warmer weather works toward its eventual demise.

All the birches like a good, moist, well-drained soil in full sun. *Betula* is the classic name of the birches.

Carpinus caroliniana, the American hornbeam, is a medium-size tree that reaches a height of 20 to 30 feet, with a 20-foot spread. The dull green foliage is simple, toothed, about 3 inches long, and turns yellowish in the fall. It's recommended for the winter garden because the trunk is ridged with dark gray bark that is very handsome when the leaves have fallen, and in the spring the trees are hung with 4-inch catkins. These trees do well in sun or shade and are tolerant of most soils. *Carpinus* is an ancient name of the hornbeam. The hard wood was once prized for mallets, cogs, and levers.

Cercidiphyllum japonicum, the Katsura tree, has beautiful heart-shaped leaves that change color from red in spring to blue-green in summer, to a lovely clear yellow and red in the autumn. The leaves emit a spicy fragrance said to resemble cinnamon just before they fall. The Katsura tree also has a special charm in the winter time, because as the trees age, the bark becomes channeled and begins to peel. The trees, originally from China, can grow to 100 feet in the wild but usually stay about 40 feet with a 20-foot spread in cultivation. A weeping form, *C. japonicum* 'Pendula', known as the weeping Katsura, resembles a weeping willow. The tree, with its arching branches that bend down to the ground, becomes a great piece of sculpture in the winter garden. For trees with such beauty, they are not temperamental, as long as the soil is good and laced with plenty of humus.

Corylus avellana 'Contorta', Harry Lauder's walking stick

Cladrastis lutea, the yellowwood, has a mature height of 50 feet with a 55-foot spread. After the leaves of the yellowwood turn yellow and drop in the fall, the trunk and branches, with their gray-white bark, become visible—an almost circular silhouette that transcends most garden sculpture. Add to this the periodic hanging blossoms of spring that resemble those of wisteria and the eventual hanging seedpods that often persist for years, and you have a special subject for the winter garden. The yellowwood does best in full sun and tolerates poor soil as long as there is ample moisture for its deep root system. This tree can also withstand difficult city conditions. The common name comes from the yellow color of the wood, which yields a dye once used by industry. *Cladrastis* is from the Greek for "branch" and "fragile."

Cornus spp., the dogwoods, are a diverse genus of trees and shrubs native to North America, Europe, and Asia. They are held in high esteem not only for their beautiful spring flowers and often colorful autumn berries, but also for their bark, which resembles the rough skin of an elephant, and for the shape of their intricate branches against the winter sky.

Cornus alba, the Tatarian dogwood, is especially useful for the scarlet color of its whiplike stems in winter. This shrub grows from 7 to 9 feet in height and roughly in the shape of a fan. Though the color is beautiful on a lone specimen it can be very special when mixed with other shrubs that have colored bark. 'Sibirica', the Siberian dogwood, has bright coral-red stems; 'Elegantissima' adds white-margined gray-green leaves to the mix; 'Kesselringii' has branches of a bright purple-red that shades almost to black; and 'Spaethii' has stems of a bright orange-red. *Cornus kousa*, the Chinese dogwood, exhibits an attractive lace-bark pattern with age. Another dogwood with colored stems is *Cornus sericea* (*C. stolonifera*) 'Flaviramea', the red-osier dogwood, a cultivar with bright yellow twigs. Another cultivar, *C. sericea* 'Kelseyi', is actually a ground cover, its thin, upright, 8-inch stems stained a bright orange-red. These shrubs need a moist, well-drained acid soil under a high canopy of open shade. *Cornus* is from the Latin for "horn," referring to the toughness of the wood.

Corylus avellana 'Contorta', or Harry Lauder's walking stick, is a must for every winter garden. This contorted cultivar of an English hazel bush was originally found growing by the side of a hedgerow, and luckily some sharp-eyed person spotted it. It could be included in the chapter on winter-flowering shrubs, but the twisted twigs and branches, which resemble writhing snakes of various sizes, are this shrub's most eye-catching feature.

Cytisus scoparius, the Scotch broom, is studded with bright yellow pea-blossom-like flowers in April and May. But there is a definite winter use for this shrub, because the chaotic swing of the green stems whipping out in all directions makes it a beautiful sight, not only alone, but planted in groups. Brooms also make excellent background shrubs. Height is from 5 to 7 feet, with a 5-foot spread. Brooms do well in sun or shade and will adjust to most soil conditions but need decent drainage. If you're looking for a plant to grow on clay banks, try the brooms. Provide poor, dry soil in sun or light shade. Cut them back by about a third after they bloom in the spring, and also prune in the early spring to remove dead wood. The genus refers to cloverlike plants with three leaflets. *Cytisus* × *praecox*, known as the Warminster broom, grows to a height of 10 feet and makes an even larger statement in the garden.

Diospyros virginiana, the American persimmon tree, is a deciduous member of a large genus of trees used for ornament, fruit, or the wood alone. Because the fruit on the American tree is small and pulpy when mature, the tree used for persimmon culture today is the Japanese persimmon, *D. kaki*, and its cultivars. The native persimmon reaches a height of 40 to 60 feet, with a 30-foot spread. The bright yellow to orange-red fruits will cling to the tree well into the winter, ripening after being touched by frost. But for the winter garden, it's the almost black bark that calls the shots. The bark is deeply cut into smooth-cornered rectangles, and in young trees the spaces between are often tinted with orange. That in conjunction with the overall shape of the tree, with its rounded crown and crooked branches, make it a beautiful tree to grow. Provide full sun and good, well-drained garden soil with added organic matter. Because of a long taproot, the trees are difficult to transplant, so use containerized specimens. *Diospyros* is from the Greek word for "the grain of Jove," referring to the edible fruit.

Dirca palustris, ropebark or leatherwood, is a little-known shrub of American origin that is extremely rare in cultivation. It's a stocky plant that grows about 8 feet high, with dull, light green leaves about 3 inches long. But its winter value lies in its thick, often gnarled dull brown trunk and symmetrically branching stocky twigs that appear to be stuck together rather than gradually tapering to the tip. Pale yellow flowers,

enclosed at their bases with hairy bud scales, appear in early spring before the leaves begin to open. These shrubs need high overhead shade and a good moist soil. The American Indians used the strong, fibrous bark for thongs and heavy twine. There are only two species, the second being a California shrub, *D. occidentalis*. The genus is said to be named for the Greek fountain Dirke.

Edgeworthia papyrifera, the rice paper plant or mitsumata, is a deciduous shrub originally from China that has long been cultivated in Japan as a source of special papers for handicrafts. It reaches a height of 8 feet, and the young branches are tough and supple, bearing oblong leaves about 5 inches long. The twigs branch regularly in threes, and the 1-inch white clusters of nodding flower buds are unique and attractive all winter. Half-inch long, rich yellow tubular flowers (rarely orange), clothed with white silky hairs, appear in the early spring before the leaves begin to open. They are hardy only in Zones 7 to 9, but in colder climates they make great greenhouse plants. The shrub was named in honor of M. P. Edgeworth (1812–81), a botanist with the East India Company.

Euonymus alata, the winged euonymus or winged wahoo, is a deciduous shrub originally from the temperate parts of Asia. It grows to a height of 8 feet, with a 5-foot spread. Because of rampant seedlings, in untended gardens you can often find a grove of these plants where once there was only one. The shrubs grow in an upright manner, with simple leaves about 3 inches long and inconspicuous greenish white flowers that become scarlet fruits in the fall. Because of the brilliant reddish pink fall color, another common name for this shrub is the burning bush. But it's the bark that makes it a candidate for the winter garden. The twigs and branches bear corky ridges like soft wings, which make it a most interesting garden subject when the leaves have fallen. 'Compacta' is a dwarf form. These plants like full sun or partial shade, soil with medium drainage, and a good supply of moisture. That's why the winged euonymus does so beautifully in a wooded setting. Old-time gardeners recommend using the species and steering away from the cultivars, because these new varieties have traded the corky texture for larger and more brilliant leaves. The genus is from ancient Greek, "having an honorable name."

Fagus spp., the beeches, are majestic trees valuable both to gardens and commerce, providing beauty, nuts, and timber. *Fagus grandifolia*, the American beech, reaches a height of 90 feet, and coming upon

Edgeworthia papyrifera, paper plant

one of these huge trees in a forest setting is, at least to a gardener, an emotional sight. In addition to its attractive overall form, another good reason to use this tree in the winter garden is its smooth gray bark, which never furrows, even on the oldest of trees. Its toothed leaves (used in trademarks, including a brand of coffee) turn a beautiful yellow-bronze in the fall but persist in hanging on the branches until well into winter. This tree is hardy in Zones 6 to 9. *Fagus sylvatica*, the European beech, also tops out at 90 feet but differs from the American species in that the lower branches often sweep the ground. There are a number of cultivars, but the most effective in the winter garden is 'Pendula', a form with weeping stems and branches that grow out horizontally from the trunk. Both are

hardy from Zones 6 to 10. *Fagus* is the ancient Latin name for the genus.

Halesia carolina (*H. tetraptera*), the silverbell, is a choice tree for the small garden, producing numerous 1-inch bell-shaped flowers in April. *Halesia diptera*, which has larger flowers, is a bit showier. Both species grow fairly fast, making attractive trees, and both have distinctive striped bark and shredding twigs, which add to their winter appeal. Large (1½-inch), interesting dry fruits persist on the twigs through the winter. The species are hardy throughout our range and are readily available from several nurseries. They add a distinct charm to the garden with their flowers and fruits. *Halesia* is named for Stephen Hales (1677–1761), an English physiologist.

Hydrangea anomala petiolaris, the climbing hydrangea, should probably be in a category devoted to winter vines, but because a healthy specimen can grow to a height of 50 feet, with an indeterminate spread, and because it's a vine that is particularly attractive in the winter months, we're including it here. Originally from Japan, this deciduous climber uses aerial roots for support. The vine blooms with typical white hydrangea flowers in early summer, and the dark green, almost heart-shaped leaves turn bright yellow in the fall. But it's during the winter months that the texture of the reddish, shedding bark is visible. This, coupled with the green of the spring buds, makes for a fine effect, especially attractive when growing on stone. The vine will also cling to masonry and trees without support and can be a glorious thing when climbing up a massive chimney or a tall pine tree. Provide partial shade, and plant the vine, hardy in Zones 6 to 8, in a soil of medium to high fertility with added humus. Only mature vines will flower well. *Hydrangea* comes from the Greek *hydor*, "water," and *aggeion*, "vessel," alluding to the cup-shaped fruit.

Kerria japonica, the Japanese rose, is the only member of the genus, first described in 1712. Although long cultivated in Japan, where the pith is used to make tiny replicas of buds and flowers for floating in cups of sake, the kerria is a native of China. The light green, toothed leaves are 2 inches long. Because the 3- to 5-foot arching stems remain green all winter, the Japanese rose is a pleasant addition to the winter garden. The many-petaled flowers are yellow-orange, about 2 inches wide, and bloom in April. Provide sun or partial shade; the variegated form does better in some shade. Plants are tolerant of most soils but need good drainage. Prune old stems and any results of winterkill. 'Picta' is the variegated form; 'Aureo-variegata' has leaves edged with yellow; and 'Aureo-vittata' has branchlets striped with green and yellows. The genus is named in honor of William Kerr, who introduced the double-flower form to England in 1805.

Kolkwitzia amabilis, the beautybush, is a one-species genus native to China. These shrubs can grow to a height of 10 (or more) feet and in early May are festooned with cascades of pink flowers with yellow throats. But few gardeners ever mention the exfoliating bark of winter, which peels off in long pieces that are pale tan on the outside and almost white within. If this bark was a bit sturdier and did not have minute longitudinal tears, it would be a great substitute for birch bark for canoes. Grow the beautybush in full sun or light shade in any reasonable garden soil with good drainage, in Zones 6 to 8. The shrubs do not transplant well, so start with a containerized plant. The genus was named in honor of Richard Kolkwitz, a German botanist.

Lagerstroemia indica, the crape myrtle, has become one of the pop plants of the last decade. These large deciduous shrubs or small trees originally hailed from China, where in nature they reach a height of 25 feet, with a 15-foot spread. The flowers appear in the summertime and bloom in a number of colors. Their multiple trunks, open silhouette, and pale gray-brown bark that shreds to expose a lighter tan underneath make them a stunning addition as a specimen tree, planted in groups. Provide full sun and soil with excellent fertility and good drainage. They can be pruned to the ground each year to keep them as shrubs rather than allowing them to mature into their tree form. There are a number of cultivars in various sizes; try to buy them when in bloom so you can get the exact shade you want for summer flowers. 'Zuni' is a semi-dwarf form, 'Acoma' grows from 4 to 6 feet, 'Hopi' from 7 to 9 feet, and 'Near East' from 18 to 20 feet. The finest bark forms are the newer *L. fauriei* 'Fantasy' (selected by the J. C. Raulston Arboretum in Raleigh) and the hybrid cultivar *Lagerstroemia* 'Natchez' (*L. indica* x *L. fauriei*), both of which are hardy to –10°F, have white flowers, are disease resistant, and have winter bark that is an unmatchable rich cinnamon tan. Crape myrtles are hardy in Zones 6 to 9. The genus is named for Magnus von Lagerstroem of Göttenburg (1691–1759), a friend of Linnaeus's.

Leycesteria formosa, the Himalaya honeysuckle, flowering nutmeg, or Elisha's tears, is not widely known in gardening circles. When it is noted in books and articles, it's only as a summertime shrub that bears pendant flowers, followed by fruits that resemble very dangling earrings. Originally from the Nepal area of the Himalayas, where it's known as *Nulkuroo*, this plant was sent to England in 1824 in a shipment of seeds from some gardens in India. Gardeners of the day generally regarded it as a background shrub. But on a chilly morning in early January, the bunches of 6-foot stems that make up this shrub are a bright grassy green. They resemble a grove of equisetum or horsetails, only lacking the rings found on the stems of the latter. The berries appear in the fall, but by the time of the winter garden, unless protected by nets, they will have been eaten by the birds. These deciduous shrubs need shade, especially in the warmer parts of the

Lagerstroemia 'Natchez', crape myrtle

South, and a soil with reasonable fertility. Unfortunately, the near-zero temperatures in the mountains of Asheville can turn the bright green stems a dismal brown, but new shoots appear in the spring. The seeds are generally available from the various seed exchanges (see Plant Sources).

Magnolia macrophylla, the bigleaf magnolia, is a multi- or single-trunked deciduous tree reaching a height of 30 to 40 feet, with a 25-foot spread. It has the largest single leaf in all the temperate zones of the world, growing up to 40 inches long, so in the autumn you don't rake the leaves, you gather them up! This tree's winter appeal is in the stout twigs and sparsely branched trunks, which add a unique coarse texture to the garden. The soft, 6-inch buds are also quite evident and only hint at the elephantine leaves and flowers that will appear in late spring. Provide full sun or partial shade in rich, well-drained soil. It is hardy well beyond our region to the north.

Metasequoia glyptostroboides, the dawn redwood, is a beautiful deciduous evergreen tree, first described in 1941 from fossil material and brought back from Szechwan, China, shortly after the end of World War II. This tree can reach to 70 to 100 feet in height, with a spread of 30 feet and a trunk up to 9 feet in diameter. The needles turn a glorious orange-brown in the autumn, then promptly fall from the tree. This tree's winter interest lies not only in its overall form, but also in the red-brown bark that becomes gray with age. Soft brown plumelike flowers appear on older trees in February and March, and the resulting cones ripen the following December. This tree needs full sun in a good garden soil with adequate drainage. Dawn redwoods grow rapidly and need plenty of room. In our Asheville garden, a tree planted at the edge of the road has sent roots 50 feet or more down toward the lake in search of water. Metasequoias may grow on moister soil than most trees. Older bark may be deeply ribbed, and the roots may enlarge at the base of the trunk like buttresses. Older specimens can only be described as striking, especially in winter. The genus name is from the Greek for "changed" and "sequoia," referring to this tree's close relation to that forest giant.

Close relatives are our native bald cypress (*Taxodium distichum*) and pond cypress (*T. ascendens*). Both are deciduous conifers with interesting bark, trunk, and twig features in the winter landscape. In addition, taxodiums can grow in very wet soil, or even standing water (though that slows their growth). When the water levels fluctuate, they produce knees, upright extrusions of the roots that may reach 3 to 4 feet with time. Although cypress knees are interesting in the wild, when formed in the garden they can create a nuisance for the lawn mower or disturb the paths.

Ostrya virginiana, the American hop hornbeam, is a small deciduous tree found growing from Virginia to the western part of northern Florida. In nature they reach a height of 30 to 40 feet. *Hillier's Manual of Trees and Shrubs* describes the hop hornbeam as an "attractive, small tree of elegant, rounded, or pyramidal habit." The tree produces two types of catkins: the male, which persist from the year before, and the inconspicuous female blossoms, which appear in very early spring, at maturity developing into pendant catkins that look exactly like a head of hops, each pouchlike bract holding a small nut at its base. Because the branches tend to grow upright, this is a good small tree for use in limited space. The fall color is an unremarkable yellow, but the bark is exceptional and looks as though a cat has scratched the surface into narrow, shredded strips with its sharp claws. This tree needs partial shade and good, moist, fertile soil. The wood is very hard and was used for edges, mallets, tool handles, gears, and wheel cogs. The genus is the ancient Greek name for this group of trees.

Parrotia persica is discussed in the chapter on flowering trees, but the texture of the bark is so attractive that it deserves mention here as well. As the tree ages, the bark becomes a mottled mix of gray and brown, flaking away to show tints of green, like a patchwork quilt. The cultivar 'Biltmore' is propagated from a hundred-year-old specimen at Biltmore House and Gardens in Asheville. It is an upright, multitrunked beauty with an exceptional bark pattern.

Paulownia tomentosa, the princess tree or cotton tree, reaches a height of 30 to 50 feet, with an average 25-foot spread, and is strikingly handsome when in bloom. Unfortunately, it garners mixed reviews from many conservationists, who view it as an oriental threat that is pushing out many native species. As you drive along North Carolina's I-40 in April, these trees are covered with glorious fragrant, tubular flowers that resemble gloxinias. But these trees do sprout up like weeds, clinging to rocky clefts where most other trees could not take root. Their numbers result from seedpods that each contain about two thousand seeds, giving a mature tree a seed count of about 21 million. Once established, princess trees immediately send up

Pinus bungeana, lacebark pine

32

rank growth topped with heart-shaped leaves up to a foot long. The wood of the tree is very light and is valued in Japan and China for cabinets, tea chests, and wooden shoes. In fact, it's so valuable that poachers are now taking these trees from the forest to sell abroad. All this being said, the tree does make a statement in the winter garden, with the brownish black pods that appear in the fall covering the coarse, gray branches and persisting throughout the winter.

Physocarpus opulifolius, the ninebark, is another shrub whose winter appeal lies in its shredding bark. It is a coarse, thick, untidy shrub that grows to 8 feet tall, with arching stems producing 2-inch clusters of white spiraealike flowers in late spring. It likes well-drained moist soil and does well in Zones 6 to 8. There are certainly many better shrubs, but it is native throughout eastern North America and is tough once established.

Pinus bungeana, the lacebark pine, unlike most conifers, is usually multitrunked, and its trunks often reach heights of 40 to 50 feet, with 40-foot spreads. This evergreen is grown not only for the year-round 4-inch bright green needles, but especially for the multi-colored trunks whose bark peels off in irregular pieces like an unfinished jigsaw puzzle. Before being introduced to common gardens, these trees were found only in Chinese temple gardens, their trunks glowing with shades of green, creamy white, gray, and brown, all visible because of the exfoliating bark. Unfortunately, this fantastic color show is usually not present until the tree is at least twenty years old, so be sure to save up to buy a reasonably mature balled-and-burlapped specimen. Plant the lacebark pine in full sun in a fertile, well-drained acid garden soil.

Platanus occidentalis, the sycamore, buttonwood, or American plane tree, found its popularity increase when it was featured in American popular music. In an ideal setting this stately tree can reach a height of 100 feet, producing several large secondary trunks and massive spreading limbs. We're including it here for two winter features: its interesting bark, with a thin brown outer layer that continually exfoliates to reveal inner layers of white, yellow, and dark green, and the soft-prickly, inch-wide seed balls that last through the winter before greeting spring by breaking apart and releasing hundreds of fluffy seeds. For sycamore success, water is the key. Plant in full sun or partial shade in a well-drained situation, but make sure the soil is fertile and stays moist. The sycamore can withstand severe city conditions and smog, making it a useful park tree. The tree has a few deficits, however, includ-

Platanus orientalis, plane tree

ing its poor fall color; its habit of shedding leaves, seed balls, and bark, making occasional cleanups necessary; and its fast growth (up to 3 feet a year), making it unsuitable for the small garden. The famous London plane tree, (*Platanus* × *acerifulia*), a tree bred to withstand the worst of city conditions (at one time London had the most polluted air in the world), is a form derived from hybridizing our native *P. occidentalis* and the European *P. orientalis*. This tree also has bark that flakes off in large patches, and it has twin seedpods instead of single ones. *Platanus* is the classic Greek name for the plane tree.

Poncirus trifoliata, the hardy orange, is surprisingly hardy for a deciduous tree with orangelike fruits. These fruits have been used as stock for citrus to make the trees more hardy. Mature trees reach a height of 10 to 15 feet, with a maximum spread of 12 feet. The new twigs are green and produce vicious green thorns, suggesting that one use would be to make an animal-proof hedge around a garden. In the South, the white flowers appear in late March or early April, producing yellow-orange fruits up to 2 inches in diameter that persist on the trees well into the winter. They are often gathered for fall fruit bowl decorations because of their delicate fruity fragrance. This is a fas-

Poncirus trifoliata 'Flying Dragon', contorted trifoliate orange

cinating and beautiful winter tree. Provide full sun and a good acid garden soil with good drainage. There is an old but striking cultivar called 'Flying Dragon', which has even more effective twisting stems and sharply curved thorns. *Poncirus* comes from the French word for a kind of citron.

Prunus spp., the cherries, are generally viewed as spring-flowering specimens that also have great fall color. The fruits may ripen profusely in midsummer and get the birds drunk with delight as the juicy drupes ferment in the heat. There are several cherries that also have winter appeal that do well in our region. One of the best ornamental cherries is *Prunus* 'Okame', a hardy hybrid between *P. incisa* and *P. campanulata*. 'Okame' has beautiful shiny, mahogany-colored bark with typical horizontal streaks that are very conspicuous in winter. The tree grows straight and tall with a rather narrow crown, making it useful for the small garden. The bark has such a tactile quality that these trees should be planted where they may be touched by admirers. The beautiful frostproof, carmine-pink flowers are produced in profusion in February to March, but the tree does not produce viable fruits. The summer foliage is handsome, and the fall color is very good. This is truly a tree for all seasons.

The *Rubus* genus, the white-barked or white-washed brambles, (members of the great rose family) has over 250 species. Two species are noted for the bloom on their canes, a white, waxlike material that coats both stems and twigs. On still winter days they look like frozen fountains of ice, and make no mistake—these plants are spectacular in the winter garden. *Rubus biflorus* is a deciduous shrub that reaches a height of 8 to 10 feet, with 4- to 8-inch leaves and white midsummer blossoms, followed by flavorful yellow berries. This shrub was first brought to England in 1818 from the Himalayas. *Rubus cockburnianus* is the same height but has a bushier top. Small, starlike purple flowers are followed by small black fruit. This species was introduced from China in 1907. Both species like full sun and any good garden soil. As with most raspberries, the stems should be cut back to the ground every second year after fruiting is over, allowing for new, more vigorous canes. New plants are easily started by division or from cuttings. *Rubus* is the ancient Latin name for the brambles.

Rubus phoenicolasius, the wineberry, is a naturalized species found east of the mountains from Georgia into Pennsylvania. Its arching 10-foot stems are covered with sharp prickles and fine, sticky 1/4-inch hairs

Prunus incisa 'Okame', Okame cherry (bark)

that are exquisite when backlighted on a winter morning. A characteristic feature is the pure white undersides of the leaflets. As with other members of the clan, the vegetative proliferation of the canes and the numerous seedlings that result from bird disperal of the fruits have the potential to make them, if ignored, a garden nuisance.

Sorbus alnifolia, the Korean mountain ash, is one species of a genus of about eighty-five deciduous trees or shrubs from the Northern Hemisphere. This tree is grown for a number of reasons, including its dense, rounded habit of growth, flat clusters of scarlet to orange fruits, and autumn leaf color shading from brilliant orange to scarlet. But for the winter garden, it's the smooth, dark gray bark with twigs of reddish brown tint, slightly pubescent when young, that takes front stage. Provide full sun in any good garden soil with decent drainage. *Sorbus* is the ancient Latin name for this genus.

Stewartia spp., the stewartias, represent some six species of deciduous shrubs and small trees from eastern Asia and eastern North America. They are usually grown for their camellia-like blossoms, but they also have great winter interest. *Stewartia koreana*, the Korean stewartia, reaches a height of 45 feet and bears 5-inch leaves that turn a brilliant orange in the fall. Large white flowers resembling camellias appear in summer. In winter, the bare branches create a beautiful pattern, and the exfoliating dark brown bark peels away in irregular patches to reveal a lighter brown

35

Ulmus parvifolia, lacebark elm

bark underneath. *Stewartia pseudocamellia* is similar to *S. koreana*, but the young stems are gray-green, often with a reddish orange sheen in the spring. The flaking bark is more like that of a sycamore, peeling off in large pieces to reveal lighter tints underneath. *Stewartia ovata* var. *grandiflora*, the mountain camellia, is a rare plant of the mountains of the Carolinas, having 4-inch white flowers with purple stamens in the center. The bark flakes off in irregular patches, leaving interesting combinations of light and dark, similar to the sycamore but far more beautiful. Provide partial shade and an acid soil, with plenty of moisture and additional humus. The genus is named for John Stewart, earl of Bute (1713–92).

Styrax obassia, the bigleaf snowbell, is a deciduous tree from Japan that reaches a height of 20 to 30 feet. The leaves are oval, up to 8 inches long, and

(Left) *Rubus cockburnianus*, ghost bramble

densely downy beneath. The fragrant flowers are bell-like and hang down in terminal racemes up to 8 inches long. Half-inch-long ovoid fruits with a velvety surface add interest, along with the coarse twigs and peeling bark. The main appeal of this attractive species is its form. Michael Dirr says; "Architecturally, the smooth gray branches with numerous twists, turns and sinuations are handsome for winter effects." The oval buds and peeling bark on the twigs make for interesting details. The thin outer bark may peel off the entire length of a season's growth of a twig, usually the second year. Plant in rich, moist soil where observers can have a dramatic close encounter with the pendulous flowers, large oval leaves, and winter bark. This tree is hardy to –25° F.

Ulmus spp., the elms, are trees of great beauty and stately elegance. Most American towns have an Elm Street, named for the American elm (*U. americana*), a magnificent tree that grew to a height of 125 feet and was once widely planted along broad streets and parkways. Because of rampant destruction by Dutch elm disease, however, they have now mostly passed from the American scene. But, there are other elms that are more resistant to the disease, and a few are known for their winter beauty.

Ulmus alata, the winged or wahoo elm, is an American native with corky wings on many of its branches. A small southern elm, it reaches a height of 40 feet. It has small, narrow, deep olive green leaves, smooth above and downy beneath, and a light brown bark with flat, broken ridges. The fruits give the tree a reddish color, and that, along with the texture of the wings, makes this a lovely tree for the winter. Provide moist, well-drained soil in full sun to partial shade. Currently there are no named selections of this tree in the nursery trade, but the J. C. Raulston Arboretum at Raleigh is developing a weeping form called 'Lace Parasol'. Originally found in Texas, this selection promises to be a beautiful tree for the small garden, both winter and summer. According to Cocker and Totten in *Trees of the Southeastern States* (Chapel Hill: The University of North Carolina Press, 1934), it is one of the few trees that lightning does not kill.

Ulmus parvifolia, the Chinese lacebark elm, reaches a height of 30 to 40 feet, with a 30-foot spread. This species grows rapidly. Graceful in habit and rounded in growth, this tree has shiny green, elliptical leaves that are a little over 2 inches long and inconspicuous flowers that appear in late summer. But it's the mature gray bark that is especially beautiful, for it peels irregularly to reveal inner shades of green and orange. Several cultivars exist, many with attractive exfoliating bark that reveals various shades of gray, green, and orange. The cultivar 'Drake' (Drake's elm) is smaller, with a somewhat upright form, and is recommended for the South. It is still too large for the small garden but would make an effective lawn tree. It seems to be resistant to Dutch elm disease and is a tough tree for urban conditions, because once settled in, it tolerates drought. Provide sun or partial shade in good garden soil with adequate moisture. *Ulmus* is the classical Latin name for the elm.

4
PODS, FRUITS, PLUMES, AND BERRIES

On the motionless branches of some trees autumn berries hung like clusters of coral beads, as in those fabled orchards where the fruits were jewels; others, stripped of all their garniture, stood, each the centre of its little heap of bright red leaves, watching their slow decay; others again still wearing theirs, had them all crunched and crackled up, as though they had been burnt.

—Charles Dickens, heralding the entrance of the immortal Mr. Pecksniff in *Martin Chuzzlewit*

IT IS AMAZING JUST HOW MANY PLANTS, SHRUBS, AND TREES bear interesting, attractive, or just plain beautiful pods, fruits, and berries that will add sparkle and drama to a winter garden.

These structures are all part of the reproductive devices of plants that bear and disperse the seeds, and each has a separate strategy for success. Some use parachutes, wings, or other inflated appendages to release the seeds to the open air. Others depend on gusts and gales of wind to throw the seeds about over a long period of time. Some tiny seeds are actually held in the pods until late winter so that tiny shoots can fall to the top layer of leaf litter in the field and forest and not be covered by falling debris.

The juicy sorts of fruit are meant to be eaten by birds and animals, the seeds to be spit out or excreted well away from the parent plant. Fleshy fruits like beautyberries, honeysuckle, dogwood, and cherries are devoured as quickly as they ripen; others, like holly, pyracantha, cotoneaster, nandina, and chokeberries, hang on the plants well into winter. These latter fruits are low in nutrition and flavor (try eating one!) and are utilized by birds only as a last resort in late winter, but from the human point of view, they make the finest winter garden ornaments. So without further ado, here are the plant descriptions.

Aronia spp., the chokeberries, are deciduous shrubs that bear fruits so bitter that birds and animals let them be, and they remain on the trees well into the winter. *Aronia arbutifolia*, the red chokeberry, is cov-

ered with thousands of bright red 1/4-inch berries that develop from spring-blooming 1/2-inch pink or white flowers. The bushes grow from 8 to 12 feet tall. *Aronia melanocarpa*, the black chokeberry, reaches a height of only 3 feet and bears black berries. *Aronia prunifolia*, the purple chokeberry, grows between 10 and 12 feet tall and bears purple berries. The black and purple chokeberries do not keep their fruits as long as the red. All three shrubs are hardy in Zones 6 to 9. Provide good garden soil (they will tolerate soil that is periodically wet) in partial shade. Pinch new spring growth to promote branching. The genus name derives from Aria, the ancient name of *Sorbus Aria*, the beam-tree of Europe.

Baccharis halimifolia, the groundsel tree, is really a shrub belonging to the aster tribe that reaches a height of 12 feet. The evergreen elliptical leaves are a dull gray-green and grow on light gray-brown stems, the lower bark incised with perpendicular seams. The white or yellowish flowers appear in September and are tubular, blooming in a compound head. They are notable for their silky seedheads, which consist of a white pappus made of glistening bundles of white hairs. Individually, these are untidy plants, but they are unique when displayed in masses. Groundsels are common in salt marshes and along the beaches and sand dunes from Massachusetts to Florida and are spreading inland for hundreds of miles. They are quite at home in the gardens of Zones 7 to 9. *Baccharis* comes from the Greek word *bacchus*, for "wine," alluding to the spicy odor of the roots.

Smilax walteri

Baptisia australis, the wild indigo, has long been grown as a deciduous garden shrub, although it's really a herbaceous perennial plant belonging to the pea family. The leaves turn black after exposure to a killing frost, but the main drama provided by this plant belongs to its attractive seedpods, once called Indian rattles. Either gilded for dried flower arrangements or left *au naturel* in the garden, these pods are both interesting and attractive. The plant blooms in late spring with dark blue pealike flowers. *Baptisia alba* is a beautiful white-flowered form. 'Blue Smoke' is a new

PLANTS WITH PERSISTENT
WINTER BERRIES FOR THE BIRDS[†]

Alexandrian laurel or poet's laurel (*Danae racemosa*), red

Barberry (*Berberis thunbergii*), red

Carolina cherry-laurel (*Prunus caroliniana*), black

China berry (*Melia azedarach*), yellow

Chokeberry (*Aronia arbutifolia*), red or black

Clerodendron (*Clerodendron indicum*), blue-black

Coralbeads (*Cocculus carolinus*), red (rarely persistent)

Coralberry, Indian current
(*Symphoricarpos orbiculatus*), red

Cotoneaster spp., red

English ivy (*Hedera helix*), black

Firethorn (*Pyracantha* spp.) red-orange

Gold-dust tree (*Aucuba japonica*), red

Greenbrier (*Smilax* spp.), most are blue or black;
S. *walteri*, red

Hackberry, dwarf (*Celtis tenuifolia*), black

Hawthorn (*Crataegus* spp.), red

Hawthorn, Indian (*Raphiolepis* spp.), purple-black

Holly (*Ilex* spp.), esp. winterberry, Yaupon, and possum-haw, red; inkberry, gallberry, Japanese holly, black

Honeysuckle, Japanese (*Lonicera japonica*), black

Jerusalem cherry (*Solanum pseudocapsicum*), orange

Mistletoe (*Phoradendron serotinum*), white

Mondo-grass (*Ophiopogon japonicus*), blue

Monkey-grass (*Liriope spicata*), black

Nandina (*Nandina domestica*), red

Privet (*Ligustrum sinense, L. japonicum*), purple-black

Red cedar (*Juniperus virginiana*), blue

Rose (e.g. *Rosa carolina*), red, orange

Sarcococca spp., red or black

Skimmia japonica, red

Sparkleberry (*Vaccinium arboreum*), black

Sumac (*Rhus typhina, R. glabra*), red

Viburnum (*Viburnum lentago, V. trilobum*, etc.),
red, blue, black

Wax-myrtle, bayberry (*Myrica* spp.), blue

[†] (at least in the South)

40

hybrid between the two species. All of these plants will seed about. Their roots are excellent for holding a bank of soil in place. Allow plants to mature and enlarge without undue disturbance. Provide an exposure in full sun with good, well-drained garden soil. *Baptisia* comes from the Greek *babto*, "to dye," because some species were used as a safe alternative to the poisonous indigo; unfortunately, these dyes were not fast.

Berberis spp., the barberries, are known for their prickly stems, attractive leaves, and beautiful berries. For years, planting barberry hedges has been a popular approach to foundation planting. *Berberis vulgaris*, the common European barberry, is a deciduous shrub that has naturalized in many parts of East Coast, but

as it is an alternate host for wheat rust, it is not sold by nurseries today. *Berberis julianae*, the wintergreen barberry, is a native of China that arrived in England in 1907. The height of a mature bush is 6 feet, with a 5-foot spread. The branches are armed with thorns, and the long, thin 3-inch evergreen leaves, of a deep glossy green, are also edged with short spines. Small, yellow waxy flowers bloom in early April, followed in the autumn by bluish black oblong berries that persist into winter. This is a most attractive shrub. 'Nana' is a cultivar that grows about 4 feet tall and has dark green foliage that turns a wine red in winter.

Berberis thunbergii, the Japanese barberry, grows about 5 feet tall, with a 5-foot spread. The deciduous, medium green, spineless simple leaves turn scarlet in

Berberis julianae, **wintergreen barberry**

the autumn before they fall to reveal the fruits. Creamy white flowers bloom in April, followed by reddish orange fruits in autumn, which hang on the bare branches throughout the winter. *B. thunbergii* var. *atropurpurea* bears dark red leaves; 'Kobold' forms a perfect mound about 2 feet high with yellow leaves; 'Minor' also grows about 2 feet high; 'Rose Glow' is a dwarf form with young leaves that begin a deep red, mottled with silvery pink, and turn bright scarlet in the fall. *Berberis × mentorensis*, the mentor barberry, is a hybrid between *B. julianae* and *B. thunbergii*. It grows about 6 feet tall with a 7-foot spread. It has slender, thorny branches; leathery, spiny dark green leaves; and yellow flowers that appear in March and April. So many dull dark red berries develop in the fall that they give the shrub a colorful glow.

Berberis verruculosa, the warty barberry, reaches a height of 4 feet, with a 4-foot spread. This shrub has pronounced arching stems. The twigs of this most refined barberry bear little warts, hence the popular name. Evergreen 1-inch leaves have spiny edges with the margins rolled under. Yellow flowers appear in April, followed by autumn fruits of a rich black with a bluish bloom. 'Compacta' has a dwarf habit.

Provide barberries with sun to very light shade and soil of medium fertility with good drainage. All of these barberries are hardy in Zones 6 to 8, except for *verruculosa*, which dislikes the heat of Zone 8. *Berberis* is the ancient Arabic name for these plants.

Callicarpa spp., the beautyberries, are deciduous shrubs that grow to a height of 4 to 10 feet, with a 4- to 8-foot spread. The toothed yellow-green leaves reach a length up to 6 inches, and the flowers open in clusters located at the leaf axils. *Callicarpa americana*, the American beautyberry, has pinkish blue flowers and clusters of shiny, conspicuous, and unique bluish purple berries that encircle the stems. 'Russell Montgomery' is a cultivar with especially effective white berries. *Callicarpa japonica*, the Japanese beautyberry, is identical in habit, but the leaf edges are smooth, the flowers pinkish white, and the fruits violet to dark purple. 'Leucocarpa' bears white fruit. 'Luxurians' is larger than the noncultivated *japonica* and has larger, showier fruit clusters. Note that the berries are readily eaten by birds and may not last too long. Plant these bushes in groups for maximum effect. Provide full sun to partial shade in good garden soil of medium fertility and reasonable drainage. *Callicarpa* is from the Greek for "beautiful" and "fruit."

Castanea pumila, the Allegheny chinquapin, belongs to the chestnut genus. The chinquapin can be either a large shrub or a small tree, bearing slender spreading branches. Its smooth, light brown bark often has tints of red, and on old trees is a brownish gray. The leaves are deep green and smooth above and have a whitish down beneath. They flower in June, the blossoms becoming burs slightly over an inch in diameter, each containing a solitary nut that ripens in September. These nuts look more like small acorns than chestnuts. The opening burs hang on the tree well into fall and early winter, but eventually they are eaten by wildlife because the nuts are very sweet and tasty. These plants need a good well-drained soil in partial shade. *Castanea* is the Latin name for the chestnut.

Celastrus spp., the bittersweets, are evocative and bring memories to Peter of bitter winters up north, as winds from Lake Erie battered downtown Buffalo and American Indians stood huddled in doorways, selling bunches of the glorious orange-yellow pods that open to reveal the red fleshy seeds of *Celastrus scandens*, the American bittersweet. Gardeners are of two minds regarding bittersweet because of the mixup between the native and the Japanese import, *C. orbiculatus*. Elizabeth Lawrence says of oriental bittersweet, "I spent thirty-two years in an unequal struggle with roots that suckered in all directions, branches that rooted wherever they touched the ground, and seedlings that popped up everywhere." She added that perhaps it would be better to enjoy it on rambles through the countryside. The problem is that many nurseries selling the American are mistakenly selling the invasive pest. But the berries of the bittersweet are among the most beautiful that the American woods have to offer. So if you do plant the oriental, cut off all the berries for decoration before the pods have a chance to split open and scatter their seeds about your property. You must have male and female plants growing together to get the berries, but they are rarely sold as matched pairs, so you take your chances when buying seedlings. As to growing conditions, bittersweets will do more than well in average soil and are hardy throughout the United States.

Cercis canadensis, the redbud, is also noted in chapter 6 for its flowers, little pealike blossoms that bloom in clusters all over the bare branches of these small trees before the leaves appear. In late summer, the blossoms mature into long, flattened brown pods that hang on the trees well into winter. After the leaves fall, the clustered pods are readily apparent, and some gardeners view the redbud as being more messy than attractive. Provide sun or partial shade in

Cotoneaster dammeri 'Lowfast'

average garden soil with good drainage, although red-buds will do very well when planted by the side of a moving stream. The genus name comes from the ancient Greek word *kerkis*, which refers to the European relatives of this tree.

Clethra alnifolia, the sweetpepper bush, summer-sweet, or white alder, should have a far greater following in garden circles than it does. Hairy twigs and 4-inch leaves appear on 10-foot shrubs that bear their flowers in midsummer. Round grayish pods about an ¹/₈ inch long weep over the branches and persist well into winter. The peeling bark is also of interest. Provide good soil, somewhat moist, in light to partial shade. *Klethra* is the Greek name for the alder.

Cocculus carolinus, Carolina snailseed or coral-berry, actually gets a mention in *The Royal Horticultural Dictionary of Gardening* (Oxford: The Claredon Press, 1974) as a member of a small genus with about twelve species of deciduous evergreen climbers or shrubs. This prostrate or twining vine bears leaves in

the shape of an arrowhead, with the bottom lobes turned outward and yellow-green flowers borne in panicles, each with six petals and six sepals. The plant blooms through August, and the flowers are followed by very decorative fruits that are round red drupes the size of small peas, which last well into winter. Provide well-drained garden soil (they do well in sandy soils) in partial shade. Hardy from Zone 7 south. Be aware that snailseeds form thick, creeping roots and may strangle other vegetation. They are best grown on a fence or arbor. *Cocculus* comes from the Greek word *kokkos*, for "berry," referring to the fruit.

Cotoneaster spp., the cotoneasters, represent some fifty species of woody shrubs that have long been important in landscaping because of their good looks, their interesting blooms, and their often fascinating fruits.

There are many cultivars ranging from dwarfs to standard sizes. *Cotoneaster bullatus*, originally from western China, is a deciduous shrub growing about 10 feet tall. The glossy dark green leaves turn orange and

43

red in the fall. Rosy pink flowers blooming in late spring become blood red berries in the fall. *Cotoneaster lacteus*, the Parneyi cotoneaster, is a fountain of mahogany-colored branches up to 12 feet tall bearing large, medium green leaves up to 3 inches long. White flowers bloom in clusters and are followed by egg-shaped red berries.

Cotoneaster dammeri, the bearberry cotoneaster, is a prostrate, rooting evergreen shrub bearing 1-inch leaves that are a shiny dark green above and light green beneath. The small, white five-petaled flowers open in early June and are followed in the fall by bright red berries about 1/4 inch wide that last for months. 'Lowfast' is a good selection for warmer parts of the South, and 'Streib's Findling' is a dwarf with tiny, dense evergreen leaves. *Cotoneaster horizontalis*, the rockspray cotoneaster, grows about 3 feet in height, with a spread up to 8 feet. This is a great plant for the border or the edge of a wall or for carpeting a bank, and if you choose one plant for a condo garden, this might be it. The whitish pink flowers bloom in mid-April, followed by bright red berries in the fall. Buy cotoneasters as container-grown plants, then set them out in any good garden soil in sun to partial shade. They are hardy in Zones 6 to 8. *Cotoneaster* is from the Greek for "like a quince."

Crataegus phaenopyrum, the Washington thorn, is a beautiful tree in wintertime that reaches a height of 25 to 30 feet, with a 20-foot spread. It has been used as a staple in landscape design for years, and those years have not diminished its beauty. Reddish brown twigs with straight or slightly curved thorns about 2 inches long also bear simple leaves, about 3 inches long, of a deep glossy green, turning orange to scarlet in the fall. White flowers bloom in late spring, and in late summer they produce pendulous clusters of glossy bright red berries, about a 1/4 inch wide. Because they are quite weatherproof and very resilient, they persist through the winter. Provide full sun and a reasonably moist, good garden soil with medium drainage. *Crataegus* is from the Greek word meaning "strength," referring to the hard wood.

Danae racemosa, the Alexandrian laurel, is a one-species genus of evergreen shrubs from southwest Asia. The plant resembles an attractive dwarf bamboo. Its gracefully arching stems bear dark green, 3-inch long, bractlike "leaves" that are actually flattened stems known as cladophylls. The tiny white flowers appear in spring, blooming in terminal racemes that are not showy. But in the fall, orange-red berries appear, each about the size of a cherry, making this plant a true delight in the winter garden. Branches can be cut for winter bouquets, and Alice M. Coats remarks in *Garden Shrubs and their Histories* (New York: Simon and Schuster, 1992) that "this is [an] elegant and pliable evergreen, and quite suitable for wreaths." These laurels fill an important role as a delicate, graceful, and refined evergreen of small stature. Provide shade and a moist garden soil of high fertility, with plenty of added humus. Once established, they can withstand dry soil. The genus is named for Danaë, daughter of King Acrisius of Argos.

Dioscorea villosa, the wild yam, is a herbaceous perennial vine native to the eastern United States, found in rich deciduous woods and floodplains. The twining stems are up to 10 feet long and bear alternate or whorled leaves that may be 3 to 4 inches across. The flowers are inconspicuous, and males and females are found on separate plants. The dry seedpods on the female plants (you need both sexes to have fruits) are unique and very attractive in winter. They are dangling clusters of brown, papery pods with three divergent wings. Provide any rich soil in light shade where they may climb on other plants or structures. They are hardy throughout the area, the vines arising from a large underground tuber that may be the size of a tennis ball. The tubers of tropical wild yams are widely used as a staple starchy food, and some are the source of chemicals used in birth-control drugs. The genus name commemorates Dioscorides, the Greek naturalist and physician.

Diospyros virginiana, the persimmon, is mentioned in chapter 3 for the interesting effect of its winter bark. But the fruit, which persists on the trees until well into winter, is also quite interesting in the winter garden, not to mention its attractiveness for both wildlife and use in home cooking. The inconspicuous white, bell-shaped flowers appear in late spring, followed in the autumn by round orange-red berries, about an 1 1/2 inches in diameter. Although some books suggest that you must plant both male and female trees for fruit production, the persimmon is really polygamodioecious (male and female flowers appear on separate trees, along with a few bisexual blossoms), so it's a good idea to buy a named cultivar for fruit production. Fruits are edible when fully ripe or, on wild plants, after the frost comes. Provide full sun in good, well-drained garden soil with added organic matter. Because of a long taproot, the trees are difficult to transplant, so use containerized specimens.

Eriobotrya japonica, the loquat, is an evergreen shrub or small tree with great looks, especially when planted against a wall or other architectural background or grown in a pot. It can reach a height of 20 feet, with an average 10-foot spread. The thick, ruffled, oval leaves grow up to 10 inches long and are dark green above and rusty beneath. The fragrant white 1/2-inch flowers appear in 5- to 7-inch panicles, blooming in November. They are followed by edible, pear-shaped, orange-yellow fruits that ripen in the spring. Unfortunately, loquats are hardy only in Zones 8 and 9 and bear fruit only in Zones 9 and 10. Plant in sun or partial shade, providing reasonably fertile garden soil with good drainage. For Zone 9, try 'Champagne', a cultivar with excellent fruit quality. 'Coppertone' bears new copper-colored foliage, and 'Variegata' has white variegated leaves. *Eriobotrya* is Greek for "woolly cluster," referring to the hairy flower clusters.

Euonymus americanus is known as hearts-a-burstin' by gardeners with imagination and strawberry bush, wahoo, swamp dogwood, or spindle bush by all the rest. This is a beautiful native shrub growing between 5 and 10 feet tall, with a 5- to 7-foot spread. The crown is rounded and upright, with trailing

Crataegus aestivalis, winter-flowering hawthorn, is a small tree with a unique profusion of pure white flowers in late winter. It may have colorful fruits to accompany its 2-inch lobed leaves. The hawthorn should be grown in well-drained soil in full sun to light shade. Like its crabapple and firethorn relatives, it may be susceptible to several pests and diseases.

45

branches. The simple dark green leaves are about 3 inches long. In early summer, inconspicuous brownish green flowers open, drawing little attention. But in early autumn, the leaves turn red, then pendulous bright pink pods burst open to reveal brilliant orange-red seeds, which last until the first great frosts of winter. The green stems are also very attractive at that time. Grow in shade with soil of medium fertility and good drainage. The shrubs can be pruned to shape.

Fatsia japonica, the Japanese fatsia or Formosa rice tree, belongs to a one-species genus consisting of this Japanese native. This evergreen shrub or small tree is generally between 4 and 6 feet in height, with a 4- to 6-foot spread, although older specimens can be much bigger. The leathery, glossy, dark green leaves can reach a foot in diameter, consisting of seven to nine lobes. This plant is valuable where a bold texture is desired and is especially effective when grown in front of a wall or other architectural feature. Terminal spherical clusters of white flowers bloom in the fall, followed by very persistent dark blue winter fruits, berries about 1/4 inch in diameter. Although very tropical in appearance, the fatsia is hardy in Zones 7 to 9. Provide shade in a protected spot. Fatsia does well in any good moist garden soil, but add some humus and make sure there is good drainage. These plants are very tolerant of city conditions and salt spray. Fatsia comes from a Japanese vernacular name for the plant.

Feijoa sellowiana, the pineapple guava, is an evergreen shrub with a height of 15 to 18 feet and a 10-foot spread. The 2- to 3-inch gray-green leaves are silver beneath and cover a loose, sprawling habit. The four-petaled flowers, which bloom in May, are a little over an inch long and are red in the center and white at the margins, with crimson stamens. By fall they become 1- to 3-inch egg-shaped fruits that are green tinged with red; these soon turn to a pale yellow and are very attractive during mild winters. To ensure fruit production, plant several varieties close together for cross-pollination. The fruits make a great jelly. Native to Argentina and Paraguay, pineapple guavas are sensitive to cold and are reliably hardy only to 10°F. Provide full sun, good drainage, and a soil of medium fertility, with added humus. 'Coolidge' and 'Pineapple Gem' are self-fruiting selections; 'Variegata' has variegated leaves. The genus was named for Don da Silva Feijoa, a San Sebastian botanist.

Firmiana simplex, the Chinese parasol tree, Chinese bottle tree, Japanese varnish tree, or phoenix tree, can reach a height of 60 feet in nature but is about half as tall in American cultivation. The foot-long leaves (or even longer on young specimens) are very tropical in appearance, and terminal panicles of yellow flowers up to 20 inches long appear in June. For the winter garden, this tree is noted for its seedpods, which resemble miniature parasols. These are actually the tissue-paper-like outer skins of the fruit. During the fall, these pods are a cream color stained with pink and green tones; by late fall to early winter, they turn a warm cinnamon tan. The bright green bark is very attractive. Young plants grow straight and tall, as much as 6 feet in one year. Hardy in Zones 7 to 9, these trees need full sun, a soil of medium fertility, and good drainage. The genus was named in honor of Karl Joseph von Firmian (1716–82), a governor of Lombardy, in Northern Italy.

Halesia carolina (*H. tetraptera*), the Carolina silverbell, is usually a small tree—up to 40 feet high, with a 20-foot spread—when cultivated throughout most of the Southeast, but there are specimens in the Smoky Mountains that have reached a height of 100 feet. The 5-inch-long, simple leaves are light green, turning yellow in the fall. The white, pendulous, bell-shaped flowers bloom in mid-April, with two to five flowers in a cluster, each about a 1/2 inch long. In the fall, 2-inch fruits in the form of dry, winged pods appear, starting out a translucent yellow and turning brown with age. Younger trees show attractive striped bark, and in older specimens the bark grows in large, loose, gray to brown scales. The irregular open form of the tree is very effective in the winter landscape. The year-round appeal of the Carolina silverbell makes it a choice selection for any garden. A close relative, *H. diptera*, the coastal silverbell, equals or surpasses it in beauty. Provide light to medium shade and a good garden soil with excellent drainage. The genus is named in honor of Stephen Hales (1677–1761), an early botanical writer.

Hippophae rhamnoides, the common sea buckthorn, has long been a popular shrub or small tree for seaside plantings. It grows to a height of 30 feet, bearing willowlike leaves that are gray-green on top and silvery green beneath. Twigs are thorny and in spring bear small, inconspicuous yellow flowers that appear before the leaves. Quarter-inch-wide, bright orange fruits appear in late summer in great quantities and, because they are very acidic tasting, are not immediately eaten by the birds. Both sexes must be present to ensure pollination. These plants look especially good

(Right) *Fatsia japonica*, Japanese fatsia

against architectural features. Provide full sun to partial shade in reasonably good garden soil with good drainage. The genus name comes from the Greek *Hippophaës*, meaning a "prickly spurge."

Hydrangea quercifolia, the oakleaf hydrangea, is a magnificent native American shrub that should be found in every garden. Reaching a height between 4 and 6 feet, with a 4- to 5-foot spread, the shrub is spreading and irregular in form. Its oaklike leaves are dark green above and light green beneath, up to 10 inches in both length and width. The leaves turn orange and red in the fall, with all shades in between. The shrub has flat panicles, up to a foot across, of small white flowers that take on a purplish cast at maturity. The dried flowers and small pods persist into early winter and are not only beautiful on the shrubs, but marvelous in winter bouquets. In addition, the tannish brown bark exfoliates with age. Provide partial shade in good soil with plenty of added organic matter and good drainage. 'Harmony' has large white flower clusters; 'Snow Flake' bears large double flowers; and 'Snow Queen' forms dense, upright panicles packed with flowers.

A number of other hydrangeas are grown, many of which have persistent fruiting heads that dry well, such as *Hydrangea paniculata* 'Pee Gee'. Other familiar types are the "mophead hortensia" selections of the species *H. macrophylla*. These are usually not very attractive in winter. The "lacecap" types, however, can be interesting because they produce a more delicate head that dries well. These include *H. arborescens*, a hardy North American native, and the Japanese *H. serrata* and *H. aspera*.

Idesia polycarpa, the iigiri tree, represents a one-species genus of deciduous trees native to Japan and China. This tree grows in a pyramidal shape, eventually reaching 50 feet in height. The toothed leaves, about 6 inches long, resemble those of a catalpa tree and turn yellow in the fall. The fragrant yellow-green flowers bloom in large terminal panicles and eventually

Ilex verticillata 'Winter Red', Winterberry

Ilex decidua 'Warren's Red', possum haw

become grapelike clusters of brilliant orange-red berries that persist well into the winter. Only the female tree produces berries, so be sure to buy a sexed tree from a reliable source. Train young trees to one leader by pruning competing branches. Provide full sun in any good, well-drained garden soil. The genus was named in honor of Everhard Ysbrant Ides (c. 1720), a Dutch traveler in China.

Ilex spp., the hollies, are known not only for their glossy evergreen, spiny leaves, but also for the marvelous berries they produce. Many of these shrubs and trees are beloved for their colorful, and persistent, berries. Because of their general taste, the birds eat the berries only in late winter. Most hollies require separate male and female plants to cross-pollinate for berries. Very important: You *must* have the appropriate male for each named female cultivar, or they may not bloom at same time and you won't get berries. ('Burford' is the exception, fruiting without cross-polli-

nation.) Deciduous hollies include *I. verticillata* and *I. decidua*. *I. pedunculosa* is evergreen, with great leaves. Its berries, which are on long stalks, are very cold hardy and are not injured even at below-zero temperatures. There are other many wonderful cultivars of varying heights and colors.

Iris foetidissima is known to some as the Gladwyn iris, others as the stinking iris, and the more enlightened as the roast beef iris, because the leaves, when crushed, actually do smell like cooked meat. The flowers are not all that marvelous—rather small and of an undistinguished blue—but in winter, the large seedpods open to display brilliant, coral red seeds, like the rarest of coral jewelry. Plants grow about 18 inches tall by 2 feet wide. The rhizomes want a shady spot in moist, but not wet, soil, and once in place can be left alone.

Itea virginica, the Virginia sweetspire, is another little-known, but delightful, native shrub of the Southeast. The sweetspire will reach a height of about 5 or 6

Iris foetidissima, Gladwyn iris

feet if grown in the sun and up to 9 feet in the shade. The 2-inch leaves are elliptical and come to a sharp point. They are deep green above and paler beneath, in the fall turning various shades of reddish pink to scarlet to burgundy. The leaves persist on the branches until well into winter. Except in very warm areas, this shrub is semideciduous. Its arching branches, which may be a rich green or, in sunlight, burgundy, will add to winter appeal. Small white, fragrant flowers bloom in 6- to 8-inch racemes, opening from the base to the tip. Brown seed capsules replace the individual flowers. 'Henry's Garnet' has longer flower spikes, up to 8 inches, and its autumn leaves have even deeper colors. Plants will exhibit better fall color and produce more flowers when given at least a half day of full sun. With their long underground runners that may grow 2 to 3 feet a year in rich soils, sweetspires may be invasive. They adapt to most soils, even surviving moist soils that would hamper other shrubs. *Itea* comes from the Greek for "willow," which the sweetspire leaves somewhat resemble.

Kadsura japonica, the scarlet kadsura, is a twining vine that can reach a length of 12 feet, with an indeterminate spread. The evergreen leaves are a thick, glossy green and have red petioles. Sulfur yellow flowers appear in summer and are followed in the fall by clusters of 1-inch-wide scarlet fruits. Provide partial shade and good garden soil with plenty of moisture. *Kadsura* is the Japanese name for the plant.

Koelreuteria paniculata, the goldenrain tree or varnish tree, is native to China and Korea and has nat-

uralized in Japan. Tree height is between 20 and 30 feet, with a 20-foot spread. The dark green leaves are pinnately compound and about 14 inches long. The fragrant four-petaled yellow flowers bloom in June in pyramidal clusters up to 18 inches long. From midsummer to fall, clusters of 2-inch papery pods appear, at first pink, then a rusty brown, lasting through the winter. In addition, mature trees have attractive rough bark. 'Fastigiata' is columnar in growth with a 7-foot spread; 'September' blooms in August and September and bears pinkish bronze fruit capsules. These trees adapt to city conditions and may readily spread by seeds. Provide sun or partial shade in good garden soil; excellent drainage is necessary. The genus was named in honor of Joseph G. Koelreuter (1733–1806), a professor of natural history.

Ligustrum japonicum, the Japanese privet or waxleaf privet, hails from Japan and Korea. These evergreen shrubs have dark green, simple leaves up to 4 inches long. In May, the pungent white flowers bloom in panicles up to 6 inches long; these are followed in the fall by ¼-inch blue-black berries that remain well into the winter. 'Compactum' has dense leaves of dark waxy green; 'Pyramidale' is conical in form; 'Repandum' has narrow leaves with waxy edges; 'Variegatum' has leaves edged with white; 'Tricolor' has young leaves variegated with white and pink. The wild species is notorious for spreading by seeds and becoming an invasive nuisance; avoid it in favor of the cultivars. Provide sun or partial shade, in a lightly moist, good garden soil with medium drainage. These privets withstand salt spray and make effective subjects for topiary. They are hardy in Zones 7 to 9. *Ligustrum* is the classic Latin name for the privet.

Liquidambar styraciflua, the sweet gum tree, reaches a height between 60 and 100 feet, with a 50- to 75-foot spread. The habit is upright and semiconical. The star-shaped dark green leaves turn a brilliant scarlet and purple in the fall. The inconspicuous greenish yellow flowers bloom in the spring, followed by inch-wide, prickly round fruits that are often used to make Christmas decorations. 'Burgundy' turns a deep wine red, and 'Moraine' becomes a brilliant red in the fall. Because of the sharp, spiny fruits, many southeastern gardeners consider the sweet gum a great nuisance. Nevertheless, the trees are shapely, fast growing, and of exquisite fall color, and the twigs may have interesting corky wings. A new cultivar, 'Rotundiloba', has all the other characteristics of the species, but no sweet gum balls. Plant in full sun or partial shade in a good fertile garden soil with good drainage, and provide plenty of water. Trees are difficult to transplant when large. *Liquidambar* comes from the Latin for "liquid" and Arabic for "amber," in reference to the resin of Asiatic species.

Lonicera sempervirens, the trumpet honeysuckle, is a twining vine that can reach lengths up to 50 feet. Its thin, gray-green leaves are up to 3 inches long. In warm winters, the 2-inch-long red and gold, trumpet-shaped blossoms begin to open in mid-March, and then bloom on and off throughout the summer. Quarter-inch translucent red berries appear in the fall. Provide full sun to partial shade, in any good garden soil. These fast-growing vines can be kept in check with vigorous pruning. The genus was named in honor of Adam Lonicer (1528–86), a German botanist.

Lonicera alseuosmoides is an evergreen honey-suckle vine from China with shiny evergreen leaves and small, paired, yellowish flowers in early spring. In the fall, 1/4-inch purplish black berries with a whitish bloom appear on the stems, making this an exceptional vine for the winter garden. *Lonicera henryi* is a semi-evergreen vine whose leaves curl around the edges as temperatures drop, but it continues to bear dark blue berries that persist through the winter.

Malus spp., the flowering crab apples, can grow to 30 feet, depending on the species. These deciduous trees have oval leaves and in the spring are covered with usually fragrant white or pink flowers, followed by small red or yellow fruits that are liked by the birds. *Malus* 'Red Jade' is an attractive weeping form, about

Kadsura japonica 'Variegata'

Nandina domestica 'Alba', white-berried heavenly bamboo

15 feet tall and 10 to 15 feet wide. In spring it is covered with white flowers, which are followed by bright red fruits that persist long after the leaves have fallen. It was developed at the Brooklyn Botanic Garden and patented in 1956. 'Sugar Tyme', an 18-foot tree with a 15-foot spread, has spring blossoms that become 1/2-inch vibrant red fruits that last from late September until they drop in the spring. 'Zuni' has large white, fragrant flowers and bright red fruits that stay on the tree until December. Provide full sun and a good, moist, well-drained garden soil. *Malus* is the ancient Latin name of the apple.

The reputation and enjoyment of the colorful, shapely crab apples are marred by their susceptibility to diseases, notably apple scab, fire blight, mold, and mildew. These diseases are especially troublesome in the South and, along with their general need for a long, cold winter, keep crab apples from being characteristic of the southern landscape, joining lilacs as typical of the North. They require periodic pruning to remove the numerous water sprouts within the canopy that

reduce flowering and mar the shape. Nevertheless, they are still popular trees and may be especially useful in the small garden. 'Callaway' is considered by Michael Dirr to be the best crab apple for the South. It has white flowers, persistent red fruits, and is highly disease resistant. Another disease-resistant favorite is 'Donald Wyman', which also has white flowers, but smaller persistent bright red fruits.

Matelea carolinensis, the milkweed vine or angle-pod, is a wildflower of the Southeast belonging to the milkweed family, found in dry woods and roadside ditchbanks throughout the Southeast. The coarse, hairy vines twine over other vegetation, producing large, ovate, paired leaves. Clusters of greenish or dark brown to almost black, inconspicuous (but interesting) 1-inch flowers appear at upper leaf nodes. Under good conditions, the vines will produce numerous large seedpods, up to 6 inches long, of thick texture and tapered to a sharp point. These hang on until fall, when they dry out, split open in typical milkweed fashion, and release numerous silky-parachuted seeds.

Seedlings establish readily in disturbed soil. The pods dry well and are attractive all winter as the vines die but remain entwined on their supports. Hardy throughout our region, they grow extremely well and fast in almost any well-drained soil in full sun to light shade.

Myrica cerifera, the wax myrtle or bayberry, is a native American evergreen aromatic shrub or tree, common to the coastal plain from New Jersey south to Florida. The average height ranges from 10 to 12 feet (with occasional specimens up to 30 feet), with a 10-foot spread. The narrow, leathery, yellowish green leaves are dotted with orange glands beneath and are up to 4 inches long. The inconspicuous flowers bloom in spring and are located on short catkins that originate in the leaf axils. They are followed in the fall and winter by 1/8-inch grayish green, globular berries (really drupes) covered by a whitish resin. A delight in the winter garden is to brush against the leaves and smell the sweet, pungent aroma of bayberries. When the resin is melted from the berries, it can be used to make fragrant candles of a greenish wax. You will, how-ever, need at least 6 pints of berries to produce enough wax for one 8-inch candle. Myrtle Beach, South Carolina, got its name from this plant. Wax myrtle is hardy in Zones 7 to 9. The sexes are separate, and the berries are found only on female plants, so for pollination both male and female are needed in a ratio of at least four females to one male. Purchase plants in the fall when berries can be seen, to ensure that you get an attractive specimen. Provide sun or partial shade in any good garden soil with medium drainage but plenty of moisture. Older books recommend that mature plants be cut back to the ground every ten years. Though this shrub grows well along the coast, it will not tolerate salt spray. The genus was named for an ancient Greek shrub, possibly a tamarisk.

Nandina domestica, heavenly bamboo or nandina, is a member of the barberry family that when mature reaches a height of 5 to 6 feet, with a 2- to 3-foot spread. It's an upright shrub with many canes bearing evergreen, compound green leaflets, each about 1 1/2 inches long. The creamy white flowers appear in clus-

Nandina 'Atropurpurea' and 'Harbor Dwarf' (left)

ters on terminal growth blooming in summer. The ¼-inch berries appear in the fall, borne in large clusters at the branch tips, and persist throughout the winter. A full-berried plant is a beautiful sight, especially at Christmas, when the bright red fruits are viewed against the dark green foliage. These plants are a must for the winter garden. 'Alba' has white berries; 'Atropurpurea' has leaves that turn a reddish purple in winter; 'Fire Power' is a compact miniature with leaves that are tinged with red during the growing season and even brighter in the winter, but it has no berries; 'Gulf Stream' is a compact plant to 3 feet with striking reddish orange foliage in winter but no berries; 'Moyer's Red' can reach a height of 8 feet and has brilliant red leaves in winter; 'Royal Princess' is tall like the species but with a finer-textured foliage and brilliant red-orange berries; 'San Gabriel' bears delicate, lacy foliage but no berries; and 'Woods Dwarf', which has orange-scarlet leaves in winter, is excellent for the small garden, staying about 18 inches high. Though hardy only from Zone 7 up, farther north a well-mulched plant might lose its top but the roots will survive. Provide

(Right) *Nandina domestica* 'San Gabriel'

sun or partial shade in good garden soil with added humus and good drainage. Older plants can be rejuvenated by cutting back the canes every two or three years. The genus is from an old Japanese name.

Onoclea sensibilis, the sensitive fern, has a reputation for fast growth and is often termed a thug, but this tough fern, which lives through most summers without any problems, shrivels at the first touch of frost. Plants grow about 2½ feet tall and can carpet a damp, sunny spot with pale, sea green, wavy-edged fronds in no time flat. This plant's best feature is its fertile fronds, which look like feathers made of large brown sori that resemble beads strung on very straight stems. The rhizomes prefer a sunny to partially shaded moist to wet spot, with neutral to acidic, humus-rich soil. Because of their unique appearance, the fertile fronds have been used for centuries in all sorts of dried flower arrangements and Victorian shadow boxes. *Onoclea* comes from the Greek *onos*, "vessel," and

Nandina domestica 'Gulfstream'

Opuntia phaeacantha, prickly pear

kleio, "to close," referring to the closely rolled fertile fronds.

Opuntia spp. the prickly pear cactuses, are represented by a number of species, chiefly *O. humifusa* and *O. polyacantha*. In colder parts of the Southeast, their fleshy joints begin to dehydrate in colder weather, and they are not particularly attractive. But where temperatures are higher, they hold moisture throughout the winter and provide touch of green, and the larger plants generate a great deal of architectural interest as well. The plants flower with lovely yellow to peach-colored blossoms in early summer. These cactuses are very attractive when growing surrounded by rocks or gravel. The red, ovoid fruits remain colorful until very cold temperatures freeze them. They have a red juice and are often eaten, some cultivars having a sweet, beetlike flavor. Provide very well-drained soil in full sun. The genus is named for a Greek town where cactuslike plants once grew.

Oxydendrum arboreum, the sourwood, is a small deciduous tree reaching a height of some 30 feet, with a 15-foot spread. Sourwoods are found growing wild only in the midsouthern states and have no close relatives anywhere else in the world. These trees are fast becoming popular and adaptable street trees for cities. This is a beautiful all-season tree. It has an erect habit, with a graceful trunk and slender upright branches. The 5- to 7-inch simple, toothed leaves are a shiny green, turning a unique and pleasing red in the fall. In early summer, terminal clusters of one-sided racemes

produce white, bell-shaped flowers that resemble lily of the valley. The nectar is the basis for mild-tasting sourwood honey, made only in the southern Appalachian mountains. The flowers are followed by brownish gray seedpods that persist on the branches until well into winter, giving the tree a lacy silhouette. The bark is a reddish gray and is creased with furrows as the tree ages. Provide sun or partial shade in a moist, well-drained garden soil. Sourwoods can be grown readily from seed or easily transplanted when young, but for larger specimens, buy a containerized plant. *Oxydendrum* comes from the Greek for "sour tree," referring to the taste of the leaves.

Prunus caroliniana, the Carolina cherry laurel, is a small evergreen tree that reaches a height of 20 to 30 feet, with a 20-foot spread. This tree was originally native only to a narrow strip of land along the coast, but birds scattered the seeds, and it's now quite common in the Carolinas. Its 2- to 4-inch oblong leaves are a glossy dark green. In March and April, fragrant white flowers bloom in short, dense racemes, followed by black oblong fruits about 1/2 inch long that persist through the winter, although they are very popular with birds. This is a beautiful, year-round ornamental tree. It is related to the European cherry laurel, *P. laurocerasus*, a species with many evergreen cultivars used in foundation plantings, but that rarely produces flowers and fruits. Provide full sun or partial shade in moist, well-drained garden soil with added humus. The wilting leaves of the cherry laurel produce hydrocyanic acid, a deadly poison. *Prunus* is the classic name of the plum.

Pyracantha coccinea, the scarlet firethorn, is an evergreen thorny shrub that reaches 6 feet in height, with a 6-foot spread. It bears bronzy green leaves 1 1/2 inches long. In early May, 1/3-inch white flowers bloom in clusters, followed by 1/4-inch reddish orange berries that persist well into winter. There are dozens of cultivars. 'Aurea' has yellow fruit; 'Mohave' bears large masses of orange-red berries. *Pyracantha koidzumii* 'Low-Dense', the low-dense pyracantha, grows to 6 feet high, with a 6-foot spread. It has dark green foliage, the new leaves being light green. Quarter-inch white flowers bloom in May, followed by bunches of 1/4-inch orange-red berries. It is not hardy in Zone 6 or below. For both shrubs, provide full sun and well-drained moist garden soil with added humus. Note that pyracanthas are susceptible to many problems, including aphids, scale, and scab. In early summer, watch out for

(Right) *Pyracantha coccinea* 'Navajo', a dwarf

Rosa sericea pteracantha, red thorn rose

lacewing bugs on the leaves. With proper treatment and careful cultivar selection, resistant plants are well worth adding to your garden. *Pyracantha* comes from the Greek for "fire" and "thorn."

Pyrus calleryana, the Callery pear, is a small tree that reaches 30 or 40 feet in height, with a 30-foot spread and an upright, conical form. The simple, 3-inch leaves are a glossy green, turning red in the fall. One-inch white flowers bloom in early April, followed by 1/2-inch orange-brown fruits in the fall. There are many cultivars, including the very popular 'Bradford' pear, selected in the late 1940s by John Creech, former director of the National Arboretum. Because of its cold-tolerant blossoms, this tree has been overused by municipalities and developers. Older trees are especially prone to ice and wind damage. We strongly rec-

ommend choosing a more sturdy selection, such as 'Capitol' or 'Aristocrat'. Provide sun or light shade in good, moist, well-drained garden soil. The genus is named for J. M. M. Callery and was originally introduced from Japan.

Rhus typhina, the staghorn sumac, is termed a trash tree or shrub by highway departments yet wins awards in England at the Royal Horticultural Society. William Robinson, the man mainly responsible for changing the look of the English border and pioneering the concept of the wild garden, advised using the sumac for its summertime tropical look, its brilliant orange and scarlet autumn color, and its dark crimson fruits that persist throughout the winter. The leaves are large and bear eleven to thirty-one leaflets. The late-spring flowers are small and yellowish green, borne in dense panicles. The fruits are red globose berries covered with red hairs and are borne in large panicles at the ends of the branches. The young branches bear many fine hairs and look like a stag's antlers in velvet. Provide full sun in good garden soil. Sumacs may be pruned to shape. This species is native to northeastern North America. *Rhus* is the ancient Greek name for the genus.

Rosa spp., the roses, are valuable to the winter garden, not only for their tangled form, but mainly for their brightly colored fruits called hips. *Rosa moyesii* has attractive but simple wine-red flowers on 10-foot shrubs. Come the fall, equally bright orange-red hips, shaped like 2-inch flagons, appear and persist into the winter. *Rosa multiflora*, the Japanese rose, though termed a weed by many (especially because some nurseries oversold the bushes as living fences during the 1970s), still has great winter beauty, especially when the arching branches, often reaching 10 feet, tumble about like a brown fountain, all displaying

thousands of 1/4-inch red hips. *Rosa sericea pteracantha* is a sight for winter-worn eyes when this 8-foot shrub is covered with bright red, pear-shaped hips and the beautiful but flattened, translucent crimson thorns shine in the warming winter sun. The trailing stems of *Rosa wichuraiana* bear evergreen foliage in Zones 8 and 9, fading out as the weather gets colder in Zones 6 and 7, but the tiny red hips remain. Provide full sun and a good, moist, well-drained garden soil. *Rosa* is the old Latin name for the rose.

Ruscus aculeatus and *R. hypoglossum*, the butcher's-brooms, are Mediterranean evergreen shrubs with dark green stems covered with sharp-tipped flattened branches called cladophylls. Cladophylls look like leaves but are really modified branches that actually bear tiny greenish flowers in late winter. If pollinated, the flowers produce 1/4-inch orange-red berries that persist all winter. These odd plants add an unusual texture to the winter garden and are quite happy in shade in dry, well-drained soil. They are also adaptable

Ruscus aculeatus, butcher's broom

to sunny sites. Each plant forms a slowly enlarging clump, but these plants may also seed around the garden. The clumps produce sturdy roots that are nearly impossible to extract intact, making division of the plant difficult and risky. Divisions and seedlings are slow to become established, but are long-lived. *Ruscus aculeatus* is the more well known, having short, stiff, very sharp, ovate cladophylls to 1 inch long. Florists sometimes spray the dried stems of *R. aculeatus*, sharp as they may be, in various colors for use in flower arrangements. *Ruscus hypoglossum* has cladophylls to 3 inches long, curving and pliable, and not as sharp. Both species are hardy to at least 0°F in protected sites.

Sarcandra glabra, the sarcandra, is a member of the Chloranthaceae family, from Southeast Asia and very new in America. It is almost unknown in cultivation, and there is little to be found in the literature (see Plant Sources). Woodlanders Nursery, in Aiken, South Carolina, grows these plants in well-drained, sandy soil, where they have proved hardy to about 10°F. They

form low, irregular, evergreen shrubs less than 2 feet high, with 4-inch glossy leaves. Summer flowers are very inconspicuous, but they readily produce clusters of small, bright orange fruits that persist all winter and are very attractive against the foliage. This is a choice plant, unfortunately limited by its hardiness.

Skimmia japonica, the Japanese skimmia, is an evergreen shrub originally from the Himalayas, Japan, and China. It reaches a height of about 5 feet, with a 2- to 3-foot spread, exhibiting a rounded moundlike form. Its elliptical dark green leaves are between 3 and 5 inches long. In April, small, fragrant white flowers bloom in large terminal panicles, with the female flowers on separate plants, the male flowers being larger and more fragrant. By the fall, 1/3-inch scarlet berries appear in large clusters. 'Formanii' has larger clusters of fruit; 'Rubella' is a male clone with red flower buds that persist through the winter, blooming in the spring. *Skimmia reevesiana*, the Reeves skimmia, is a compact bush about 2 feet high, with a 3-foot spread and 1/2-inch red berries.

Sarcandra glabra

Skimmia japonica, female berries

Skimmia japonica, male flowers

Skimmias are hardy only in Zones 7 and 8. Provide partial shade and a good, moist but well-drained garden soil with added humus. *Skimmia* comes from the Japanese word *skimmi*, "harmful fruit," because the fruit is thought to be poisonous.

Stranvaesia davidiana, the Chinese stranvaesia, is an evergreen shrub or small tree from western China. The medium green, lustrous 2- to 4-inch oval leaves are tinted with red in spring and pick up ruddy tints again in the fall. Small white flowers appear in spring, blooming in 4-inch-wide clusters. By autumn, large clusters of red fruits appear on the branches and remain throughout winter. The variety *undulata* has leaves with wavy margins; 'Flava' has yellow berries; 'Painter's Palette' presents its red fruits surrounded by leaves splashed with green, pink, and white. Provide partial shade in good, well-drained garden soil with added humus. The genus is named for William Thomas Horner Fox Strangways (1795–1865), earl of Ilchester and English botanist.

Symphoricarpos spp. are little-known native American shrubs of great interest for the winter garden. *Symphoricarpos albus*, the snowberry or waxberry, is found in the Midwest, where Jefferson talked of its beauty, remarking that the large fruits were "as white as snow which remain through the winter . . . making it a singular and beautiful object." The shrub reaches a height of 3 feet and has elliptical leaves about 3 inches long. Pink flowers bloom in spring and form the white fruits from summer to early autumn. *Symphoricarpos orbiculatus*, the coralberry, is a southeastern native sent back to England in 1730. It is an erect shrub from 2 to 5 feet high with purplish brown stems. The oval leaves are a dull gray-green and a little over an inch long. The very small, inconspicuous five-lobed yellow flowers of spring develop into purplish red coral-like berries that appear in the fall and remain on the branches well into the winter. Larry has noted a little-observed feature, that the long stolons produced under good growing conditions reach out up to 6 feet from the base of the plant, allowing it to eventually form dense colonies. 'Leucocarpus' has white fruits; 'Variegatus' has yellow areas on the leaves. Provide partial shade in a good, well-drained but moist garden soil. When established, these plants are very tolerant of dry shade. The genus name comes from the Latin *symphoreo*, "to bear together," and *karpos*, "fruit," referring to the berries' being clustered.

Viburnum dilatatum, the linden viburnum, reaches a height of 7 to 9 feet, with an 8-foot spread. The 4-inch-wide rounded leaves have hairs on both sides and are a medium green, turning a russet red in the fall.

White flowers bloom in May and are followed by clusters of scarlet red fruits, often so heavy they bend the branches. *Viburnum trilobum*, the cranberry bush, is a deciduous shrub that can reach a height of 12 feet. Elizabeth Lawrence quoted A. M. Leonard, of American nursery fame, as writing back in 1935: "Its translucent, orange-red fruits borne in flat, terminal clusters are not eaten by birds. They remain until spring, a beautiful sight when snow is on the ground." 'Compactum' is dense and compact, staying about 4 feet high; 'Wentworth' has leaves tinted with red in the spring and very large clusters of berries. Provide full sun or partial shade in a good, moist but well-drained garden soil. *Viburnum* is the classic Latin name for the genus.

The Ornamental Grasses

Ornamental grasses had a great surge of popularity during the Victorian era. At that time, these tough, but beautiful, perennials were used in fairly liberal interpretations of wild gardens, while their flamboyant seed heads enjoyed a great vogue as highlights in winter bouquets. Then, as a class, the grasses fell into a long period of disuse, finally to be resurrected in the 1970s. Twenty years ago there were probably just five species available, and then only at specialty nurseries. Today there are hundreds of species and cultivars available.

The grasses listed here not only are desirable in the summer and autumn garden, but they assume an entirely different kind of mantle during the winter. For then their green blades turn various shades of browns, buffs, and yellows, highlighted with occasional reds and oranges, and their billowing seed heads wave in the winter winds.

Andropogon glomeratus, the bushy bluestem, is a grass that likes to grow near water. A native of the eastern and southern United States, this is a clumping deciduous grass with shiny green leaves about a 1/2 inch wide and up to 18 inches long. The cottony flowers emerge in early September and rise from 2 to 3 feet above the foliage. In fall, the flower spikes turn orange and the leaves become a reddish purple. *Andropogon ternarius*, the red broomsedge, grows all the way from Florida to Texas. In the 1930s, it was planted for erosion control. This grass is not planted for the leaves but for its fluffy flower spikes, sometimes reaching 4 or 5 feet tall. Plant in full sun in a good, well-drained garden soil. *Andropogon virginicus*, or just plain broomsedge, is widely distributed in the eastern United States and is grown for both the bronze fall leaf color, which persists well into winter, and the beautiful

Oat grass (*Arrhenatherum bulbosum*), thyme, and geranium. The ornamental oat grass is very unusual in that it grows from underground tubers, likes some shade, and goes dormant in hot weather. The thyme is evergreen, helping to mark the spot for the dormant grass. There are many fine-leaved geraniums with various colors and textures.

seed heads up to 3 feet tall. It is especially attractive when grown in clumps. Plant in full sun in moist garden soil. *Andropogon* comes from the Greek *aner*, "man," and *pogon*, "beard," referring to the flowers.

Calamagrostis acutiflora, the feather reed grass, is a cool-season grass that is evergreen in warm climates, where the leaves reach up to 2 feet in height. In summer, tall 3- to 4-foot flower spikes emerge, and in a soft breeze this grass sounds like rustling skirts. In the fall, the leaves turn yellowish orange, and the spikes dry to a golden color, persisting well into the winter. *Calamagrostis arundinacea* var. *brachytricha*, Korean feather reed grass, is a warm-season grass with 2-foot

leaves that turn bright yellow with the coming of fall. This grass is also blessed with lovely flower spikes that look like embroidered lace on stiff stems. They begin as green touched with pink, and turn a light tan as the frosts arrive. Provide full sun in a good, moist garden soil. The genus is from an ancient Greek name for a type of reed.

Chasmanthium (Uniola) latifolium, the wild oats or sea oats, is another native American grass that should be familiar to those who love to walk the beaches of the East coast. This clumping, deciduous grass has long been prized by flower arrangers for the beautiful drooping stems that hold dozens of flat,

1-inch-wide flower spikes that look like stylized oats. The flowers begin as green, then age to copper, and when winter comes, turn a lovely shade of grayish tan. This grass seeds about but is never invasive, and gardener friends will gladly take your extra seedlings. Sea oats look especially grand when planted by the waterside. Provide partial shade and a good, moist garden soil with added humus. *Chasmanthium* comes from the Latin *chasma*, "gaping," and *anthe*, "flower," alluding to the open spaces in the flower spikes.

Cortaderia selloana, the pampas grass, has become a cliché in many gardens, especially at the front entrances to southern motels. But this in no way should detract from the beauty of the plumes, especially when massed and not left to one or two specimens stuck next to brick or concrete pillars. The 5-foot leaves arch and wave in the slightest breeze, and the great white plumes often rise up to 12 feet above the ground. 'Carminea Rendatleri' is the pink pampas grass, with 6-foot plants and pink plumes rising above the foliage; 'Pumila' is a new dwarf cultivar with a grassy clump only 3 feet tall and 6-foot plumes. Pampas grasses prefer full sun in a good garden soil with plenty of moisture. The genus is the Argentine name for this grass.

Deschampsia caespitosa, the tufted hair grass, is a cool-season plant that forms dense tufts of graceful, thin, dark green foliage, usually reaching a height of 3 feet. But the icing on the cake is the inflorescence: loose, airy panicles of flowers that grow so close together they often obscure the leaves. In Zones 8 and 9, these grasses are usually evergreen, but in colder areas, the leaves turn shades ranging from bright yellow to burnished gold, with all sorts of bronzy tints and highlights. Provide light shade and a good, moist garden soil with added humus. Because they resent hot and dry situations, siting is very important in most southern gardens. The genus is named in honor of Dr. Deschamps of St. Omer, a French naturalist.

Erianthus ravennae, the Ravenna grass, comes from southern Europe, where it often grows along the edges of streams or ponds. The dense gray-green foliage rises about 5 feet above the ground, and in the late summer, flower spikes like tan feathers rise 10 to 12 feet into the air. In the fall, the leaves turn various shades of brown, with tints of orange and purple. Both blossoms and leaves persist well into the winter. As with many of the larger ornamental grasses, you should be absolutely sure about placement before planting out. For the first two years, Ravenna grass will look as if it's been overstated by the garden writers, then growth really kicks in, and by the third summer you will have a major landscape statement on your hands. Provide full sun and a good, well-drained garden soil. *Erianthus* comes from the Greek *erion*, "wool," and *anthos*, "flower," referring to the blooms.

Miscanthus spp., the eulalia grasses, are represented by three species and a number of cultivars. *Miscanthus giganteus* (*M. floridulus*), the giant Chinese silver grass, is the largest species, producing arching clumps of medium green leaves a little over an inch wide and up to 3 feet tall. In September, foot-high flowers appear on top of 10- to 14-foot canes that closely resemble bamboo. They begin as a reddish tan but soon turn to fluffy silver feathers. With the coming of frost, the foliage turns brownish with purple tints, and the leaves begin to fall from the canes, lying at odd angles on the ground. But the canes persist through the winter, often looking like an oriental sculpture. They also make great garden p-sticks, an English invention used to support weak-stemmed plants. Place the canes in an upright position in the garden, usually early in the season. Plants will grow up through them and eventually cover them with foilage. *Miscanthus sacchariflorus*, the silver banner grass, is a creeping grass rather than a clumper, so it can sometimes become a threat to the well-ordered garden. The 4- to 7-foot olive green leaves each bear a clearly marked white midrib, especially prominent on the underside. The flowers are silky panicles on top of 7-foot stems, beginning the season as light green but turning silvery white with age. The golden brown of the leaves in fall is most attractive, and the leaves and flowers persist well into the winter. 'Robustus' is a cultivar that reaches 8 feet with ease. Because this grass moves across the landscape, contain the plants by surrounding the rhizomes with a barrier. Or if you have clay soil, dig a big hole, fill it with good sandy soil, and plant the grass within. Both of these grasses do beautifully by the water's edge. Provide full sun and a good, moist, fertile soil. Without adequate moisture these grasses might not flower. *Miscanthus* comes from the Greek *miskos*, "stem," and *anthos*, "flower," referring to the stalked spikelets.

Miscanthus sinensis, the Japanese silver grass, has been cultivated in Japan and China for centuries. These are the plains grasses you see in Japanese art films. The species is getting harder to find in nurseries,

(Right) *Miscanthus* in winter

as the number of cultivars continues to increase. In the garden, its medium green, arching blades reach a height of 5 to 8 feet. The inflorescence is a terminal plume, touched with metallic tints of purple before opening, then turning white touched with tans and yellows at maturity. Depending on the climate and the summer, the leaves vary from tan and brown to reddish orange and a mellow yellow.

As to the cultivars, 'Cabaret' has 6-foot-high, inch-wide, ribbonlike foliage striped with various bands of creamy white, and pinkish flower stems. 'Gracillimus', the maiden grass, has been in the trade since 1878 and is probably still the best in the clan. The narrow, silvery green leaves have pronounced midribs and form beautiful, stylized clumps of foliage about 6 feet tall that wave in the wind. The copper-colored flowers appear in late September, rising about 2 feet above the leaves. Fall color varies from orange to burnished tan to faded green, depending on the garden's location. 'Morning Light' has very narrow leaves with a narrow band of white on the leaf margins, giving the effect of shimmering light. The leaves reach a height of 4 to 5 feet, and turn a light tan. The flowers are up to 6 feet tall, opening a reddish bronze, then aging to a light tan. 'Purpurascens' forms 3- and 4-foot clumps, with flowers on 5- and 6-foot stems. The medium green leaves have tints of red, but in the fall, the entire clump becomes a mass brilliant orange-red. This particular cultivar does best in Zones 7 and 8. 'Variegatus' is still one of the best cultivars, its white-striped, arching leaves forming graceful clumps of foliage that are marvelous in the summer garden. The leaves turn to tints of light buff and brown in the fall, while the flowers are tan. 'Zebrinus' has 3/4-inch-wide leaves brushed with creamy white bands of color that develop as the temperatures warm in late spring. The clumps are usually about 6 feet tall and turn a light brown with frost. The flowers are a pinkish copper when they first open, becoming fluffy tan as they mature.

Panicum virgatum, the switch grass, is a native American clump-forming grass from the prairies and open woods. The 4- to 7-foot stems bear deep green to gray-green leaves that turn various shades of yellow in the fall, becoming beige in the winter. The flowers form airy panicles that hover about 2 feet above the foliage. From a distance, they look like patches of silvery mist. 'Heavy Metal' has stiff, metallic blue leaves to about 3 feet tall that turn yellow in the fall; flowers bloom on 4- to 5-foot stems. Both flowers and leaves persist well into the winter and can be picked for winter bouquets.

Provide full sun with a moist, fertile soil. This grass will withstand some salt spray. Because the rhizomes tolerate water, this is another great grass for planting by the waterside. *Panicum* is an old Latin name for one of the millet grasses.

Pennisetum spp., the fountain grasses, have an apt common name, as the plants do look like controlled spouts of water. The species in general garden use is *P. alopecuroides* (*P. japonicum*). Originally from East Asia and Australia, this is a well-behaved, clumping grass, with 2- to 3-foot mounds of gracefully arching leaves, about 1/2 inch wide and up to 30 inches long. With the coming of frost, the foliage turns an almond-brown, then continues to fade to a straw color as winter advances. Showy flowers resembling stiff foxtails bloom in midsummer, measuring 1 to 3 inches wide and 4 to 10 inches long. They open creamy white but age to reddish brown. In areas of high winter winds, the seed heads break apart, and by winter's end all that's left are the flower stems, looking like straight jets of frozen water spouting from the mounded fountain below. In warmer areas, plumes persist until spring. Fountain grasses are beautiful as specimens or planted out in odd-numbered groups.

'Hameln' is identical to the species, only it's about 2 feet tall and likes moisture; 'Japonicum' is the largest of the fountain grasses, producing a mound of foliage between 4 and 5 feet high; and 'Little Bunny' is the smallest fountain grass, looking exactly like the others but only growing a foot high. None of these grasses do well south of Zone 8. 'Moudry', the black-blooming fountain grass, was originally touted as being from New Zealand but turns out to be an American introduction from Cincinnati. This is a magnificent late bloomer that bears almost black flowers, but it has a tendency to shatter in bad weather and seed about. It's hardy in Zones 7 to 9. For all these grasses, provide full sun and a good, moist, well-drained garden soil.

Pennisetum orientale, the oriental fountain grass, is smaller then *P. alopecuroides* and bears showy pink plumes instead of white. The foliage fades to a yellowish brown in the fall, then becomes straw-colored for the winter. This grass is hardy in Zones 7 to 9. Provide full sun or partial shade and well-drained garden soil. *Pennisetum setaceum* (*P. ruppelii*), succeeds only in Zones 8 to 10. The purplish pink, very showy flowers and the leaves fade to a soft straw color before producing new leaves in late winter. 'Rubrum' (*P. setaceum* 'Cupreum') is a beauty with its burgundy leaves and reddish purple plumes, but it is successful only in

Zones 9 and 10, although it can be grown as a pot plant in colder areas. *Pennisetum* comes from the Latin *penna*, "feather," and *seta*, "bristle," referring to the long, feathery bristles of the inflorescence.

Schizachyrium scoparium, the little bluestem grass, has long been a favorite of grass aficionados. Also known as prairie beard grass and broom sedge, this is one of the most prevalent wild grasses in the eastern United States. It's found growing on prairies, in open woods, on the sides of dry hills, and in many areas where it was planted as an erosion control. Little bluestem is a deciduous, clumping, warm-season grass that grows between 2 and 5 feet tall, averaging at 3 feet. The 1/2-inch-wide, light green leaves darken with age. Beginning in July and on through September, these grasses send up lovely fluffy flower spikes. When frosts come, the leaves turn colors ranging from flaming orange to a burnished bronze. The tints are highlighted by the silky spikes of the ripening seed heads. Little bluestem holds its color well into the winter and looks its best when planted in masses. Provide full sun in good, well-drained garden soil. *Schizachyrium* comes from the Greek *schizo*, "to cut," and *achyron*, "husk," referring to the seed heads.

Spartina pectinata, the prairie cord grass, is yet another American native that is just as beautiful in the winter as it is in the summer. The glossy green leaves can reach a length of 6 feet and look like hair from a giant's head. In the fall, the leaves turn a brilliant golden yellow, persisting through the winter months. 'Aureomarginata' has leaves with a golden edge and is the type usually sold by nurseries. Provide full sun and a good, moist garden soil. This grass is a spreader, not a clumper, so a barrier of some sort is usually called for. The genus name comes from the Greek word *spartine*, a rope or cord.

Stipa tenuissima, the Mexican feather grass, is fairly new to the garden scene. Our original plants came from the seed exchange for the Scottish Rock Garden Society. This is a spectacular grass, and southerners are blessed to have the climate to support it. The needle-thin leaves grow in dense clumps about 18 inches high and wide. The flowers appear in early summer and bloom like green silk, becoming golden as they age. This grass becomes a lovely shade of tan in the winter, and the leaves persist until spring, when you should cut them off with a scissors in preparation for the new growth. Feather grass reseeds with ease but is easily removed if you have too many plants. Provide full sun or partial shade and well-drained garden soil. *Stipa* comes from the Latin *stupa*, "rope," and refers to the flowers.

5
FLOWERS FOR THE WINTER GARDEN

See, Mary, what beauties I bring
    from the shelter of that sunny shed,
Where flowers have the charms of spring,
    Though abroad they are frozen and dead.
While earth wears a mantle of snow,
    These pinks are as fresh and as gay
As the fairest and sweetest that blow
    On the beautiful bosom of May.
    —William Cowper, *A Winter Bouquet*

HE SOUTHEAST HAD A SNOW IN JANUARY 1996. THE Northeast did, too. For northerners, snow is a normal winter occurrence, but for southerners it's unusual. And especially so when it adds up to inches of snow in Raleigh and Charlotte and a couple of feet in Asheville, not to mention frost warnings in Florida.

But on the bright, sunny morning of January 17, I put on my rubber-soled shoes and went for a walk in the winter garden. The lake below our house was still frozen, but the ice had that look that ice cubes get when their clear outer layers melt and the air-fizzed centers begin to show. There were little piles of snow throughout the rhododendron thickets and at the sheltered edges of the walls, but the mosses were clear and shining green. In the rock garden, a few heaths (*Erica carnea* 'Springwood White') were in bloom, and underneath the wall, a leaf-denuded winter daphne (*Daphne odora* 'Variegata') still boasted dozens of tight-fisted buds that would surely bloom in a few weeks. Then, in the front of the garden, the branches of the winter-blooming honeysuckle (*Lonicera fragrantissima*) were lined with leaf buds that closely resembled thumbless boxing gloves and were full of fragrant white flowers ready to bloom at month's end. And in John Cram's garden next door, the snow melted to reveal the nodding waxy white blossoms of the Christmas rose (*Helleborus niger*). Spring may have been far away, but the rewards were already there to be enjoyed.

Winter-Flowering Bulbs

Louise Beebe Wilder, a very popular garden writer of the 1930s and 1940s, wrote in her delightful book, *Adventures with Hardy Bulbs* (New York: The Macmillan Company, 1936), the words to an old triplet:

Clean and round,
Heavy and sound,
In every bulb a flower.

And that's how it is with bulbs—at least for the first year. The problem for the gardener is allowing the foliage to ripen and still living with ratty greenish brown leaves as they slowly die but, at the same time, nourish the bulb for the production of the next year's flowers. Hundreds of pages could be written about bulbs (Mrs. Wilder's book came to 363), so all we can do is hit the highlights with our favorite bulbs that bloom in the Southeast before April Fool's Day.

Anemone spp., the anemones or windflowers, belong to the buttercup family (Ranunculaceae). They are not really bulbs, but shriveled and blackened tubers usually put in the bulb section by catalogers. *Anemone blanda*, the Grecian windflower, blooms early in the season with daisylike flowers and is quite beautiful when naturalized under trees or on a grassy hillside. Flowers come in shades of blue, pink, and white, or mixed colors. They are usually inexpensive, so don't stint when planting them about. These plants need excellent drainage to succeed. Ev Whittemore reports that *A.*

Anemone blanda

blanda blooms in her garden near Brevard, North Carolina, in early February. *Anemone pulsatilla* (*Pulsatilla vulgaris*), the pasque flower, has soft, silvery-haired stems and bears 2½-inch-wide flowers of great beauty. It has bloomed in our Asheville rock garden in early March, with its cup-shaped, violet-purple flowers opening flat to over 2 inches in width. The leaves are finely cut and fernlike, usually developing after the flowers have gone to seed. Even then they are of interest, as they form silvery plumes that wave in the early-spring winds. These plants must have perfect drainage and do best in a limy soil with plenty of grit. There are many cultivars, including 'White Swan', 'Barton's Pink', and a deep red called 'Red Cloak'. *Anemone* is derived from the Syrian word *Nana'an*, a cry of lament for Adonis when the blood-stained earth became scarlet wildflowers after his side was pierced by a wild boar.

Bulbocodium vernum, the spring meadow saffron, is one of two members of the genus. Both are crocus-like perennial cormous herbs originally found growing from the Alps to the Caucasus. They flower shortly after the snowdrops and are often mistaken for an off-pink crocus. There are usually two flowers to a corm, and the leaves appear after the flowers fade. They are far more expensive than windflowers, but still deserve to be spread about as much as the pocketbook allows. They do well in the rock garden.

Chionodoxa spp. were originally named glory-of-the-snow by the French botanist Pierre Edmond Boissier (1810–85), who one spring came upon thousands of *C. sardensis* sporting sky blue flowers with a background of melting snow near the summit of Boz Dagh in Turkey. The bulbs are small and pear shaped, not too expensive, and bear six-petaled, starlike flowers, the petals joined at the base. The largest flowers, of a rich gentian blue, are found on *C. gigantea*, appearing on 8-inch stems. The best-known species is *C. luciliae*, which has bright blue flowers with a white center on 6-inch stems. There is a white form called 'Alba' and a beautiful pink cultivar known as 'Pink Giant', having eight to ten rose pink flowers on every stem.

Colchicum spp. are popularly known as the autumn-flowering crocuses, and most of them do so. *C. luteum* blooms in late winter and early spring, however, and is one of the last species to bloom. Hailing from 6,000 feet up in the Himalayas and northern India, it does its best in well-drained soil. The narrow-petaled flowers are bright yellow and, when naturalized, open like a sprinkling of snowy stars. The 5-inch-long leaves appear in spring after the flowers have faded. English books suggest hiding the ripening foliage under a carpet of winter-flowering heathers.

Crocus spp., the crocuses, are bulbous plants—technically termed corms—and are members of the iris family, a fact not readily apparent until you look at the structure of the flowers.

According to Greek legend, these flowers were named after a beautiful youth of the Grecian plains, known far and wide as Crocus. As so often happens, the lad was smitten with a shepherdess of the hills called Smilax (the differences between the mountain folks and those who live down below began long, long ago). Smilax did not return his love, but she did bestow her name on the genus *Smilax*, a large group of mostly vining plants in the lily family, many with thorny stems. As for Crocus, he pined away and died, so, the story goes, the gods changed him into the flower that bears his name.

The ancients often used this flower to adorn their marriage beds because, according to the Greek poet Homer, the crocus was one of the flowers used to decorate the couch of Zeus and Hera. At the time of Nero, crocuses were considered to be a great cordial, a tonic for the heart, and a potent love potion. Those Romans with more money than tact would strew the blossoms throughout their banquet halls, and the flowers also tumbled on the waters of fountains and the small streams that rippled through the gardens. But caution was advised, because they closely resembled colchicums, which were full of the deadly poison colchicum. Then, for gourmet dining, there was the saffron crocus (*C. sativus*), a flower that, along with flax and wheat, is one of the oldest cultivated plants.

Some biblical scholars believe it is the Karkom mentioned in the *Song of Solomon*.

There are many more species and cultivars than those listed below (the current seed list of England's Alpine Garden Society lists over forty species alone), but a catalog search has shown that the following crocuses are those most often available from specialty nurseries in the United States.

Crocus aerius grows at 7,000 feet in the mountains of northern Asia Minor, blooming in February. The flowers are lilac in hue with yellow throats.

Crocus ancyrensis, the Ankara crocus, is a native of Turkey, blooming in late winter. The vase-shaped flowers are a rich orange-yellow with yellow anthers. The leaves appear with the flowers.

Crocus asturicus is a native of the *Sierra de Ancares* of northern Spain. The 4-inch violet-purple flowers have orange stamens and bloom in early winter or late fall, sometimes before Thanksgiving. 'Atropurpureus' has flowers of dark mauve.

Crocus biflorus has naturalized in parts of Scotland as a garden escape and is now known as the Scotch crocus. Known to gardeners since 1629, the flowers are silvery white with purple stripes and narrow grayish leaves, generally appearing in February, but much depends on the severity of the winter.

Crocus chrysanthus, the snow crocus, was discovered in Bulgaria and resembles *C. biflorus* in its flowering time, usually blooming when the snow melts. The flowers typically are globelike and yellow, but there are many variations. 'Advance' has flowers that are yellow inside and violet outside; 'Blue Bird' has outside petals of violet-blue with a white margin and a pure white interior surrounding deep orange stamens; 'Cream Beauty' is entirely Naples yellow with the base sprinkled with a bronze-green; 'E. P. Bowles' is lemon yellow with a bronze base; 'Gypsy Girl' has bright yellow flowers with maroon tiger striping on the outside; 'Lady Killer' has unique pointed petals that are deep purple, edged with white, on the outside and white within; 'Princess Beatrix' is a clear lobelia blue with a golden yellow base; and 'Snowbunting' has scented flowers of glistening white with golden throats and feathered purple on the outside. This species is very easy to grow, multiplying yearly, and reliable even in the shade.

Crocus etruscus usually flowers in mid-March. The color is a soft lilac, and the outer segments are feathered with reddish purple, surrounding yellow anthers. According to Mrs. Wilder, this crocus was discovered by a Professor Palatore in the oak woods by a roadside as he walked up the Salita del Filetto in Tuscany. Any flower with that kind of pedigree belongs in everyone's winter garden.

Crocus flavus (*C. aureus*) bears golden yellow to orange, cup-shaped flowers. This crocus was originally from Yugoslavia and Turkey but was a stalwart member of Elizabethan gardens and the first yellow crocus to be cultivated. Gerard's *Herbel* describes the flowers as resembling "a hot glowing cole of fire." This plant was the basis for the large Dutch yellow crocus, which is sterile, but the species sets seed with ease.

Crocus imperati, the Italian crocus, blooms in January and February with large, vaselike, fragrant

Crocus tomasinianus

flowers that change color from bud to bloom. The buds are buff-yellow feathered with reddish violet, opening to an interior of mineral violet tinged with rose. The flower was named in honor of the Italian botanist Ferrante Imperato. English books advise growing this crocus as a pot plant for Christmas bloom. It is especially recommended by plantsman Graham Stuart Thomas in his book *Colour in the Winter Garden* (London: Dent, 1957; 3rd ed., 1984).

Crocus korolkowii was named for the Russian general Korolkow, who found the plant blooming in Turkestan. The small flowers are star-shaped, ready to open their golden petals, faintly tinged with green, wide to a warming spring sun. The leaves lay flat upon the ground.

Crocus laevigatus comes from Greece, bearing small, white, sweetly scented flowers with orange throats, the outer segments feathered with purple. This crocus can bloom anytime between November and March, depending on the severity of the weather and the microclimate.

Crocus sieberi is a native of the White Mountains of Greece and has been described as one of the most beautiful of all the species. The globular blossoms are bright lilac with orange throats and tipped with purple-maroon. As pot plants, they bloom from January to March; outside, they open in January, except in the mountains. Until opening, 'Firefly' has white flowers with gray veining; they open to a rich lilac color with a yellow base. 'Tricolor' has a broad golden band at the base of the flower, then a band of white, and finally petals of a deep lilac-blue.

Crocus susianus, the cloth of gold crocus, is a native of Crimea. It's an early bloomer, usually greeting the February sun with rich orange flowers, the outer petals feathered with bronze.

Crocus tomasinianus, is one of the hardiest species and one of the earliest to bloom. This species seeds freely, and as a result, there are many natural variations and cultivars. In its native homeland along the eastern coast of the Adriatic, this crocus blooms in February. Many horticulturists have recommended it as one of the best for naturalizing. 'Barr's Purple' has large blooms of amethyst violet; 'Ruby Giant' is a deep violet-purple with a lighter base; 'Whitewell Purple' has reddish purple blossoms.

Crocus vernus is a native of the higher mountains of Europe, including the Pyrenees, the Alps, and the Carpathians. In *My Garden in Autumn and Winter* (London: T. C. & E. C. Jack, 1915), E. A. Bowles wrote

Crocus tomasinianus and *Eranthis hiemalis* (right)

that he has "often seen the Crocus flowers pressing upward against a thin layer of almost transparent snow, and a few hours afterward, widely open in the sunshine which melted away their last film of winter covering." On the slopes of Little Mont Cenis in Southwest France, Bowles saw flowers in an endless variety of white, lavender, and striped forms. This is the species most responsible for the large-flowering Dutch crocuses, although in the wild they are much more petite. 'Haarlem Gem' has flowers of mauve-gray on the outside, with an amethyst violet interior.

Cyclamen spp., the cyclamens, consist of nineteen species, all of which are native to parts of Europe, western Asia, and North Africa. If gardeners knew how easy it was to raise cyclamen from seed, it would be a

far more popular flowering plant in the Southeast. *Cyclamen persicum*, for example, will flower within nine months of germination, and most of those grown for southern gardens will flower during their second season. The seeds must be kept in the dark until germination takes place.

Although grouped with bulbs, the cyclamens are really cormlike tubers that produce heart- or kidney shaped leaves on long stalks, many with pronounced silvery markings and maroon undersides. The flowers of pink, white, or shades of red or purple have reflexed petals held on long, slender scapes over the foliage. Many have a delicious scent.

In her book *Successful Southern Gardening* (Chapel Hill, The University of North Carolina Press,

Cyclamen coum

1989), Sandra Ladendorf tells of moving south and having garden writer William Lanier Hunt tell her, "You must raise some cyclamen on your hill." After hiking over Hunt's property, where thousands of cyclamen were flourishing, she became an enthusiast. "By careful selection of species, you can have some cyclamen in flower in your garden twelve months of the year," she said.

These are shade-tolerant plants, easily grown in a well-drained soil with plenty of leaf mold. Plant them on the shallow side, no more than 1½ inches deep, putting the smooth, slightly convex side down. Then mulch with more leaf mold. Good drainage is the key to success. All the species do beautifully when grown in pots, and Peter has one plant of *Cyclamen persicum* that is over twenty-five years old and two tubers of the same species collected in Israel's Negev that are over twenty years old. All of the cyclamens bloom every year with hundreds of fragrant blossoms. *Cyclamen* comes from the Greek *kyclos*, "circular," referring to the flower stalks, which twist spirally after fertilization, with some species actually pulling the ripened seed onto the ground.

Limiting the choice to the winter garden cuts down on the species, but still leaves the following (in order of bloom):

Cyclamen hederifolium (*C. neapolitanum*) begins blooming in Asheville and Charlotte around August, but it will continue to bloom (depending on the weather), off and on, well into November and December. Its many flowers are pink with darker eyes, and there is also a white form, *album*. The arrow shaped foliage has serrated edges and is deep green, spotted with silver. This cyclamen is a native of southern Italy and Greece, and old tubers can eventually measure over a foot across. We might add that even if it didn't flower in the winter, this is one plant worth having just as a beautiful ground cover.

Cyclamen coum blooms around Thanksgiving then, depending on the winter, off and on until April. The stems are about 3 inches high, and the unmarked leaves begin to appear in the fall. The flowers are a magenta-purple, and with time, they begin to seed about. It is considered a choice winter bloomer.

Cyclamen pseudibericum bears large, fragrant flowers of a vivid purple-magenta with a dark blotch of color, like an ace of spades, at the base of each lobe. There is also a very attractive form with pale pink flowers. Both bloom in late winter or early spring. The serrated foliage has silver mottling on the surface, with a pale crimson, almost brownish, underside. This plant was first described in 1901 from tubers collected in Turkey, close to the Syrian border. They need mulch protection in the mountains.

Warning: When buying cyclamen plants, make sure your sources use nursery stock grown from seed and not plants collected in the wild by unscrupulous plant scavengers.

Eranthis hyemalis, the winter aconite, is truly a herald of spring. These are tuberous-rooted perennials that bear large, globular, lemon-gold buttercups that float above palmately cut foliage. *Eranthis* comes from the Greek *er*, "spring," and *anthos*, "flower."

In 1629, John Parkinson wrote of the winter aconite in *A Garden of Pleasant Flowers* (New York: Dover Publications, 1976), "There are diverse forms of Wolfebanes which are not fit for this booke . . . yet among them there are some, that notwithstanding their evil quality, may for the beauty of their flowers take up a roome in this Garden." Although Parkinson confused the winter aconites with their more deadly relatives, including the poisonous aconites used by hunters to

poison wolves, he loved them. In England, these flowers bloom in January, and the colder the weather and deeper the snow, the larger the flower. Here in America, they do the same, appearing in the mountains in late February. After the blossoms fade, the leaves make a charming carpet of green, but they, too, soon disappear. Plant plenty of these beauties for the carpet effect. It's best to leave them undisturbed so they form large clumps of bloom. Aconites like a well-drained soil, preferably under the shade of trees and shrubs.

Galanthus spp., the snowdrops, represent some twenty species that range over Europe, including the British Isles, as far east as the Caucasus, and then from northern Russia down into the Greek archipelago. These delicate, drooping, bell-shaped flowers, with their conspicuous trio of outer white petals with emerald-green markings, have been garden favorites for centuries.

Snowdrops usually bloom a bit earlier than the crocuses but carry over and produce fresh blossoms for weeks. They often bloom through the melting snow

Eranthis hyemalis, winter aconite

Galanthus byzantinus, snowdrop, is one of several species of dwarf bulbs from Asia Minor. The pure white pendant flowers bloom in mid-winter, often with *Croccus tomasinianus* and *Eranthis*. The three inner "petals" are short, thus differentiating *Galanthus* from *Leucojum*. In situations of rich, well-drained soil, they will multiply into striking clumps.

and make February walks through wooded gardens a late-winter delight. They are included here only for the northern part of this book's range because snowdrops do not do well in hot climates.

We first learned about moving snowdrops in *Merry Hall* (New York: E. P. Dutton, 1953), a charming English garden book by Beverly Nichols, who wrote about getting a spade and transplanting the snowdrops in mid-February to another part of his garden by lifting the plants in a solid chunk of soil when they were in full flower.

Last weekend we had a garden visitor who said she assembled wonderful centerpieces for the table by digging up clumps of snowdrops, surrounding the plants with an assortment of dried mosses and ferns, and then plunking everything into a charming old basket—and her dinner guests were delighted.

You will need a number of these bulbs to make a decent floral display, at least 180 per square yard. Since they are not very expensive, here's one place not to stint. Plant new bulbs in the fall, in a shady spot with good, woodsy, well-drained soil. When your time-honored plants become crowded, dig them up and divide them in the late winter or early spring. This procedure does not harm snowdrops at all. But because their roots form in August, digging them up at that time can be fatal.

Galanthus caucasicus, the Caucasian snowdrop, is a very hardy species with broad glaucous leaves up to 9 inches long. The flowers lack any green markings and generally come into bloom earlier than the other snowdrops. *Galanthus elwesii*, the giant snowdrop, is a large-flowered species from the mountains of Asia Minor bearing white blossoms, each petal marked with emerald green at the base. The plants are 6 to 8 inches tall. *Galanthus nivalis*, the common garden snowdrop, is a smaller version of *G. elwesii*, growing between 4 and 6 inches tall and excellent for naturalizing. Snowdrops should be planted in large drifts and are especially attractive when lining wooded pathways through clumps of rhododendrons or other small trees. 'Flore Pleno' is the double-flowered cultivar. The variety *viridapicis* is a robust form with beautiful green markings on the tips of both the outer and inner petal segments. *Galanthus* comes from the Greek for "milk flower."

Hermodactylus tuberosus, the snake's head or widow's iris, has long, narrow, quadrangular leaves that appear in gardens in early winter. There is only one species, obviously related to the genus *Iris* but differing in the shape of the tubers and other minor botanical characteristics. There is only one flower per stem, about 2 inches in diameter, with velvety plum purple or brownish violet blades, pea green inner segments, and a slender green bract that hangs over the top of the flower like a hood. A native of the Mediterranean regions from southeast France and North Africa eastward to Israel, it flowers in our Asheville garden in mid to late March, earlier in years of mild winter temperatures. These plants are best divided in August and September before growth begins.

Ipheion uniflorum (*Brodiaea uniflora*), the spring starflower, originally from Peru and Argentina, is not widely known among gardeners. The flowers appear very early in the spring, the blooming stems emerging from grasslike leaves that appear in the fall and lie upon the ground until late spring. The leaves smell of onion when crushed. The charming, pale blue, starlike

Hermodactylus tuberosus, widow's iris

Ipheion uniflorum

flowers are an inch across and smell of mint. Each stem produces only one flower, but a single bulb will, over the course of days, produce many stems. Both old flowers and tired leaves quickly disappear after blooming. It should be planted in drifts, like other small flowers, and given the shade of tall trees, especially in the South. 'Wisley Blue', originally found in the gardens of the Royal Horticultural Society, bears 2-inch flowers of the deepest blue.

Spring starflowers do well in pots for indoor winter flowers. Pot the bulbs 1 inch deep in a mixture of one-third sterile potting soil, one-third sharp sand, and one-third shredded peat moss. Keep the potting mix moist until the leaves finally wither away in late spring. Then keep the bulbs dry until you repot them in fresh soil the following fall.

Iris spp., the irises, represent a large genus with more than 200 species, including a number of winter-blooming flowers. Although most irises have rhizomes, many of the winter bloomers arise from pear-shaped bulbs and belong to the category of bulbous irises.

Unlike the typical garden iris, which seems to take any amount of punishment, the bulbous irises are pickier about their environment. There are three main groups of irises. For the winter garden, we are interested in those of the reticulata group, which bloom in February, and the juno group, which bloom in early spring. The third group consists of the Dutch, English, and Spanish irises, which do not bloom until late spring.

The reticulata group is composed of very hardy small, bulbous irises that, if given proper drainage and a summer baking, will persist in the garden for years. They come from Asia Minor and are characterized by the bulbs' wearing a netted tunic and the plants' dwarf habit. The grasslike leaves come to a sharp point, sometimes hiding the flowers, but that's a minor fault. Take time to examine the falls on the flowers and notice the conspicuous bee guides, usually not important in American gardens but extremely useful for pollination in the Caucasus mountains. The group name refers to the

(Right) *Iris reticulata*

78

reticulate, or netted, coat on the bulbs. Most of the flowers are fragrant, and Louise Beebe Wilder wrote in *Adventures in Hardy Bulbs* that a few flowers would perfume an entire room. Sow the seeds out in the open, but depending on the location, if seedlings appear in December to February they might need protection.

Iris bakeriana has leaves up to a foot long, with 2- to 3-inch flowers that are smaller than the type. The color is a medium violet, with a white streak on each fall that is streaked with yellow. Although not always easy to find at bulb nurseries, the seed is often available from the various rock garden societies.

Iris danfordiae was introduced from Asia Minor, specifically in central Turkey, in 1876. The color is a rich yellow, with brown spots on the rounded part of the fall. These irises are usually not expensive, so here's a case where more is better, although Roger Phillips and Martyn Rix in their book *Bulbs* (New York: Random House, 1989) warn that they "will flower well the first year after planting but [are] difficult to keep going in the open garden." Ev Whittemore, our garden friend in Penrose, North Carolina, reports having this iris in bloom in her garden at the end of January during a warm winter.

Iris histrio is a native of southern Turkey, where it grows on stony hillsides, flowering in February and March. It's another beautiful flower of a light violet hue, veined with darker blue, and having yellow falls dotted with purple. There is a form called *I. histrio* var. *aintabensis* found growing in pockets of limestone rock, described by Louise Beebe Wilder in *Hardy Bulbs* as "haunting the foothills of subalpine regions." It is like the species but smaller and more delicate in coloring.

Iris histrioides blooms very early in the year in its native Turkey, but according to Mrs. Wilder, a month later than *I. histrio* in her northern garden. The color is variable and close to *I. histrio*, but the bulbs usually offered by nurseries have much larger flowers and are called 'Major'. For such a rare beauty, three other varieties are usually offered. 'Frank Elder', a hybrid of *I. histrioides* var. *major* × *I. winogradowii*, has large, pale blue flowers subtly overlaid with yellow and suffused with pale yellow, the falls veined with a darker blue. 'Katherine Hodgkin' is similar to 'Frank Elder', but the flowers are more yellow and suffused with pale blue, then lined and dotted with a darker blue. 'Lady Beatrix Stanly' has more than the usual number of spots on the falls.

Iris kolpakowskiana was found in Central Asia growing on stony or grassy slopes. Not usually offered by the nurseries, it is available from the rock garden societies as seed. The color is a purple-lilac, with snow-tiger stripes on the falls.

Iris reticulata is the true species. The upright petals, or standards, are usually a slightly paler lilac than the deep violet falls. The falls have golden yellow crests surrounded by wide patches of white and violet splatters. This is the tried-and-true winter-blooming iris. It has been growing in gardens since its introduction in 1829 and has given rise to a number of cultivars. 'Cantab' was originally raised by E. A. Bowles. He wrote in *My Garden in Spring* (London: T. C. & E. C. Jack, 1914); "So far, then, my turquoise treasure which I call Cantab has thrived, and besides two clumps here, I have been able to send it out a little way into the world, by sharing its offsets with a few friends whose openly expressed raptures have convinced me it would find a good home and loving care in their gardens." The flax blue flowers have a pale yellow splotch on each petal. 'Clairette' has been termed a possible hybrid with *I. bakeriana* by Phillips and Rix. It has sky blue standards and deep indigo falls, with white stripes. 'Harmony' is a hybrid of *I. reticulata* and *I. histrioides* 'Major', bearing sky blue standards and royal blue falls touched with gold. 'Natasha' has ice blue petals that are almost white, with orange marks on the falls.

The juno group hails from Bokhara, Afghanistan, and Turkey. These plants want to be baked in summer's oven, and while resting, look at water with the same contempt that W. C. Fields did. These irises resemble small corn plants. Unlike the other bulbous irises, the junos have persistent fleshy roots that need special handling to prevent damage when planting, lifting, or storing. But any inconvenience is more than compensated by their magnificence. Junos are usually represented in the trade by just three species, although once again, if you search the seed lists of the various rock garden societies, you should find most of the species offered. The following are the most beautiful. As to care, once again the secret is good drainage, some overhead protection from too much rain, and the required summer baking.

Iris bucharica is a native of Central Asia, especially Tajikistan and the northeast of Afghanistan, where, like all the junos, it grows on sparse, rocky soil and grassy hillsides. The creamy white flowers are about 2 inches across and have patches of yellow on the falls. Give it well-drained soil in full sun.

Iris caucasica was a success for Mrs. Wilder, for it survived the cold of Rockland County, New York, under a mulch of salt hay. The soil she described was light,

Iris stylosa (I. unguicularis), winter iris

well-drained, and limy, and the bulbs were planted by a south-facing wall. The flowers are a greenish yellow and certainly not up to the beauty of *I. persica*.

Iris magnifica really does look like a corn plant, but with flowers coming up from almost every leaf joint. In the wild, plants reach a height of 16 inches or more. The 2-inch-wide flowers vary from a light lilac to almost white. This is the largest juno species and is easily grown in good, deep, well-drained soil, in full sun.

Iris orchioides, or the orchid iris, is a native of central Asia and grows in the kind of soil that the uninformed call bomb-blast rubble. Its wide, foot-long leaves are a glossy green and surround flowers of a deep yellow with darker stains on the falls. The bulb is often as large as a hen's egg.

Iris persica is a native of southern Turkey, Syria, and Lebanon, where it grows on rocky hillsides and among scrub oak. It grew in Mrs. Wilder's northern garden for many years, and she said of this beauty, "In certain regions of the South, in old gardens, *Iris per-sica* has long been established and flourishes freely. One would like to know the history of its introduction into these gardens, and why it apparently did not reach northern gardens, though perhaps it did, and simply perished for lack of warmth and a sympathetic understanding of its needs." The solitary flowers are a combination of greenish white and brownish yellow, with a purple area on the falls that surrounds a brilliant orange ridge. The bulbs are expensive but worth the cost, if you have the patience to grow them.

In addition to the reticulata and juno irises, there is also a winter-blooming rhizomatous iris known as *Iris stylosa* (*I. unguicularis*), the so-called winter iris. Plants grow from a thick, creeping rootstock and produce tufts of narrow, bright green, swordlike leaves. The flower stem reaches a height of about 6 inches and bears a beautiful 3-inch-wide flower of a bright pale blue, with falls having golden yellow patches in their centers and spotted with purple. There is a white form called 'Alba'; 'Speciosa' is deep blue; and 'Violacea' has violet-colored flowers. They bloom from January to April.

Narcissus with *Forsythia*

Leucojum vernum, the spring snowflake, is a larger, more robust relative of the snowdrop. These bulbs have been popular for more than four hundred years. The nodding, bell-like flowers resemble lily of the valley and, depending on the type, are borne on stalks from 9 to 14 inches tall. In late February, while visiting at Sea Island off the coast of Georgia, we've seen marvelous collections of this easily naturalized bulb. *Leucojum* needs sandy, well-drained soil and should be planted in fall. The name is derived from the Greek for "white violet."

Muscari spp., the grape hyacinths, generally flower in March, sometimes extending into April. Originally they were lumped in with the other hyacinths, but botanist and plant hunter Joseph Pitton de Tournefort (1656–1708) gave them their own genus. He chose the name from the Latin *moschus*, or "musk," referring to the scent of some species. They are not fussy when it comes to soil and are easy to grow. Many will seed about with ease, and they are sometimes perceived as a pest by more fastidious gardeners.

Muscari armeniacum is the time-honored grape hyacinth, a native of Bulgaria, Yugoslavia, Greece, and the Caucasus. These plants will often reach a height of 6 or more inches, and a good, healthy bulb will pro-duce four or five flower spikes. And they do seed about. 'Blue Spike' has flowers of a flax blue, but these are sterile and do not produce seed; 'Early Giant' bears white-rimmed florets of a deep cobalt blue. 'Cantab' has sweetly scented, clear sky blue flowers and is a bit shorter than the other cultivars. *Muscari azureum* (*Hyacinthella azurea*), is a native of Asia Minor and bears a dense head of bright, sky blue flowers that are bell shaped and sweetly scented. *Muscari botryoides* is the original grape hyacinth. It has been in cultivation for more than four hundred years, appearing in England in 1576. 'Alba' is the white-flowered form.

Muscari comosum, the tassel hyacinth, is called by many a weed of cultivation, and is really not that attractive. But it is worth noting for two rather strange cultivars, both called the feathered hyacinth. 'Monstrosum' produces sterile blossoms of violet-blue, each flower cut into shreds, and 'Plumosum' has shredded flowers of a ripe reddish purple. As Mrs. Wilder put it, "[They] doubtless appealed to the Victorian taste."

Narcissus spp., the daffodils and narcissus of poetic glory, can bloom from January to May, depending on the variety and species chosen. We are listing only those

(Right) *Narcissus bulbicodium*

that bloom in the first three months of the year, and we know we are missing dozens of varieties. But entire books can be devoted to these glorious flowers that prompted Shakespeare to write in *The Winter's Tale*:

> Daffodils,
> That come before the swallow dares, and take
> The winds of March with beauty.

All the daffodils and narcissus listed below are hardy in Zones 6 to 8. In Zones 9 and 10, most such bulbs must be precooled for eight to ten weeks at 40°F to 45°F before being planted out in December. If unsure, check the Plant Sources list for growers that deal with warmer areas of the South.

Plant these bulbs in midautumn in well-drained, sandy, humus-rich soil. Put a bit of bulb food in the bottom of each bulb hole before you add the bulb. In order to guarantee next spring's flowers, daffodil and narcissus foliage must be allowed to ripen after blooming, regardless of how ratty it looks. Always remove the spent flower heads so the bulbs will not waste energy in making seeds and will increase in size. These bulbs should generally be planted from 6 to 8 inches deep, less with smaller bulbs.

Trumpet daffodils produce flowers with one blossom to a stem. The trumpet is as long as or longer than the petals.

Narcissus 'Golden Harvest' is 14 inches tall and blooms with golden yellow trumpets.

Narcissus 'Little Beauty' is a miniature at 8 inches, perfect for the rock garden, and blooms with creamy white petals and bright yellow trumpets.

Narcissus 'Rijnveld's Early Sensation' is one of the earliest daffodils to bloom, sometimes just after Christmas in the warmer parts of the South. It is 14 inches tall and blooms with bright yellow trumpets.

Narcissus 'W. P. Milner' is another miniature, at 7 inches, also perfect for the rock garden. It produces sulfur yellow trumpets.

Cyclamineus daffodils are the first hybrid daffodils to bloom in spring. The petals are reflexed and stand away from the slender trumpet.

Narcissus 'February Gold' has yellow, trumpetlike flowers on 10-inch stems.

Narcissus 'February Silver' blooms with white petals and a bright yellow crown, which quickly fades to pure white, on 10-inch stems.

Narcissus 'Jack Snipe' has bicolor flowers with lightly swept-back white petals and primrose yellow, medium-length crowns on 8-inch stems.

Narcissus 'Jetfire' has a bright orange trumpet emerging from reflexed golden yellow petals on 12-inch stems.

Other daffodils include *Narcissus* 'Waterperry', in the **jonquil group**, which includes daffodils of garden origin, most with a sweet scent and more than one flower on the stem. This cultivar has flowers with white petals framing a cup of light yellow that blushes to pink at maturity.

Narcissus 'Grand Soleil d'Or' is a member of the **tazetta group**, the most widely distributed and the oldest known forms of the *Narcissus* genus. They do well in the warmer parts of the South. This cultivar has flowers with yellow petals surrounding an orange cup and are extremely fragrant. They force well indoors without cooling.

Narcissus 'Jumblie' is included in a division made up of daffodils that do not fit in the twelve divisions published by the American Daffodil Society. It's a miniature on 7-inch stems, with yellow petals that flare back from a pencil-thin yellow-orange trumpet.

Narcissus 'Tête-à-tête' has fragrant golden blooms, often two per stem, with reflexed petals and a long, slender cup on 6-inch stems.

Narcissus minor is a charming daffodil with canary yellow trumpets surrounded by pale yellow petals on 8-inch stems.

Paperwhites also belong to the tazetta group of daffodils. They do not require a cold period before blooming. For this reason, they are prized as indoor forcing bulbs farther north. In Zones 9 and 10, these bulbs will grow outside where other classes of daffodils will fail to produce buds.

Nerine spp., a genus of twenty or more species of plant belonging to the amaryllis family, are named for a water nymph in Greek mythology. The flowers consist of umbels with up to twenty or more blossoms on erect scapes between 16 and 20 inches tall. The leaves appear during the summer, after the flowers, then ripen and disappear, followed by the next set of flowers from October into February, depending on the exposure and the winter temperature. Bulbs need a deep, rich, sandy loam and, once planted, should be left on their own. They also do well in the garden or in pots.

Nerine bowdenii was found in the Drakensberg Mountains of South Africa, where it grows in dry soil, sometimes even under an overhanging cliff. Six to twelve rose pink flowers appear on 12-inch scapes. In

(Right) *Narcissus* 'Tête-à-Tête'

warm, sheltered spots, nerines will bloom up to Christmas, as long as the bulb and foliage are protected from hard frosts. When grown in a very warm spot, the plant appears to be evergreen.

Nerine filifolia was discovered in 1879 in Africa's Orange Free State and Natal (now South Africa). The bulbs grow in wet meadows and along the edges of streams, where they flower in January and February. The plant's twelve to sixteen flowers are a bright rosy red with incurving petals.

Puschkinia scilloides (*P. libanotica*), the striped squill, is a native of the Caucasus, where it grows in scrub and stony places and, depending on the weather, usually blooms at the end of March and sometimes April. The flower is named for Count Apollos Apollosovich Mussin-Puschkin (1760–1805), who left Russia in the year 1800 for the Caucasus in search of mineral wealth and never returned. This is a gem of a flower, resembling a small hyacinth, but slim and refined with porcelain blue flowers, not gaudy in the least. There is also a pure white form called 'Alba' that is just as beautiful. A green form is as yet unnamed but has been collected growing in the same area as the common form. Use these bulbs everywhere you can.

Scilla spp. is a genus name used by the Greeks and Romans for *Urginea maritima*, the sea squill. These flowering bulbs are popularly known as squills, bluebells, wild hyacinths, and jacinths, the last name being an old French word for hyacinth. Their starlike blossoms appear very early in the spring and often carpet a still-sleeping lawn with gemlike dots of color. Most of the species self-sow with ease and are great when naturalized along garden pathways to accompany the snowdrops.

Scilla bifolia, the two-leafed squill, appears with the crocuses and winter aconites. The tiny, gentian blue flowers are borne on 6-inch stems and gyrate like rock stars in the slightest breeze. Native to central and southern Europe, they grow in the woods, taking advantage of the early sunset under the spring's leafless trees. There is a great deal of variation in the flowers, and two cultivars are offered, 'Alba' which has white flowers, and 'Rosea', with flowers of ivory pink.

Scilla siberica, the common Siberian squill, will soon carpet your bare late-winter garden with thousands of delicate prussian blue flowers. This flower was introduced from Russian Siberia in 1796 and is probably the most popular of the early-blooming bulbs. Because the foliage is grasslike and goes unnoticed by most gardeners, its ability to seed about should be a

blessing. If it does bother you, the plants are easily pulled up. Mrs. Wilder suggests planting Siberian squill about the base of *Lonicera fragrantissima* and *Magnolia tomentosa*, or shaded by shadblows or forsythia. There is a white form called 'Alba' that comes true from seed and is just as prolific as the blue. The two could make a stunning combination if mixed in a definite pattern.

Scilla miczenkoana (*S. tubergeniana*) has been the unfortunate victim of a name change, but that shouldn't stop the planting of this very-early-blooming species that bears larger white flowers than usual, with petals of the palest blue or often pure white. The stamens are a bright yellow.

Sternbergia spp. are known by most gardeners as the autumn-flowering crocuses. The bulbs are native to the Caucasus and Asia Minor and named in honor of Count Kaspar Maria von Sternberg (1761–1838), a famous German botanist. They have long-necked, black, tunicated bulbs; straplike leaves; and flowers that have six stamens instead of the three found in crocuses. For cultivation, they need an open, sunny spot with well-drained, sun-baked soil, as many of the species come from Turkey, Syria, and Iran. Use plenty of leaf mold when planting. We've found that they do quite well near a wall, so it's obvious they do not object to some lime. They should be left undisturbed for years so that they will form large clumps. Early writers called these flowers autumn or winter daffodils, and some have thought it to be the original lily of the field of biblical fame.

Sternbergia lutea is well known and, in our experience, always blooms in late fall, but we are still including it here. *Sternbergia fischerana* grows on stony hillsides and slopes, in nature flowering in February and March. It's a lovely thing, but it needs plenty of summer baking to be successful in the garden. *Sternbergia candida* was discovered in 1976 in southwestern Turkey, where it flowers in January and February. The flowers are a pristine white, and a plant in bloom is a truly beautiful thing. It is still a rare find at the nurseries, but seeds are occasionally available from the various rock garden societies.

Winter-Blooming Herbaceous Plants

When winter winds blow drifts of snow through barren forests and temperatures plummet below zero, plants seldom bloom. But throughout the Southeast, winter is never quite the awesome threat that it becomes in colder parts of the country (although recent events might prove otherwise). The herbaceous perennial plants listed below actually bloom during the winter months, although not all at the same time. Their flowering schedule will vary according to the local weather.

There are a number of wildflowers that bloom in late winter to early spring, including skunk cabbage (*Symplocarpus foetidus*), the small heartleaf ginger (*Hexastylis minor*), columbine (*Aquilegia canadensis*), and bloodroot (*Sanguinaria canadensis*). Unfortunately, many of these flowers do well only in the mountains and piedmont, where they revel in cooler temperatures, so they are not all listed in the following collection.

Adonis spp., the pheasant's eyes, represent some forty species of Eurasian herbs, a few of which are found blooming in the winter garden. *Adonis amurensis* is rare in winter gardens, only because many gardeners do not know of its adaptability. But in Japan, the plant is lifted from the garden in late fall and forced for winter bloom. The type bears golden-green flowers about 2 inches across, with twenty to forty petals, that

appear before the feathery leaves. Today there are many cultivars, some with double flowers, in colors ranging from a bright yellow to white to pink. The plants reach a height of about 10 inches. They completely disappear by high summer. *Adonis vernalis* is another early bloomer native to Europe. It has been in general cultivation since the 1500s. The golden yellow flowers, which are held above the feathery foliage, are often 2½ inches in diameter. This plant has medicinal uses and has been known to transfer its toxic effect to the milk of goats and cows.

Antennaria plantaginifolia, the early everlasting, pussy-toes, or cat's-foot, belongs to a genus of low woolly perennials. It is between 2 and 12 inches tall and bears solitary heads of compacted flowers that resemble fuzzy buttons. The basal leaves are roundish with 3 to 5 prominent veins, cobwebby above and covered with silvery hairs beneath. It grows in dry woodlands or on well-drained soil above mountain streams, usually blooming in very early spring. The genus is

Adonis amurensis

named for the Latin antennae because the scales on the male flowers look like a butterfly's antennae.

Aquilegia canadensis, the columbine, is a charming flower for any garden setting and often begins to bloom in late March. The red and yellow flowers have elongated tubular petals that harbor nectar for spring-migrating hummingbirds. Perfectly hardy and not fussy as to soil, columbines are readily grown from seed, in fact one of the easiest native wildflowers to grow. A single plant may last only two years in your garden, but it will usually seed itself around. The name *Aquilegia* has various interpretations but may refer to the similarity between the talons of the eagle and the pointed nectar tubes.

Arisarum proboscideum is commonly called the mouse-tail plant, and a group of blossoms looks exactly like a bunch of mice at a cheese convention. This is one of three species of plants with creeping rhizomes that are native to the Mediterranean region and in Zones 7 and up are green all winter. The plant blooms in late winter to early spring. The flowers are hooded, with dark brown tops and whitish bottoms, and at the end of each shoot, there is a long tail that winds about. Plant in good, moist soil with plenty of compost.

Aster grandiflorus belongs to a great plant family, Compositae, and in particular the aster tribe. With more than two thousand species of mostly perennial plants in this tribe, we do not know just how many are winter bloomers, but we do know of one cold-hearted beauty, and that's *A. grandiflorus*. West of the piedmont in North Carolina, it's only been recorded in Burke County and as yet has missed Asheville. In *Gardens in Winter* Elizabeth Lawrence mentioned this aster blooming around Christmas and, as such, called it the Christmas daisy. As with so many plants, it has more cachet in England than America, having been introduced there in the early 1700s. Miss Lawrence notes that Canon Ellacombe (1822–1916), owner of the famous garden at Bitton Vicarage in Gloucestershire and author of *In a Gloustershire Garden* and *In My Vicarage Garden*, called it "a most desirable plant; in colour it is even a deeper blue that *Aster amellus*, and it has the great advantage of flowering so late that in mild seasons it will give good flowers in December and even at Christmas." He also suggests picking it in bud, then bringing it indoors for winter cheer.

Bergenia cordifolia, the heartleaf bergenia, has thick, leathery leaves that remain green during the

(Left) *Aquilegia canadensis*

Arisarum proboscideum, mouse-tail plant

winter in the South and turn red from Zone 6 down. Large 8- to 10-inch-wide leaves have wavy, serrated edges coming from a basal rosette. Bergenias are more than just ground covers (although in Portland, Oregon, their strong winter growth borders on the obscene), because they also bloom. In early spring, 3- to 6-inch clusters of bell-like waxy flowers appear, in shades from pale pink to rose to white, blooming above old foliage. In the mountains, they can take a lot of sun, but at lower altitude they need semishade. They do not do well in the heat along the Gulf Coast or in Florida.

Helleborus argutifolius (*H. corsicus*)

like) seldom stop very long for freezing weather. They bloom steadily and defiantly through our meanest winters, and even after a drop to 10°, mild weather brings out more buds. In good winters they are a mass of color, dragon's-blood-red buds and Indian-yellow flowers, and the air all about is perfumed with the most delicate and delightful of all scents." For mountain dwellers, we add that wallflowers will bloom in greenhouses and plant windows in February, the secret being the temperature. When kept in a spot at 60°F or less, the plants will set buds. They always want perfect drainage and a bit of lime, hence their fondness for growing in walls.

Chrysanthemum arcticum, the arctic daisy, is not in our ken but has been mentioned by Mrs. Wilder, as blooming in her November rock garden in upstate New York. Writing in *Adventures in My Garden and Rock Garden* (New York: Doubleday, Page & Company, 1923), she mentions having it for a time, "but never its mass of white lilac-tinged daisies, for it went off in a wet spell."

Chrysogonum virginianum, the green-and-gold, is a native American genus of one species found growing at the woodland's edge from southern Pennsylvania down to Florida. A perennial of neat habit, this plant reaches a height of about 8 inches. The golden-yellow blossoms, which resemble small sunflowers, bloom from early spring, then off and on until late fall. Sometimes, when the weather cooperates, they blossom well into December. Give these plants ordinary, well-drained garden soil with added humus. Two cultivars are sometimes available: 'Allen Busch', which grows more rapidly than the species, and 'Mark Viette', a long-blooming form from the Andre Viette Farm & Nursery in Fishersville, Virginia. *Chrysogonum* comes from the Greek *chrusos*, "golden," and *gonu*, "knee," and has no obvious applications.

Euphorbia amygdaloides var. *robbiae*, Miss Robb's spurge, is a perennial evergreen ground cover with rosettes of dark green leaves that reaches a height of 15 inches and slowly spreads to a 3-foot diameter. Bright chartreuse flowers appear in late March and remain until May. Provide full sun or partial shade in any reasonable garden soil. The genus is named for Euphorbus, a physician to King Juba of Mauritania.

Euphorbia helioscopia, the sun spurge, is an annual (and weedy) plant, a native of Europe, introduced to the States from eastern Canada, blooming in late March. It often persists as an old-fashioned garden escape and is considered an undesirable nuisance.

Bergenia crassifolia, the Siberian tea, is like *B. cordifolia*, but the leaves are more oval in shape. Plant in moist soil with plenty of humus, and remove damaged leaves and faded flowers in spring.

Calendula officinalis, the pot marigold, is mentioned here for the warmer parts of our region. If the seeds are planted in summer and the winter is mild, these plants will often bloom well into the winter months.

Cheiranthus cheiri, the English wallflower, brightens with both scent and flower, but it is the flower that really holds one's attention when winter is sweeping in. Again quoting Miss Lawrence, "Wallflowers (which I do

However, it does grow in poor soils and adds a lively yellow-green color to the late-winter garden in the South. The sun spurge does well in sun or shade—just watch out for its exuberant reproductive habits and remove unwanted seedlings.

Hacquetia epipactus is a native of the eastern Alps, the 8-inch-high plants found growing in rich woods, usually on limestone outcroppings. It blooms from March to late April, with tiny yellow flowers, resembling bright yellow balls, surrounded by yellow-green bracts, all on short stems. The one-species genus was named in honor of Balthasar Hacquet (1740–1815), author of a book on alpine plants. Provide good, moist soil in partial shade.

Helleborus spp., the hellebores, consist of about twenty species of plants that belong to the buttercup family. Hellebores have been cultivated for centuries, the botanical name being bestowed by Hippocrates and used by other Greek writers.

The soil should be well drained and enriched with leaf mold or compost, and all species appreciate a neutral to slightly alkaline soil and do especially well when planted near mortared steps or walls. Plants that naturally start from seed will do well even in heavy clay soil. A thin layer of leaf mulch is beneficial because it keeps the roots cool in summer and, in colder areas, protected in winter. The spent leaves from the previous season should be removed in early spring.

When planting hellebores, dig a good-size hole so that the roots can be carefully spread apart, with the crown placed about 1 inch below the soil surface. The Christmas rose needs special care, as it resents being moved, but the others seem to have little problem with adapting to a new home.

Hellebore seed loses vitality quickly, and after six months germination can be disappointing. Flowering plants will develop from seed in about three to four years and should be left undisturbed so they can become large specimen plants. If division is needed, do so in early fall, keeping at least five growth buds to each division.

Here's a special note to flower arrangers: To keep hellebore blossoms fresh in water, slit the stem lengthwise from the bottom, at least three or four times, with a sharp razor or knife.

The following species are as listed in *The Gardener's Guide to Growing Hellebores*, by Graham Rice and Elizabeth Strangman (England: David & Charles, 1993), and have done well in our gardens in Asheville and Charlotte.

Helleborus foetidus 'Wester Flisk', stinking hellebore

Helleborus argutifolius (*H. corsicus*), reaches a height of 3 to 4 feet, and a mature plant can be 4 feet across. The stiff, leathery leaves are divided into three spined leaflets. It blooms from January until March, with the stems capped with twenty to thirty green, cup-shaped flowers up to 2 inches across. This plant came to our gardens from the North Carolina State University Arboretum.

Helleborus foetidus, the stinking hellebore, can sometimes have a sweet odor but often comes across as being foxy. The foliage smells unpleasant when crushed, hence the species name. This is a native plant in Britain, and a number of forms have been named.

Helleborus niger, Christmas rose

Helleborus orientalis, Lenten rose

The species can grow to 2½ feet high and 4 feet across. The dark green leaves are usually divided into nine toothed leaflets and add a wonderful texture to the garden year-round. The pale green flowers have a brown or reddish purple edging and are about inch wide. An extremely nice cultivar is 'Wester Flisk', whose stems, petioles, and inflorescences are tinted a bright red.

Helleborus niger, the Christmas rose, blooms in our gardens during mid to late December. It's a mountain plant in Europe, and it resents acid soil and does not do well in poor or dry soil. If your soil is acid, try adding a dash of lime, along with plenty of organic matter to hold moisture. The plant reaches a height of 9 to 12 inches. Its dark, leathery leaves are pedately divided into seven, eight, or nine segments, which are usually untoothed except at the tips. The large, showy flowers bloom on a single stem and can vary from 2 to 3 inches across. They are usually a waxy white, but may be pink on the reverse side of the petals or turn pink with age.

Helleborus orientalis, the Lenten rose, is the most commonly grown hellebore, usually blooming in early spring. It has drooping, long-lasting flowers of cream, light green, or many shades of purple to brown, often suffused with maroon spots. Many new dark-flowered selections are being produced by several nurseries. Dozens of foot-wide palmate leaves on 18-inch stems arise from a central crown and can make a 4-foot circle. The plants interbreed like the gods of ancient Greece, the baby plants visible under the plant's leafy umbrella, and your garden will eventually sport new plants, some with flowers that are classically beautiful and others with colors that are a bit of a bore. You may have to thin the plants, but do it when they are seedlings, as adults resist extractions. It's up to you to choose the best. Make no mistake about it, the Lenten rose is a superb landscape plant and should be one of the highlights of many gardens. In addition to plants scattered about various parts of our garden, one large plant resides at the top side of two low stone steps and acts as a focal point throughout the year. Once established, this plant can tolerate dry shade and will choke out all other plants—including weeds. But be warned: All parts of this miracle plant are very poisonous.

Hepatica americana is a woodland wildflower of rare beauty that blooms in late winter and very early spring. You will find it in bloom when the woods floor is still a carpet of last autumn's fallen leaves. Hepaticas are low plants with round-lobed basal leaves and several stalks bearing solitary pink, lavender-blue, or white flowers with five to nine petal-like sepals. There is also a species with sharp-pointed leaves known as *H. acutiloba*. The genus name refers to the three-lobed leaf, thought to bear a resemblance to the human liver, and according to the Doctrine of Signatures, hepatica was used to treat liver diseases in the Middle Ages.

Hexastylis minor and *H. arifolia* are two species of the birthwort family (Aristolochiaceae), sometimes placed in the genus *Asarum*. They are evergreen plants with beautifully mottled leaves. The 1-inch brownish flowers bloom from February to May and are usually hidden beneath the leaves. They are worth looking for and showing to children, who like to call them "piggies" or "little brown jugs." Slow to propagate, they are a challenge for the nurseryman but are worth seeking out for their tight winter appearance and garden persistence.

Iberis sempervirens, the perennial candytuft, flowers in southern gardens on and off throughout the winter. Elizabeth Lawrence spoke of the cultivar 'Little Gem' as blooming in her Charlotte garden from Thanksgiving to Easter. The tightly packed disks of buds soon open to masses of small white flowers, blooming in racemes that lengthen with age. These blossoms, with two petals longer than the others, turn pink with age. Use candytufts for edging, along rock walls, in rock garden clefts and crevices, and if you remember to water, in clay pots artfully placed throughout the garden. Once established, as long as they have plenty of sun and good drainage, these are drought-resistant plants. The genus is named for Iberia, the ancient name of Spain, since many wild species are found there.

Jeffersonia diphylla, the twinleaf, is a small and elegant member of the barberry family that has the great distinction of being named for Thomas Jefferson.

Although it is related to the mayapple, its solitary 1-inch-wide flowers, each with eight pure white petals and borne on leafless scapes, look more like pale anemones, or even mayflowers, than barberries. This wildflower is called the twinleaf because its leaves are divided, looking like green butterflies fluttering from flower to flower, aloft in a woodland breeze. When blossoms go to seed, the maturing seedpod has a distinctive hinged top and looks like a miniature version of a Dutch burgher's pipe. The twinleaf is found only in eastern North America. Each of its charming flowers only lasts one day, and when blooming in February, it always suffers from any climatic disturbances; even a heavy rain will shatter its petals. From this description, you can tell it's not easy to keep this plant for any length of time. But new plants are easily grown from seed, and it's worth the time and patience needed to grow this particular gem.

Mandragora autumnalis, related to the legendary mandrake (*M. officinarum*) of the forked root, said to shriek in pain when pulled from the ground, is found naturally in northern Italy and western Yugoslavia. The plant grows in rocky outcrops, specifically near pine woods and olive groves, blooming from January to April with small, purple, five-petaled flowers surrounded by coarse leaves. While not a real beauty at that time of the year, it's definitely an interesting curiosity.

Petasites japonicus, the Japanese butterbur, is grown as a vegetable in the Orient. When you see old Japanese prints depicting peasants running from rainstorms and holding gigantic leaves overhead, they are using a large form of this plant (*P. japonicus* var. *giganteus*) as vegetable umbrellas. In our gardens, however, the interest lies with their blooming in February and March. In midwinter, the roots send up stalks that bear bunches of tightly packed, chartreuse-colored buds that open as tubular flowers holding masses of pistils. During the summer, the plants make effective ground covers, especially at the edge of a pond or stream. But they are weedy, so use caution in their placement. The best way to grow this plant is to confine its roots to a large pot sunk to its rim in the ground. English books advise that they then be lifted, pot and all, and brought inside to brighten winter days.

Petasites fragrans, the winter heliotrope, is a European wildflower that blooms at the same time, with pale lilac flowers that smell of vanilla. Sometimes seeds are offered by various seed exchanges, but it's more likely that you will have to go out and search for this species. *Petasites* comes from the Greek *petasos*, "broad-brimmed hat," referring to the large basal leaves.

Phlox subulata, the ground pink, moss pink, or mountain pink, is famous for its sheets of blatant color when it bursts into late-winter or early-spring bloom, especially conspicuous when surrounded by browned grasses and leftover dead leaves. Today ground pink is so commonly cultivated that most gardeners find it difficult to believe that it's a native plant. The evergreen mats of needlelike foliage are often covered with buds standing only a few inches high. These suddenly bloom in shades of white, pink, lavender, and an occasional cerise. There are a number of cultivars, including

'Rosea', with pink flowers, and 'Scarlet Flame', a near-red form. About the only planting advice we can offer is, in order to keep your esthetic reputation, to refrain from mixing colors.

Primula spp., the primroses, can be plant problems in the South because they resent heat. But the three species listed here are reasonably reliable in most of our climate zone. *Primula denticulata*, the drumstick primrose, is a native of the Himalayas. Foot-high stems bear round heads of pale purple flowers with yellow eyes, blooming in March. A mature plant will often produce two dozen or more balls of bloom. The leaves are tufted, about 6 inches in length. Plants like moist soil with a high organic content. They slowly increase their numbers with new shoots that appear around the parent plants. And primroses are easily increased by seed or division.

Primula veris are fragrant charmers that will stand up to 8 inches tall, with a dozen yellow flowers about $1/2$ inch in diameter dangling from a peduncle, or flower stalk. Larry has a friend in Charlotte, long-time gardener Leon Gutmann, who has rows of *Primula veris* planted along his garden trails, where he invites visitors to walk down his primrose paths. While the modern hybrids may be colorful, they don't have the charm of the simple species. Larry has seen charming clumps at Woodlanders Nursery in Aiken, South Carolina, in full bloom in mid-March after surviving 15°F in bud.

Primula vulgaris is the beloved cowslip of Eastern Europe, and not to be confused with the American cowslip or marsh marigold (*Caltha palustris*). Delicate, nodding, yellow flowers appear on 6-inch stems that stand above basal leaves between 6 and 8 inches long. This species, and several varieties and selections, may bloom in late winter. In the South, the leaves may persist into summer, but they look yellowish and ragged. The species may thrive for a few years in the garden, or it may act as an annual. Well-drained but moist soil and partial shade may help it survive. It is easily grown from seed.

Pulmonaria spp., the lungworts, were used in medieval times to treat various lung diseases, not always successfully. The "lung" part of the name refers to the whitish gray spots that adorn the leaves of several species. They are more valuable as ground covers in the shade garden and for the lovely sprays of little five-lobed, tubelike flowers that appear in very early spring. The plants grow about a foot high and will do well in any fertile soil, in full or partial shade, and are reasonably evergreen in the South. The plants can be

Primula veris selection

dug up in late winter, potted up, and forced into bloom to brighten otherwise dull days.

Pulmonaria angustifolia has green leaves without the typical spots and bears sprays of small pink buds that turn a clear blue upon opening. *Pulmonaria officinalis*, the Jerusalem sage or Jerusalem cowslip, bears sprays of bright pink flowers that arch above the fledgling spring leaves, turning a lilac-blue as they age. The leaves are more or less spotted. *Pulmonaria saccharata*, the Bethlehem sage, is the most popular plant for the garden. The leaves are spotted and the flowers a bright pink, eventually turning blue. 'Mrs. Moon' is the most popular cultivar, but there are others, including 'Leopard', which has more than average spotting, and 'Cambridge Blue', named for the color of its flowers.

Ranunculus ficaria, the lesser celadine or figwort ranunculus, is a perennial buttercup that grows less than a foot high and bears inch-wide, solitary golden yellow flowers. The plant spreads by underground runners and disappears entirely as summer nears. Many gardeners think of this plant as a weed, and it probably is. But more than one plantsman has said that if the plant originally came from a remote part of Tibet rather than wet meadows just outside of suburbs in Europe and western Asia, everybody would want one. This Eurasian native was introduced into New England, where it escaped into the wild. *Ranunculus* means "little frog" in Latin and refers to the aquatic habitat preferred by some of the species. For a weed, there still are a number of listed cultivars, including the white

Ranuculus ficaria, lesser celandine

form 'Albus', a double form named for 'E. A. Bowles', 'Lemon Queen', 'Randall's White', and 'Brazen Hussy', which has winter leaves that are almost black (really a very dark purple).

Shortia galacifolia, or Oconee bells, are wildflowers with a past. In 1839, Asa Gray, America's great botanist, saw an unusual dried plant specimen in André Michaux's Paris herbarium dating from the 1790s. The label said it had been collected in the high mountains of the Carolinas. Dr. Gray returned home and hunted the heights of North Carolina for the unnamed plant, entirely without success. Two years later, he described the plant in print, naming it *Shortia galacifolia*. After that, no botanist worth his salt ever visited the mountains without searching for it. Then, in 1877, a young boy, George McQ. Hyams, of Statesville, North Carolina, picked up a plant on the banks of the Catawba River near the town of Marion in McDowell County, and the world once again had found Oconee bells. In 1886, huge fields of these wildflowers

were found and wagonloads were taken away; in fact, it was almost wiped out of existence in that spot.

Oconee bells are difficult to establish. Patience is needed when planning on using this marvelous plant as a ground cover. The plant eschews lime in any form, so if planted on a wall, keep it away from any mortar. But even when its growth is on the scant side, the flowers of late winter are worth the wait. The nodding blossoms are bell-like in form. Their white, waxy petals evidence a soft pink glow and are delicately scalloped at the edges. Add to this the shiny, rounded evergreen foliage with its autumn tints of bronzy red, and you know why gardeners around the world love to grow it.

Symplocarpus foetidus, the skunk cabbage, is the earliest wildflower in eastern North America to bloom; in North Carolina, which is its southernmost range, it often blooms in February. Being a member of the jack-in-the-pulpit family (Araceae), it has a spike of flowers surrounded by a tough, leathery, leaflike spathe, which may be reddish brown or greenish in color. This inflorescence is famous for producing its own heat to such an extent that it melts the snow immediately surrounding the plant. The flowers also produce a fetid odor to attract flies for pollination, because self-respecting bees are still asleep in the hive. The flowers are followed by large green leaves that produce a skunky smell when crushed. While not your average garden flower, it does provide a bold, hostalike appearance in the bog or wetland habitat it requires. While perfectly hardy, it is nearly impossible to transplant because of its enormous rootstock, and virtually no nurseries grow it. Yet we constantly receive inquiries as to its availability. Imaginative gardeners will try growing plants from seed.

Tussilago farfara, or coltsfoot, is a weedy perennial that grows from an invasive, creeping rhizome. Like most interlopers, this is a tough plant, and it will live in dirt that is often a combination of road salts, sand, pure clay, and rock shards. But if established in the woodland garden, in late February and on into March it will reward gardeners with bright yellow dandelionlike flowers. Blooming along the side of the road, they look like golden coins left by escaping pirates. Although the flowers have been used in folk medicine, it's the leaves that were once the most important. In the days of the flintlock rifle, the down from the undersides of the leaves was used as tinder, and birds still use the fluff to line their nests. *Tussilago* comes from the Latin *tussis*, "cough," and refers to the use of the leaves to help treat recurrent coughs.

Vinca minor, the common periwinkle, remains one of the favorite old-time evergreen ground covers. It was brought over from Europe with the colonists and is now found in every old cemetery. It's a perennial evergreen subshrub, with shiny 2-inch leaves that spread about on long stems that will root at every node. It has

Viola hybrids, miniature pansies of the 'Sorbet' strain, are currently popular as small clump-forming bedding plants for winter-spring color. They come in a variety of rich pastel colors and pleasing combinations, and they thrive in rich soil in light shade to full winter sun. Try growing them from seed in July to set out in September.

five-petaled violet flowers that bloom in spring and fall. Cultivars include 'Alba', with white flowers; 'Alpina', bearing light blue flowers; 'Azurea Flore Pleno', with double flowers of sky blue; 'Gertrude Jekyll', which has smaller leaves and large white flowers; 'Multiplex', with double flowers of purplish blue; and 'Sterling Silver', having leaves with creamy white margins and lavender-blue flowers. Common periwinkle is a great plant for clothing steep banks, carpeting problem areas, and covering rocks. Provide partial shade in good garden soil with added humus. *Vinca* (or *pervinca*) is the ancient Latin name for these plants.

Viola odorata, the sweet violet, belongs to a genus of wildflowers that takes an expert to slowly wade through its taxonomy. Some gardeners view violets as weeds, but their early-spring bloom is so delightful that we think their weedier aspects should be forgotten, at least until later in the garden year. But when it comes to blooming in the new year, nothing is more charming than a planting of this sweet violet.

Viola tricolor has been called the original Johnny-jump-up, European wild pansy, field pansy, or ladies' delight, this last name used by Alice Morse Earle in her book *Old Time Gardens* (New York: The Macmillan Company, 1901). "For several years the first blossom of the new year in our garden was neither the snow-drop nor crocus, but the ladies' delight . . . such a shrewd, intelligent little creature that it readily found out that spring was here ere man or other flower knew it." Gerard described this flower back in 1587 and bestowed the original, and still valid, scientific name. As to common names, in addition to those already mentioned, add to the list none-so-pretty, kit-run-about, three-faces-under-a-hood, jump-up-and-kiss-me, pink-of-my-Joan, and just plain kiss me.

In addition to the common form, there is a very dramatic dark purple cultivar called 'E. A. Bowles' or 'Bowles Black'. It's often available from the more sophisticated seed houses.

Viola × wittrockiana is the scientific name of the pansy, one of the South's great winter-blooming plants (some might say the *only* winter-blooming plant). It's a delightful flower that sometimes falls under the spell of the old proverb that familiarity breeds contempt. Certainly, when the pansy is used to the exclusion of all other bloomers and planted out in masses using only the brightest colors, there might be occasion to point out the possibility of design problems. But if the various cultivars are used with some restraint, and possibly find their way to window boxes, tubs, and planters, or are mixed with some ornamental grasses, pansies should be a delightful addition to the winter garden in the South.

6

WINTER-BLOOMING SHRUBS, TREES, AND VINES

Even though the shadblow may flower only briefly—three days if either rainy or hot weather sets in—some horticulturists prefer its refined, delicate display to the more flamboyant magnolias or royal azalea blooming at the same time . . . . The name shadblow recalls that spring event when shad used to swim up the pure coastal rivers to spawn. The shadblow is a first hint—along with pussy willows and skunk cabbage—that winter is almost done with.

—Judith Leet, *The Botanical Paintings of Esther Heins*

IT'S AMAZING JUST HOW MANY SHRUBS AND TREES WILL produce flowers in a southern winter. From heathers to camellias to witch hazels, there is just no excuse not to have a good selection of these magnificent plants in your garden. As Vita Sackville-West said in *Country Notes in Wartime*, "Gardener, if you listen, listen well: plant for your winter pleasure, when the months dishearten" (Freeport, NY: Essay Index Reprint Series, 1970). And if the changing weather patterns are any clue to coming winters, we should do everything possible to make those dark months a brighter time at home.

Shrubs

Berberis darwinii, the Darwin's barberry, which hails from southern Chile and the Patagonian Mountains, has 1/2-inch-long evergreen leaves with two or three coarse teeth on either side. The shrubs generally reach 5 to 6 feet high. Golden yellow flowers appear in November, numbering between ten and thirty in racemes, followed by blue berries covered with a bloom. Provide partial shade in the summer, planting in a good, moist, acid garden soil. They are not reliably hardy in the higher mountains. *Berberis* comes from the Arabic name of the fruit.

Calluna vulgaris represents the Scotch heathers, evergreen plants with small, green, needlelike leaves that are perfect for the rock garden. There is only one species, but there are many, many cultivars. Called lings in England, these subshrubs usually bloom from summer into fall. But one cultivar, 'H. E. Beale', will bloom with pink flowers in late fall, often persisting into early winter. This plant needs a poor, acid, moist but well-drained soil, and protection from late-winter sun, not to mention summer heat. They do very well in the northern and mountainous portions of our range, where summer nights are cooler. These plants are often grown for their lovely winter foliage colors (see chapter 8).

Camellia spp., the camellias, have been popular for more than a thousand years in the orient—Japan alone is said to possess over nine hundred cultivars.

In 1847, a beautiful French courtesan named Alphonsine Duplessis died at the age of 27. She loved camellias more than anything in her not unsophisticated life, so her grieving lovers—of which there were many—covered her coffin with a pall of white camellias. Alexander Dumas *fils* became enchanted with the story and wrote *La Dame aux Camélias*—mistakenly translated into English as *Camille*. In 1852, a play was produced, and the rage for camellias swept the continent. By the end of the nineteenth century, the fervor had passed, and when popularity again picked up, the interest was in outdoor cultivation. The genus is named for a Moravian Jesuit, George Joseph Kamel (1661–1706), who traveled in Asia (1704) and wrote plant histories.

In Zone 7 and up, the camellia is hardy outdoors. Some cultivars can even take short spells of −5°F, and research continues to develop varieties that will with-

Chamaecyparis pisifera 'Filifera aurea', threadleaf cypress

Berberis darwinii, Darwin's barberry

stand even lower temperatues. When winter winds blow and the temperature in Asheville is below zero, I cover our bushes with a blanket for the night, and in seven years I have never lost a bud. The buds normally open when daytime temperatures are above freezing. Most cultivars are quite specific in their blooming periods; others, like 'Lady Clare', may bloom anytime from Thanksgiving to Mother's Day.

Common camellias grow into evergreen shrubs or small trees from 6 to 10 feet tall in ten to fifteen years. *Camellia saluenensis*, originally from China, is a compact shrub growing to 15 feet. *C. vernalis* resembles *C. sasanqua* but blooms later in spring. *C. sasanqua* is a smaller shrub with an open habit, bearing thin leathery leaves of a bright glossy green above. These bushes will reach a height of 6 to 8 feet in 10 years or so, eventually topping 15 feet. There are many cultivars, including 'Floribunda', with white flowers edged in lavendar. 'Rosea' bears flowers of a deep pink and 'Cleopatra' of rose-pink petals. Originally from Japan and the Ryukyu Islands, they bloom in late autumn to winter. The seeds yield a non-drying oil of commerce. *C. olifera*, the seeds of which are the source of commercial tea oil, used in the arts and in medicine, blooms in November with lovely single, white flowers. It's the hardiest of the camellias.

These shrubs need an acid soil with a moist but never soggy location. In the spring when new growth begins, fertilize camellias with any acid fertilizer used for rhododendrons. We use cottonseed meal to great effect.

Some of the more beautiful of today's cultivars are 'Lady Vansittart', with white-striped rose pink flowers of medium size; 'Dixie Knight Supreme', which has deep red, variegated white blossoms with a loose peony form; 'Charlie Bettes', a large white semidouble; 'C. M. Wilson', an anemone form with large pink-white flowers; 'Dr. Clifford Parks', a *Camellia japonica* hybrid with a red-orange cast and a very large, loose peony form; 'Drama Girl', a deep salmon to rose pink, large semidouble; 'Finlandia', a white semidouble of medium-size flowers; and 'Cherries Jubilee', a burgundy red with red and white petaloids (a form of petal).

Camellia japonica 'Lady Clare'

Chaenomeles spp., the flowering quinces, are dependable shrubs that bloom in late winter or early spring with hundreds of blossoms on each bush. In mid-February 1996, after the toughest Asheville winter in years, the buds were burgeoning and would be in bloom in early March. *Chaenomeles* comes from the Greek for "split apple" and refers to the edible fruits, which resemble miniature apples and make great jelly.

Chaenomeles japonica, the Japanese flowering quince, bears single, 1½-inch, fragrant flowers on thorny stems before the leaves appear. The bushes reach a height of 3 to 4 feet, with a 2- to 3-foot spread. References point out that this is a good city plant, and ours are set within a foot of the asphalt of Lakewood Drive and do well every year. Plants will take sun or shade, are very tolerant of soil, and like decent, but not perfect, drainage. Prune nonflowering shoots. Among the cultivars are 'Minerva', with velvety cherry red flowers; 'Pink Beauty', with rose pink blossoms; and 'Snow', with pure white, waxy flowers.

Chaenomeles speciosa, the flowering quince, grows to a height of 5 to 6 feet, with a 5-foot spread. Masses of 2-inch flowers appear before the leaves on spiny branches. The flowers are usually rose pink, scarlet, orange-red, or white, followed by greenish yellow, fragrant fruit. It is very easy to force twigs into winter bloom indoors. 'Cameo' has semidouble apricot-pink flowers; 'Jet Trail' is a short bush with white flowers; 'Phyllis Moore' bears semidouble pink flowers; 'Snow' has single white flowers; 'Texas Scarlet' has bright red flowers that cover a compact bush; and 'Toyo-Nishiki' has blends of white, pink, and dark rose flowers. This shrub can have problems with fire blight and scale and should not be planted near orchards.

Chimonanthus praecox, the wintersweet, is a marvelous winter shrub that is valuable for its fragrant flowers. The ¾-inch-wide flowers are yellow striped with purplish brown. They appear on leafless branches, beginning to open in December and continuing to bloom on and off all winter long. Foliage is a

Chaenomeles speciosa, flowering quince

102

Chimonanthus praecox

rich, shiny green and turns a clear yellow in the fall. Wintersweet grows up to 12 feet high, with a 10-foot spread. Plant these shrubs in any good garden soil where they will get afternoon sun. Mulch plants to keep the soil moist during the winter. After the flowers fade in early spring, prune back the older canes. *Chimonanthus* comes from the Greek for "snow" and "flower", and *praecox* means "precocious."

Corylopsis spp., the winter hazels, are close relatives of the witch hazels (the genus is Latin for "like hazels"). There are about ten species, originally natives of Southeast Asia and the Himalayas. In early spring, the attractive flowers appear before the leaves. Among the most beautiful plants are *Corylopsis sinensis*, a species that reaches a height of about 8 feet and is covered by hanging racemes of sweetly scented yellow flowers with orange or yellow stamens. *Corylopsis spicata* is a Japanese native that flowers in March and April. It has narrow racemes of yellow-green flowers with red anthers. *Corylopsis pauciflora* is another

Japanese native. It can reach 12 feet and blooms in late winter with pale yellow, scented flowers in delicate racemes. Provide moist garden soil with plenty of organic matter in partial shade. Flowers can be injured by early spring frosts.

Daphne spp., the daphnes, represent some fifty species of evergreen and deciduous shrubs with lovely flowers and attractive foliage, named for *Daphne*, the bay-tree. The most common species is *Daphne odora*, the winter daphne. Reaching a height of 3 to 4 feet, with a 3-foot spread, this would be an attractive evergreen shrub even without the late-winter blooms, but the star-shaped, very fragrant flowers of a rosy purple without and white within are the icing on the cake. Unfortunately, it's not easy to establish and takes a few years to settle in. This is a slow-growing plant that likes good drainage in soil of medium fertility, in sun or shade. It's especially effective when planted against a wall. There are a number of cultivars, but the one we like best is 'Aureo-marginata', which has leaves lightly

103

Corylopsis sinensis, winter hazel

bordered with yellow and flowers of lavender-pink. In rough winters, the foliage might be burned and fall off, but the flowers usually persist and new leaves come out in spring. Avoid direct morning sun, as this also can cause frozen leaves to burn. Other cultivars include 'Alba', with white flowers, and 'Rubra', bearing wine red flowers.

Daphne bholua, the Himalaya daphne, is an erect evergreen shrub to 7 feet. Two cultivars are known. 'Gurkha' is a deciduous form first discovered in 1962 by Major Spring Smythe in Nepal, growing at 10,000 feet. The flowers are purple-rose and bloom in January and February. 'Jacqueline Postill' is an evergreen variety with reddish mauve flowers that are white within and bloom into March. *Daphne mezereum* is a little-known deciduous, winter-flowering shrub that blooms

in February and March and bears pale purple, fragrant flowers on 2- to 3-foot shrubs. These plants will do well in acid or alkaline soil but should be protected from cold, harsh winds.

Erica spp., the heaths, are evergreen shrubs originally from Africa and Europe. They range from shrubs a few inches high to 20-foot trees. Although both heaths and heathers are botanically considered to be evergreen shrubs, gardeners usually think of them as plants useful for the perennial garden and border because of their profuse flowering, their low stature, and their evergreen habit. Leaves are generally small and needlelike, and the flowers are tubular or bell shaped, ending in four lobes. And those flowers will cover the plants in winter, in addition to the wonderful leaf colors that many species and cultivars exhibit. In

Daphne odora with ice crystals

Daphne odora 'Variegata'

Forsythia

fact, today there are hundreds of choices. *Erica carnea*, the spring heath or snow heather, grows about a foot high, with prostrate branches that can eventually spread to 3 feet. 'King George' blooms in January with deep magenta flowers that enhance its dark purplish foliage; 'Springwood' bears white flowers and 'Springwood Pink' has pink flowers, both blooming from early March; and 'Pink Spangles' grows 1 foot high and bears deep pink flowers in late winter, usually from February to April.

In late autumn and early winter, *Erica × darleyensis*, the Mediterranean heaths, bloom with their small bell-like flowers on 2-foot-high mounds of tiny, dark green, needlelike leaves. 'Darley Dale' has pink flowers, and 'Silberschmelze' has white.

Gardeners in Zone 8 should look for *Erica lusitanica*, the Spanish heath, a dense, erect shrub that will top 12 feet and bears thousands of tiny white flowers

(Left) *Erica × watsonii* 'Dawn' is one of several members of the large heath genus. This hybrid is from European parentage, but most species are from South Africa. All like a cool climate and well-drained soil, making them extremely unlikely candidates for the southern garden. If one takes in a certain spot, don't try to move it. *Erica carnea* is another good species with which to try a cultivar.

with pink stigmas and stamens. *E. arborea*, the tree heath, is hardy in Zone 7 and reaches a height of 20 feet. Large panicles of white, fragrant flowers appear in late winter and early spring. The roots of this last tree are used in the manufacture of brier pipes.

Heaths like a light, sandy, acid soil and do poorly in the presence of limestone. If your garden soil is heavy or uncut clay, add pea gravel and peat moss. New blooming wood is produced by heading back after flowering. A well-planted display of heaths and heathers becomes a refined patchwork quilt of color, both from foliage and flowers.

Forsythia spp., the golden bells, have been around American gardens long enough to be considered clichés of early spring. The first of these shrubs to be discovered was *Forsythia suspensa*, a Chinese species cultivated in Japan and introduced into England as late as 1850. The second species of note is *F. viridissima*, also found in China and reaching England in 1844. They were named in honor of William Forsyth (1737–1804), a superintendent of the Royal Gardens at Kensington, England.

Since both species are variable, a number of cultivars have been produced. But for southern gardens, a hybrid between the two, *Forsythia × intermedia*, is the best form. Reaching a height of 8 to 10 feet, with a 7- to 10-foot spread, this shrub has very attractive arching branches, with the flowers appearing in early

Hamamelis mollis, Chinese witch hazel

March, well before the leaves. 'Arnold Dwarf' is a wide-spreading, low-growing plant with sparse, pale greenish yellow flowers that makes a great ground cover; 'Beatrix Farrand' has large, vivid yellow flowers; 'Densiflora' bears pale yellow flowers on pendulous branches; and 'Spring Glory' bears pale sulfur yellow blooms that cover 6-foot branches. In 1939, *Forsythia viridissima* 'Bronxensis' was first grown at the New York Botanic Garden in the Bronx. It's a wonderful dwarf form that is especially grand when planted at the edge of a wall.

Forsythia giraldiana is an upright shrub that was introduced from Gansu, China, in 1910, growing to a height of 12 feet and covered with pale yellow flowers. *F. ovata* came from Korea in 1917 and grows as a spreading shrub about 5 feet high, bearing small, amber yellow flowers.

Forsythias do well in ordinary, well-drained garden soil but flower better if some humus or composted manure is added. They require little pruning, but you can thin out old shoots by cutting branches for forcing.

Garrya elliptica, the quinine bush or silk tassel bush, was found in 1827 growing on the south side of the Columbia River in Oregon. The plant was sent to England, where it bloomed in 1834. It became the one

(Left) *Garrya elliptica*, silk tassel tree

member of a new family called Garryaceae, causing a great furor among the botanists of the day. The genus was named in honor of Nicholas Garry, a deputy governor of the Hudson's Bay Company from 1822 to 1835. In early winter, the male plants produce beautiful dangling catkins from 6 to 12 inches in length. Females bear shorter catkins, followed by purple fruits. The best form is 'James Roof', which has extremely long catkins. *Garrya × issaquahensis* was found in a private garden in Issaquah, Washington, and is a hybrid between *G. elliptica* and *G. fremontii*, a hardier wild form. The result is a hardier cultivar with flowers able to survive temperatures just above 0°F. *Garrya* is not hardy in Zone 6 but needs warmer weather to survive and bloom. It prefers good, well-drained garden soil and is both salt and wind tolerant. These plants frequently succumb to our hot, humid southern summers.

Hamamelis spp., the witch hazels, are superb winter-flowering plants, with flowers now available in a wide variety of colors and sizes. There are two American species: *H. virginiana*, a native of the eastern United States, where it often becomes a small tree, bearing flowers with four bright yellow petals, and *H. vernalis*, the vernal witch hazel, a smaller species found from Arkansas to Oklahoma and Louisiana, having carmine flowers with light yellow highlights. The

Hamamelis intermedia 'Jelena', witch hazel

vernal witch hazel has three good cultivars, 'Carnea', with red flowers; 'Lombart's Weeping', with red-orange flowers; and 'Sandra', with new leaves of a plum purple, and brilliant red fall foliage instead of the usual bright yellow. Both plants usually bloom after the leaves have fallen. Their black seeds are discharged from the drying pods with explosive force, easily heard on cold winter days. Amazingly, too, witch hazels are pollinated by winter moths, members of the subfamily Cuculliinae, and various flies. The well-known witch-hazel extract is derived from the bark of *H. virginiana*, and the early settlers used the wood for divining rods.

But when it comes to home gardens, these American species are usually replaced by Asiatic species, the first being *Hamamelis japonica*, introduced in 1862, bearing fragrant yellow flowers with petals up to $3/4$ inch long, opening from January to March. Then came the Chinese witch hazel, *H. mollis* 'Brevipetala', introduced in 1879, a plant distinguished from the Japanese form by larger flowers with straight, broad petals, of a deeper yellow color, and much more fragrant.

Finally, in 1945, the Arnold Arboretum hybridized the Chinese and Japanese forms, producing *H. × intermedia*, although there were crosses reported at a much earlier date. 'Diana' bears fragrant clusters of coppery red flowers that appear in early spring before the leaves. 'Arnold Promise' is the best-known cultivar (a hybrid between *H. japonica* and *H. mollis*), coming from the Arnold Arboretum in 1928, and bearing many large, bright yellow flowers on a spreading shrub; 'Jeleva' has exceptional bloom in Charlotte, with bright yellow-orange petals; 'Pallida' is a very popular cultivar, with large yellow flowers usually opening for the New Year; and 'Primavera' has sweetly scented, primrose yellow flowers that appear after the others bloom.

All these shrubs eventually can reach a height of 15 feet. They prefer a light, well-drained soil in the partial shade produced by a high canopy of trees. But they like the soil moist, and their biggest enemy is summer drought. In nature, they are often found grow-

(Right) *Hamamelis* 'Arnold Promise'

Jasminum nudiflorum

ing next to streams and in areas with a good amount of rainfall. Witch hazels should not be pruned except to remove dead wood, although you can cut branches to bring indoors for the flowers. One final note regarding color: If you are planting a red-flowered variety, keep them in an intimate setting so the flowers can be enjoyed. If seen in a large garden against a background of other trees, the reddish flowers do not stand out as well as the yellow cultivars.

Jasminum nudiflorum, the winter jasmine, came from China in 1844. It's a rambling deciduous shrub that can reach out for 10 to 15 feet, but its average height is between 2 and 4 feet, typically with a 5-foot spread. The flowers are bright yellow, about an inch in diameter, and bloom off and on all winter long, usually starting on warm days in January. Leaves do not appear until well into spring. These jasmines are not fussy and will adapt to most garden soil of low fertility and medium drainage. They should be pruned back

(Left) *Jasminum nudiflorum*, **winter jasmine**

every three or four years to rejuvenate the bushes. The plants are especially attractive if planted on a slope or on top of a wall so that the long, arching stems can tumble into open space.

Lonicera fragrantissima, the winter-blooming honeysuckle, was first discovered in 1845 by Scotland's great plant explorer Robert Fortune, who was searching China for plants. Soon thereafter, this plant appeared in American gardens. The maximum height is 10 feet, and the branches splay out with good form. The flowers are small and creamy white, appearing during midwinter. While not outstanding in floral might, they have a charm all their own, not to mention a marvelous fragrance, which gives this shrub its common southern name of breath-of-spring. Stems can be cut before blooming begins and brought indoors, where the partially opened buds will continue to expand and release fragrance to the inner air. William C. Welch, a noteable garden writer from Texas, reports that early southern gardeners often planted a winter honeysuckle near a frequently used gate to the garden so that both fragrance

113

Lonicera fragrantissima, winter honeysuckle

and flowers could be easily enjoyed. When not in flower, these shrubs are still attractive for their blue-green foliage. In the winter, the brown-gray bark shows up to advantage, the top layers tearing away in a pleasing manner. For planting, any good garden soil will do, but we have found that these plants appreciate moisture.

Lonicera standishii has smaller flowers but otherwise differs little from *L. fragantissima*. A hybrid between the two, *Lonicera × purpursii*, was a chance seedling that appeared in the Darmstadt Botanical Gardens in the 1920s. It is said to be superior to the species, but our seedlings are only a year old, and it's too soon to judge. Both plants need warm summers to set a good crop of blossoms.

Loropetalum chinense, the blush loropetalum, is a white-flowered, broadleaf evergreen shrub or small tree from China, Japan, and India. It has appeared in southern gardens for many years, and the late J. C. Raulston of the university arboretum at Raleigh had seen 25-foot specimen trees in Atlanta. Height is between 6 and 10 feet, with an 8- or 9-foot spread. Trees bloom in March with showy flowers bearing feathery petals about an inch long. Sun or partial shade will do, and good, moist garden soil with reasonable drainage, on the acid side, is preferred. J. C. reported that there is a new form from the West Coast called 'Sizzling Pink', with hot pink flowers, and 'Burgundy' boasts the same flowers, only hovering above purple foliage. *Loropetalum* comes from the Greek for "strap" and "petal," referring to the petal's shape.

Maesa japonica, a member of the Myrsinaceae family (African boxwood) from Eastern Asia, is a tropical evergreen shrub or small tree reaching a height of 10 to 15 feet. It is extremely rare in cultivation but has some potential in the warmer parts of our region. Some books say it is not hardy, but our gardener friend Cynthia Aulbach-Smith has grown a plant for several years at her home in Columbia, South Carolina. It is about 3 feet tall and produces interesting elongate clusters of white flowers. The plant form, leaf structure, and flowers are

Loropetalum chinense 'Roseum'

Loropetalum chinense, Pink Form

Mahonia bealei

superficially identical to the evergreen *Leucothoe fontanesiana*. The plant is variously hardy, surviving some winters and dying back to the ground in others. It requires winter protection and a well-drained rich soil.

Mahonia spp., the Oregon grapes, are not grapes but native American members of the barberry family (Berberidaceae). The most popular of these evergreen shrubs is *M. aquifolium*, the mountain grape, holly mahonia, or holly barberry. This and *M. bealei* are stalwart features of the southern winter garden. *M. aquifolium* has an irregular and informal look, producing upright stems with few side branches. Height is about 4 feet, with a 3- to 5-foot spread. The leathery compound leaves have five to nine hollylike leaflets and are a glossy dark green turning a reddish purple in winter. The fragrant little ball-like, yellow flowers bloom from March to April in erect terminal clusters about 3 inches long. They are followed by grapelike clusters of

(Left) *Mahonia aquifolium* 'King's Ransom', Oregon grape

blue-black fruits that are loved by birds. These shrubs are great in the winter landscape and excellent as foundation plantings. They are not recommended for the Coastal Plains, although they do withstand wind exposure. 'Compactum' has very glossy, dark green leaves that turn bronze in winter; 'Golden Abundance' has more golden yellow flower clusters than the species; and 'Vicarii' has young reddish leaves that turn green in the summer and last through the winter.

Mahonia bealei, the leatherleaf mahonia, is a larger shrub, reaching a height of 5 to 6 feet, with a 3- to 4-foot spread. Foliage is a bronze-green, turning a reddish green in the fall. The yellow flowers appear in March, blooming in clusters about 6 inches long. The summer fruit is blue. *Mahonia japonica* is often confused with *M. bealei* but has pendulous racemes of yellow flowers up to 10 inches long. *Mahonia* × 'Arthur Menzies' is a hybrid between *M. bealei* and *M. lomariifolia* that was found by chance in a flat of seedlings from Strybing Arboretum in San Francisco. This lovely shrub bears spectacular panicles of yellow flowers in

December and January. *Mahonia × media* 'Charity' is a hybrid form of *M. japonica* and *M. lomariifolia* with great and luxuriant foliage and soft yellow flowers on erect spikes, blooming in late February.

Provide partial or full shade for these dependable shrubs, planting in soil of medium fertility with a high organic content and good drainage. Heavy pruning of the side branches on old or neglected plants will lead to a rush of new growth. The only problem is that like the laurels, they suffer from leaf spot, but this is a small price to pay for such a lovely specimen plant. The genus was named in honor of American horticulturist Bernard McMahon (1775-1816).

Michelia figo (*M. fuscata*), the banana shrub, is a member of the magnolia family but is hardy only to Zone 7; elsewhere it must be grown as a pot plant. This shrub reaches a height of 6 to 8 feet, with a 6- to 8-foot spread (or the size of a small tree in warmer climates). It is altogether a beautiful thing, with glossy dark green foliage, each leaf about 3 inches long, and 1 1/2-inch-long magnolialike flowers that are very fragrant, smelling of bananas. It blooms from late March through June. 'Stubbs' Purple' is a cultivar with fragrant purple flowers. Elizabeth Lawrence wrote that a bad freeze in March 1960, "with temperatures down to 10°F, after a fairly mild January and February, did more damage than I have ever seen before. The banana shrub, *Michelia fuscata*, was so badly hurt that I decided to discard it." Banana shrubs have survived for Larry at 0°F but were killed to the ground at −6°F, only to grow back with great gusto from the roots.

Paeonia suffruticosa 'Kan Botan', the Japanese winter-flowering tree peony, is a rarity in most Southern gardens because so far the plants are not readily available to the gardening public outside of Japan. In Japanese, *Kan Botan* means "winter tree peony." These plants flower in spring, then bloom again from late November to January. They were developed in Japan from the original Chinese tree peonies and have been known for more than three hundred years. Japanese winters are colder in January than December, so gardeners make little cone-shaped huts of rice straw to protect the plants from severe winter winds. Though the winter flowers are smaller than those of spring, between 4 and 5 inches wide, they still manage to project the beauty of a peony. Once the winter flowers are through, the stems are pruned back to healthy buds for spring bloom. The plant will not bloom where winters are too warm.

Pieris japonica 'Pygmaea' is a distinctive dwarf Japanese Andromeda. It may reach a 2-foot height after ten years, and often exhibits twisted branches that curve about at interesting angles. The leaves are very narrow and needlelike, giving the plant a fine texture. Flowers are rarely formed but when they are, they are charming.

Rhododendron mucronulatum

Rhododendron dauricum

Pieris japonica, the Japanese andromeda or lily-of-the-valley shrub, is also in chapter 8 for its lustrous evergreen leaves. Here we include it for its tiny unopened flower buds, each with a short red stem, that hang down in long panicles. Combined with the foliage, these future blossoms make the shrub look as though you are seeing it with rose-colored glasses.

Rhododendron spp., the rhododendrons, are favored broadleaf evergreen shrubs for spring and summer bloom, but many gardeners are not aware of the winter-flowering varieties. The earliest winter bloomer is the deciduous *Rhododendron mucronulatum*, in China called *ying hong dujuan*, or "welcome red rhododendron." There it grows in thickets wandering across hilly areas. The bushes are about 6 feet high and produce many soft lavender blossoms from December to March. Two to five lateral flower buds are clustered at each branch tip, with one flower per bud that opens before the leaves. There is a pure white form called 'Album' and a larger-flowered form called 'Cornell Pink'. In the North, these bushes do well in full sun, but in the South, they prefer partial shade. The leaves turn red, yellow, and orange before falling.

Rhododendron dauricum, the *Xing'an* rhododendron of China, is a semi-evergreen shrub, reaching a height of 3 feet in cultivation but up to 7 feet in the

Sarcococca hookerana 'Humilis', sweet box

wild. These shrubs bear scattered leaves, and at branch tips there are one to two flowers that precede the new leaves. The flowers vary from lavender to reddish purple and begin blooming in January, continuing to open on warm winter days. 'Praecox' is a hardy cultivar, about 4 feet high, that bears many rich light purple blossoms (approaching mauve in some specimens) in early March and plum-colored leaves all year long.

Rhododendron moupinense, the *Baoxing* rhododendron of China, is an epiphytic, evergreen shrub about 3 feet high, found growing in the forks of tree trunks in Chinese forests at an elevation of 10,000 feet. Because it is an epiphyte, the plant does best set in sphagnum moss and grown in an orchid pot with many drainage holes at the bottom. The plants bear terminal bunches of one to three flowers that are white on the outside with red dots lining the throat and red anthers with white filaments. A hybrid between *R. dauricum* and *R. moupinense* is 'Olive', with large pink flowers blooming in February.

Finally there is *Rhododendron strigillosum*, called the prickly rhododendron because the bush is densely clad with gland-tipped bristles. This is an evergreen shrub up to 10 feet high (sometimes 20 feet in the wild),

(Left) *Salix chaenomeloides*, quince-leafed pussy willow

blooming in early March with clusters of eight to twelve flowers of deep red, with purple anthers on pale filaments. The species is found growing in forests at an altitude between 6,500 and 10,000 feet. Soil for all of these rhododendrons should be enriched with compost, on the acid side, and in hot summers, water must be provided.

Salix spp., the willows, represent more than three hundred species of shrubs and trees. They are often grown as ornamentals and along the banks of streams, where they grow with a rapidity that is sometimes alarming, especially if there are underground water pipes nearby. There are many species and cultivars well suited for the winter garden, not only for the colorful branches, but also for the time-honored and adored blossoms called pussy willows. *Salix* is the old Latin name for these plants. The Indians knew the value of chewing willow bark for pain, and it wasn't until some 150 years ago that salicylic acid was found to be the reason. When later synthesized by the Bayer Company of Germany, it was called aspirin.

Salix alba 'Snake' has fasciated, or flattened, branches, but is spectacular when the silver hairs of the individual pussies are backlit by the winter sun. *Salix caprea*, the French pussy willow, is a vigorous shrub sometimes growing to a height of 25 feet. In late winter, it is covered with the largest catkins around. Its cultivar 'Pendula', the weeping pussy willow, which was first discovered on the River Ayr in Scotland, is especially charming when its pendulous branches are covered with catkins. *Salix chaenomeloides*, the quince-leafed, giant pussy willow of Japan, has very large catkins, sometimes 3 inches long when mature. As they mature, they develop soft pink stamens, giving the pussies a dusky pink glow. The large, bright red winter buds are stunning after the leaves drop in the fall. *Salix melanostachys*, the black pussy willow, is also of Japanese origin and was introduced by the Arnold Arboretum. The catkins are so dark that they appear black and are especially dramatic against red twigs. While these willows will grow just about anywhere, they do best in full sun and moist but well-drained soil.

Sarcococca spp., the sweet boxes, represent some fourteen species of evergreen shrubs native to western China and the Himalayas. They are autumn- and winter-flowering shrubs with attractive foliage and red or black fruits that ripen in autumn. *Sarcococca hookerana* 'Humilis', the dwarf sarcococca, is a marvelous shrub of small stature with lustrous, dark green foliage and inconspicuous but very fragrant white flowers that appear in February and March, eventually producing blue-black fruits. Height is from 12 to 15 inches, and width is about 2 feet. There is a variety called *digyna* that blooms in January and February, with the most fragrant flowers in the genus. *Sarcococca ruscifolia*, the fragrant sarcococca, is composed of dense, 3-foot stems of evergreen leaves that begin to produce perfumed white blossoms in late January. *Sarcococca orientalis* has larger flowers than the rest, with just a touch of pink on the burgeoning buds. All are shade-loving plants and do their best in rich, well-drained soil. The only pruning necessary is to remove dead branches.

Spiraea thunbergii originally came from China but was extensively naturalized in Honshu, Japan, and so today is called the Japanese spiraea by most gardeners and nurserymen and bears the Japanese name *Yuki-yanagi*. This is one of the earliest-blooming shrubby spiraeas; in late February to early March, the bush will be covered with masses of white blossoms. It forms a shrub about 4 feet high with slender, arching branches covered with narrow, pale green leaves that turn orange in the fall and often stay showy until the flowers

Spiraea

122

Virburnum davidii is a lovely but touchy plant for southern gardens. It has exquisite evergreen leaves of rich color, heavy texture, and distinctive surface sculpturing. The tight flower buds open in late winter, but the flowers are not very ornamental. The plant may be tricky to establish unless it is kept evenly moist, and it may not like full summer sun.

appear in the spring. This is a beautiful plant and is one of the stars of Ryan Gainey's marvelous Decatur, Georgia, winter garden, just outside of downtown Atlanta.

Sycopsis sinensis is a shrub or small tree first collected in China by E. H. Wilson back in 1901. This member of the witch-hazel family reaches a height of 20 feet in southern gardens. These shrubs bear elliptical leathery leaves up to 4 inches long. In early spring, they bloom with clusters of deep yellow blossoms that resemble miniature tassels. The male flowers, with their yellow stamens tipped with crimson, are more colorful than the female. Provide partial shade with a good, moist, acid soil with plenty of added humus. *Sycopsis* comes from the Greek *sykos,* "fig," and *opsis,* "likeness to," referring to the shape of the fruits.

Vaccinium spp., the blueberries and cranberries, are basically plants of the North and not too adaptable to southern heat. But the dwarf mountain cranberry (*Vaccinium vitis-idaea* var. *minus*) is a marvelous plant, crowded with bell-like pink blossoms in early spring, and still small enough to be at home in a small garden. It will not do well above Zone 7. In warmer areas, choose *Vaccinium elliottii,* the deciduous Elliot's blueberry. This shrub, often found growing in colonies, reaches a height of 10 feet and produces racemes of pink flowers in early spring before the leaves emerge. In summer, dark blue or black berries appear. Give it moist soil and a partially shady spot, and it will be great in the winter garden. *Vaccinium ashei* (*V. corymbosum*), the rabbiteye blueberry, grows about 6 feet tall, with a 5-foot spread. This deciduous to partially evergreen shrub bears many small white (sometimes pink or even red) flowers and is a great addition to the early-spring landscape. Sky blue, edible berries are produced

Viburnum tinus, laurustinus

in the summer, and the leaves turn a bright red in the fall. The only problem with these shrubs is the chore of protecting the fruit in the fall. If you don't, the birds will get everything. Some cultivars are available, including 'Bluebelle', which has an upright growth habit and large berries, and 'Southland', having a compact habit.

Viburnum spp., the arrowwoods, are time-honored ornamental shrubs, valuable for flowers from late winter to summer, fruits that birds really love, and great fall colors. The genus is the classical Latin name of the wayfaring tree. With all viburnums, prune only to remove dead wood.

Viburnum × *burkwoodii* is a hybrid between *V. carlesii* and *V. utile* that reaches 6 to 8 feet in both height and width, and bears shiny, rich green evergreen foliage in the South. In late winter to early spring, domelike clusters of fragrant, waxy white flowers open. The fruits are red and gradually turn black with age. Provide sun to partial shade in a moist, well-drained soil. *Viburnum* × *bodnantense* 'Dawn' is a

(Left) *Viburnum* × *bodnantense* 'Dawn'

hybrid between *V. farreri* and *V. grandiflorum* that can grow to 10 feet in both height and width. The deciduous foliage is dark green in summer, turning a reddish purple in the fall. In late winter (anytime after January 1), extremely fragrant flowers bloom in domed clusters, appearing rose red in bud but opening to pink. Provide good garden soil with good drainage. *Viburnum* × *juddii*, the Judd viburnum (named for William H. Judd of the Arnold Arboretum), grows about 8 feet tall with a 6-foot spread, bearing deep green leaves that are downy beneath. The early-spring flowers are white and slightly fragrant, blooming in 3½-inch clusters. The fall fruits are reddish black. Provide sun or partial shade in good soil with high fertility, and good drainage.

Viburnum rhytidophyllum, the leatherleaf viburnum, bears 3- to 7-inch crinkled evergreen leaves and in the garden stays about 10 feet high with a 7-foot spread. Flat clusters of light pink flowers appear in spring, followed by red and black berries in the fall. 'Roseum' has pink flower buds. Provide shade or partial shade, with protection from too much wind. This shrub needs a moderately good soil with reasonable drainage.

125

Illicium anisatum, Japanese anise

Viburnum tinus, the laurustinus viburnum, can, with age, reach a height of 12 feet. It has dark green, glossy, evergreen leaves, and its 3-inch clusters of fragrant white blossoms (some tinged with pink) open in late winter to early spring. Metallic blue berries appear in late summer, eventually turning black. 'Eve Price' is a compact form with smaller leaves and pink flowers; 'Strictum' has a more upright form of growth; and 'Variegatum' produces variegated leaves of green and creamy white, held up with pink leafstalks. This shrub will do well in sun or partial shade and is tolerant of most soil types. It does like a moist soil, with additional water in times of drought.

Small Trees
The following suggestions for the winter garden are classified as trees, although many would pass for large shrubs.

Alnus incana, the gray alder, flowers in the late winter and early spring with 2- to 4-inch catkins, first produced in the autumn, which remain brown and scaly until they open to reveal yellow pollen. The alders tolerate sun but prefer some shade; they grow in almost any type of soil but appreciate a slightly moist aspect. For a special effect in the garden, look for 'Pendula', a cultivar that has weeping branches that are especially beautiful in the winter garden.

Arbutus unedo, the manzanita or strawberry tree, reaches a height of 30 feet in nature. It originally came from southern Europe and, of all places, the hills around the Killarney Lakes of Ireland. This is a tree of legend, with a written history that goes back to ancient Greece and Rome. Goats ate the leaves for winter forage, bees took nectar from the flowers, the fruit was eaten and was also turned into wine, and in the *Aeneid*, Virgil told of using the tender twigs of the strawberry tree to weave a bier for carrying Pallas home to his father. The plant is reliably hardy only to Zone 8, but if you live there, grow it. The pinkish white flowers bloom in terminal panicles in early spring and produce scarlet fruits in the fall. There is a small variety called 'Compact' that turns into a medium-size shrub and will do well in a container.

Cercis canadensis, the redbud, is also listed in chapter 4 for the pods that persist through the winter. We include it here for its early-spring flowers. These small trees bloom in March and April long before the leaves appear, producing small, pealike blossoms that flower in clusters all over the bare branches of the trees, giving these trees a look unlike any other. There are a number of cultivars. 'Alba' has white flowers; 'Flame' has semidouble pink flowers; 'Pinkbud' bears bright flowers of a pure pink; 'Texensis' has rose pink flowers; and 'Wither's Pink Charm' has flowers of a soft pale pink. Provide sun or partial shade in average garden soil with good drainage, although redbuds will do very well when planted by the side of a moving stream.

Cornus mas, the cornelian-cherry dogwood, is a small tree that reaches a height of 20 to 25 feet, with a 15- to 20-foot spread. The yellow flowers appear in very early spring before the leaves, producing shiny, dark scarlet fruits in late summer. The foliage is a lustrous bright green that turns a reddish green in the fall. Plant in sun or partial shade in reasonably good garden soil with good drainage. The lower branches can be removed to form a small tree for a small garden. 'Aureo-elegantissima' has variegated leaves with a creamy white edge, tinged with pink. 'Golden Glory' produces more than the average number of flowers. The North Carolina State University Arboretum has introduced an especially showy cultivar for the South called 'Spring Glow'.

Illicium anisatum, the anisetree, originally from Japan and southern Korea, can reach a height of 25 feet and is really a shrub. "On cold days," wrote Elizabeth Lawrence, "I like to pick an aromatic leaf, for the scent is so strong that it is apparent even in the frost air." The height is between 8 and 12 feet, with a 10-foot spread. The leaves are leathery and aromatic. The 1-inch white to yellow flowers have many stamens and are very fragrant. Cut branches are common Buddhist grave decorations in Japanese temple grounds. These small trees are adaptable to sun or partial shade in any good garden soil with medium drainage. They are not hardy in Zone 6. *Illicium floridanum*, the Florida

Illicium floridanum, Florida anise

Magnolia 'Ann' is one of the "Little Girl Hybrids" group from the U.S. National Arboretum. These hybrids were selected for their late flowering (to avoid frosts) and compact growth habit. They are magnificent in full bloom and grow to about twelve feet in full sun or light shade. Cultivars 'Betty', 'Rikki', and 'Susan' are very similar.

anisetree, is shorter, about 6 to 10 feet tall, with an 8-foot spread. The foliage is olive green with red-purple stems, the flowers maroon, and the fruit yellow-brown. Provide good garden soil with a high organic content. These trees will flower when very young. They are not hardy in Zone 6 or 7.

Magnolia heptapeta (*M. denudata*), the Yulan magnolia or lily tree, is a native of the central provinces of China, where it grows in moist woodland. The earliest growing records of this tree go back to the Tang Dynasty (618–906), when the flower was extolled as a symbol of purity. In the garden, this is a slow-grow-ing tree, taking a hundred years to grow to 30 feet, but the young trees will flower on three- or four-year-old seedlings. The lemon-scented blossoms have nine pure white petals (really tepals) and open from February to April, depending on the climate. Unfortunately, like many magnolias, the blooms are burned by frost and the petals are then edged with an unsightly brown. In a good year they are magnificent and are worth the wait. In the South, give this tree a lightly shaded spot with a good, moist, slightly acid soil, with added compost. Magnolias are named for Pierre Magnol (1638–1751), a director of the botanical garden at Montpellier, France.

Magnolia stellata (*M. tomentosa*), the star magnolia, is a small tree from 10 to 12 feet high, with an 8- to 10-foot spread. This tree has an attractive compact growth habit and is great for the small garden. The large and lovely double white blossoms have floppy petals tinged with pink, appearing on leafless stems, filling the garden with fragrance on late afternoons in late winter or very early spring. In colder areas of the South, the flowers are often damaged by frost, and wind up looking like pieces of dirty Kleenex pasted on the branches. Buy a star magnolia that is container grown and plant it out before growth really starts for the year. You will sometimes find a seedling tree in the vicinity of the parent; it will flower at a very early age. 'Centennial' has 5-inch flowers with white petals tinged with pink and grows into a dense, pyramidal tree that is very floriferous; 'Royal Star' has fragrant, pure white flowers with bronzy foliage in the fall; and 'Waterlily' has fragrant pink flowers.

Parrotia persica, the parrotia, is a deciduous member of the witch-hazel family that usually blooms in February around our Asheville garden. Doan Ogden, who originally designed the garden next door to Peter's, put in a parrotia back in the late 1950s. It is now a sizable tree at its mature height of 15 feet. The flowers appear in February, with male flowers that are just bunches of beautiful scarlet anthers on short stems along bare branches. The female flowers are inconspicuous. But if that's not enough, the leaves are suffused with golden and crimson tints in the fall. The tree exhibits an odd growth form: Some branches grow straight up as multiple trunks, and others grow out

Magnolia stellata (*M. tomentosa*), star magnolia

Parrotia persica

Prunus mume, Japanese flowering apricot

Prunus incisa 'Okame', Okame cherry (bloom)

horizontally to give a layered look. Leave both if you can for the full effect. Although perfectly hardy in Zone 7, parrotias should be planted in a sheltered spot to protect the flowers from cold winter winds. Good garden soil with some additional compost is all that's needed for a successful tree. The tree grows wild in its native Iran and is the only species in the genus. It was named for F. W. Parrot (1792–1841), a German naturalist and traveler, who made the first modern-day ascent of Mount Ararat in 1829.

Prunus spp., the plums and cherries, have a few species that are dependable winter bloomers. By far, the tree with the best press is *Prunus mume*, the Japanese flowering apricot. It's a small deciduous tree about 20 feet high that has been honored in Japanese gardens for hundreds of years with a respect that has resulted in more than four hundred named cultivars. There are weeping trees, ones with fastigiate branches, and others with contorted silhouettes, with very fragrant, single or double flowers of white, through shades of pink, to red, blooming from December through March, depending on the climate.

Prunus subhirtella 'Autumnalis', the winter-flowering cherry, will actually bloom anytime from October through March. This small deciduous tree reaches a height of some 20 feet, flowering with pink blossoms when winters are mild, but because of sporadic flowering, at no time is it a showstopper. The species blooms with white flowers. 'Pendula', the weeping cherry, has a forked trunk with drooping twiggy branches that are covered with pink flowers in late March on to early April.

For Zones 8 and 9, try *Prunus campanulata*, the Taiwan cherry, a tree that is laced with masses of showy deep pink to red flowers. Michael Dirr calls the flowers of *P. campanulata* "the most handsome of all ornamental cherries." A hybrid between *Prunus incisa*, the Fuji cherry, and *Prunus campanulata* is

(Right) *Clematis armandii*, evergreen clematis

132

called *P.* × *incam* and has produced an extraordinary cultivar named 'Okame'. This fast-growing tree produces a gorgeous display of frostproof bright pink flowers in late winter (February to March in Charlotte) on a very reliable basis. The narrow crown makes it perfect as a street tree or for the small garden. *Prunus davidiana* 'Alba' and 'Rubra' are free-flowering in January as long as the weather is not too severe.

Stachyurus praecox is a member of a genus of shrubs and small trees found in eastern Asia. Called *Kibushi* in Japan, this particular deciduous shrub was originally found in the thickets and mountain woodlands of Hokkaido and Honshu. Small, yellow, bell-shaped flowers, about 1/2 inch long, bloom in 2- to 3-inch racemes during March before the leaves appear. Provide partial shade and a well-drained humusy soil. *Stachyurus* comes from the Greek *stachyus*, "spike," and *oura*, "tail," referring to the shape of the racemes.

Vines

Clematis armandii, a native of central and western China, was introduced to the trade in 1900 by plant explorer E. H. Wilson. This is a very handsome, fast-growing vine—up to 15 feet in a good season—of great beauty and exuberance, with mostly evergreen leaves of a medium to glossy green, growing in groups of three. This vigorous vine climbs by twisting leaf stalks and poses no strangling threat to any host plant, though it may cover it up, so it's best on an arbor or a fence. Depending on the garden's location, flowers appear in late winter to early spring with fragrant, white, 2-inch blossoms, in showy panicles, opening on the previous year's growth. Like all clematises, the vines like a cool root run, well hidden from the sun, but do their best when the upper growth gets plenty of sunshine, or at best partial shade. It's a great accent plant for covering trellises, gateways, and pergolas, and letting the vines ramble through a neighboring tree can create a splendid effect. In the colder parts of the South, plant it on a wall that faces the sun or position the plant in a sheltered spot. 'Apple Blossom' (not a favorite of England's Christopher Lloyd) has white flowers flushed with pink; 'Farquhariana' has light pink flowers; and 'Snowdrift' bears very large white flowers.

Clematis cirrhosa is a delicate evergreen clematis from southern Europe and Asia Minor, appearing on the garden scene in 1596. The leaves are simple, narrow, and broad, sometimes lobed, and grow on a vine that reaches a length of 12 to 14 feet. The yellow-white flowers, about 1 inch across, appear in late winter to early spring. Anne Armstrong has known it to bloom all winter into spring, oblivious to the 0°F temperatures of February 1996. *Clematis cirrhosa* var. *balearica* (*C. calycina*), the fern-leafed clematis, is a variety introduced from the Mediterranean region in 1783. 'Wisley' is an English selection with larger creamy white flowers and leaves that get a bronze patina in the winter.

Gelsemium sempervirens, the Carolina jessamine, is an evergreen twining vine that can grow to a length of 20 feet, with narrow, pointed, small and waxy leaves. The fragrant yellow, tubelike flowers appear from late February to early April, blooming singly or in small, flat-topped bunches. This vine grows well in sun or shade but bears more flowers in the sun. It's tolerant of soil, has no pest problems, and should be sheared after flowering. Jessamine grows well on fences and will climb small trees without doing any harm.

Lonicera sempervirens, the coral honeysuckle, is an evergreen vine with a long period of bloom. It begins to set flowers in mid-March in the mountains, and much earlier in the warmer parts of the South. The 2-inch red and yellow tubular flowers open to greet hummingbirds as they migrate northward. The flowers are borne on the tips of long shoots and, if cross-pollinated, will produce clusters of bright red fruits. Normally, two genetically different specimens must cross-pollinate to ensure heavy fruit set. Provide as much sun as possible, in any garden soil. This plant responds well to heavy pruning after flowering.

(Left) *Clematis cirrhosa*

7

FRAGRANCE

For you there's rosemary and rue; these keep seeming and savor all winter long.
—William Shakespeare, *The Winter's Tale*, act 4

WHEN DAYS ARE CHILLY IN THE NORTH, MOST PLANTS lock up their fragrances for months on end. But with our warming sun in the South, the chill never lasts for more than a week or so, and then the air heats up enough to release the garden fragrances. An interesting thing about fragrance and the human memory is that fragrances can reach across the decades like a physical link, reminding us of an eventful time now long forgotten. The smell of boxwood on a warm winter's day or the charming odor of late-winter violets can conjure up mind's-eye visions of happy events from childhood or the time the rain leaked through the living room ceiling.

Our selection of plants for winter fragrance is arbitrary at best. We have not included the witch hazel, any of the viburnums, or *Prunus mume*, all of which have been listed in other chapters. We also have not included galax (*Galax rotundifolia*), which has a very foxy smell that many people find unpleasant. If our readers know of additional plants that should be listed here, please drop us a line.

A Letter from a Winter Gardener
"Cabin fever," wrote Ann Armstrong, "set in one day when it was twenty degrees and I took a walk in the garden. Gardeners do strange things. I came across a patch of brilliant purple violets. These were not the ordinary woods' violets but sweet violets (*Viola odorata*). I picked a few and, even in that cold, the scent was wonderful. I carried them into the house, put them

in a small vase, and their perfume filled the air. I mean to have more of these.

"Our woods' violets are considered by some to be little more than weeds, but no one would accuse *Viola odorata* of that. To my untrained eye they appear to resemble our native violets in leaf and bloom. Therefore, great care should be taken to plant these delights in their own bed away from the invasive woods' violets so you won't inadvertently weed them out.

"The sweet violet grows best in the cool seasons and in shade. It will tolerate sun if given adequate moisture, but mine in the shade look much happier than the ones in the sunnier part of the garden. They will spread by seed or runners. Once you get a patch of them going, you can divide, in the fall, the plantlets that result from the stoloniferous runners.

"You plant a bit of history with these violets. A nice touch, don't you think? They go back to ancient times, when they became the symbol of Athens. Supposedly they were used by Napoleon's supporters as a password when he was exiled to Elba. They provided fragrance for the perfume industry and, even today, are sold as fresh flowers in the European markets.

"Mine are probably the cultivar 'Queen Charlotte' in that they are dark blue. *Viola odorata* 'Rosina' is a rose pink with a dark center, and 'White Queen' has small white flowers on a 6-inch-tall plant.

"I begged a plant of winter heliotrope (*Petasites fragrans*) from a friend, who gave it to me with the dire warning of its thuggish ways. Perhaps so, but its winter foliage holds up well and its rather dull-looking bloom smells delicious. I planted it under a large oak-leaf hydrangea (*Hydrangea quercifolia*), hoping the shrub's dense foliage would slow the little plant down a bit. This winter pleasure may evolve into a love-and-hate relationship. I'll give it a few years and see how it behaves. If it romps too much, I'll have to remove it. The scent is divine. I had a little vase of the blossoms over the sink and their scent lasted a week.

"I know you have mentioned in your book the winter honeysuckle (*Lonicera fragrantissima*), a plant readily found in many old gardens. This woody shrub, with its sweet lemon fragrance, is one of the first to bloom in late winter. It blooms for three to four weeks and it will scent the entire garden. Once the bloom is over, it's just there with its tangled mass of branches. One wouldn't want it as a specimen plant, but it is nice tucked into a corner or in the shrub border. If you have inherited an old overgrown one, the best treatment could be to cut it back to the ground. It readily develops new shoots.

"I haven't grown the wintersweet (*Chimonanthus praecox*), but there is a magnificent specimen at the front of Wing Haven. Winter fragrance is the principal ornamental characteristic of this small tree. The flowers, almost a transparent yellow with a touch of light maroon in the center, open over a long period of time and are borne on the previous summer's wood. Pruners take note! It has dark green, drooping leaves in summer that change to a greenish yellow in the fall. If plants get out of hand in late winter, you can prune it to within 12 inches of the ground and it will rejuvenate itself. Of course, you will probably lose the blooms for that year, but one can't have everything.

"The darling of the winter garden for fragrance is the winter daphne (*Daphne odora*). This densely branched evergreen shrub may reach 4 feet in height and width. I say *may* because it is a temperamental plant for many, myself included. You may be clicking along with a lovely shrub, full of gorgeous scented bloom, and all of a sudden it dies. Drats! Probably too much tender loving care.

"This plant is not terribly fussy about soils, probably likes some protection from the hot afternoon sun and excellent drainage. I'm sure I killed my huge one by giving it too much water. We were going away for some time, and I was afraid the poor thing would be thirsty. I drowned it, I am sure, for I came back, and it had gone to see its fathers. A friend in California, where they grow like weeds, said that she ignored hers once it became established. They don't get a great deal of rain in California—most years.

"Having said all this, once you see or smell one of these shrubs, it is a must-have. The species has rosy-purple flowers about an inch in diameter in late winter. The flowers are long lasting. There is a cultivar called 'Alba' with white flowers. It's extremely handsome, as is the cultivar 'Variegata', this last with variegated foliage and pink flowers."

The Descriptions

Abeliophyllum distichum, the white forsythia, could possibly be listed in chapter 6 with the flowering shrubs, except that most of the year it's just a passable heap of green, achieving stardom only in very early spring. Then it bursts forth into glorious blooms, with hundreds of white, four-petaled flowers that smell of fermenting honey. Although it resembles a forsythia, this plant has a genus all its own, and deservedly so. A native of central Korea, white forsythia has been growing in American gardens since 1924, but it still lacks the popularity it deserves. Branches cut in late winter are easily forced into bloom, and the perfume is even stronger in warmer indoor temperatures. It does well in Zones 5 to 8; farther south it's too warm for decent flowering. Plants want full sun to partial shade and will thrive in any good, well-drained garden soil.

Artemisia abrotanum, the southernwood or old-man, is a subshrub growing to a height of 6 feet, bearing green aromatic leaves that are finely dissected like coarse feathers. Tiny, light yellow flowers only appear in southern gardens because the North is just too cold. This is a native of Europe that escaped from cultivation and has spread up and down the eastern seaboard. Louise Beebe Wilder wrote of this plant, also called lad's love, in *The Fragrant Path* (New York: The Macmillan Company, 1932), "[It] was found often in old gardens and once played a part in every cottager's nosegay. Few sweeter are to be devised than southernwood and white moss rosebuds. The scent of southernwood is stimulating and refreshing and in times gone by was used to keep away moths." The plants thrive in poor and dry soil in full sun or partial shade.

Azara microphylla, the box-leaf azara, has been a popular greenhouse and conservatory subject in the North because of the fragrant flowers. This is a finely textured evergreen shrub or small tree, eventually

(Right) *Buxus sempervirens* 'Elegantissima', variegated boxwood

Buxus sempervirens 'Variegata'

reaching a height of 20 feet. The flowers are too small to be considered pretty, or even interesting, just a few yellow stamens poking up among the leaves. But as described in many books on fragrant plants, the sweet scent can be detected many yards from the shrub. Daniel Hinkley, in his book *Winter Ornamentals* (Seattle: Sasquatch Books, 1993), describes the scent as redolent of white chocolate, while Mrs. Wilder says it has the fragrance of vanilla. The plant was named in honor of J. N. Azara, a Spanish patron of botany. The plants are not reliably hardy north of Zone 9.

Buxus sempervirens, the common boxwood, is beloved by some gardeners and abhorred by others, largely because of its smell. The leaves give off a strange fragrance, slightly foxy and penetrating, but quite distinctive. The odor is especially noticeable after a summer shower when the air is warm, or during the winter when, after a cold spell, the waxing sun warms the leaves on a still January day. Oliver Wendell Holmes wrote about the boxwood: "They walked over

the crackling leaves in the garden, between the lines of box, breathing its fragrance of eternity; for this is one of the odors which carry us out of time into the abysses of the unbeginning past." How true.

Callistemon citrinus,, the bottlebrush, is only successful in Zones 8 and 9. The genus consists of shrubs or small trees from Australia, *C. citrinus* usually reaching a height of 12 feet, with an 8-foot spread. The foliage is leathery and lance shaped, and the shrub looks like a creature of the desert. The flowers form 2- to 4-inch spikes, with numerous inch-long stamens. But it's the leaves that are fragrant, especially when bruised. Give plants full sun in any good soil with low moisture, because they tolerate heat and are drought resistant. Unfortunately, they are not hardy below Zone 8. *Callistemon* comes from the Greek *kalos*, "beauty," and *stemon*, "stamen." *Citrinus* refers to the lemon-scented leaves.

Calycanthus floridus, the native sweetshrub, is a deciduous shrub that grows about 8 feet tall, with an 8-

foot spread. The yellow-green leaves are smooth, about 6 inches long, and aromatic when crushed. After the leaves appear, dark red flowers bloom in mid-April, giving off the odor of strawberries. They are followed by a tannish brown fig-shaped capsule that is sweetly fragrant when crushed. Sweetshrubs are hardy in Zones 6 to 9. 'Edith Wilder' really smells of strawberries, and 'Purpureus' has purple leaves. Provide full sun or partial shade in good garden soil of medium fertility. *Calycanthus* comes from the Greek for "calyx" and "flower," referring to the colored calyx.

Camellia spp., the camellias, were also mentioned in chapter 6 for their blooms, but here we are dealing with the fragrances found in two of the species. *Camellia sasanqua* originally comes from the southern islands of Japan, where the tree grows to a height of 15 feet. In gardens it will top 6 or 7 feet in eight years. The seeds yield a nondrying oil that is important in commerce. But for the winter garden, its value lies with the small, fragrant flowers that bloom in November and December and the sweet odor of the leaves when they are picked and left to dry in the sun. Floral colors range from white to rose, and there are a number of cultivars. 'Floribunda' has white petals edged with lavender; 'Rosea' blooms a deep dusky rose; and 'Versicolor' has flowers that are white at the center, becoming pink with age, and margined with lavender. *Camellia sinensis*, the tea camellia, is a variable tree growing from 3 to 50 feet, depending on heredity and the environment. It will flower on and off all winter

Camellia sasanqua 'Pink Snow'

141

long, with small, white, fragrant blossoms. The processed leaves of this plant are the source of commercial tea, a drink that, regardless of the cachet of coffee, is the world's most popular caffeine beverage. The seeds also yield an oil used in commerce.

Calocedrus (Libocedrus) decurrens, the incense cedar, is a distinctly columnar evergreen conifer with small, scalelike needles arranged in flat branches that are held vertically. It may grow to 60 feet or more in cultivation and is taller in the wild. This cedar occurs in the mountains along the west coast of the United States, from Oregon down to southern California. The bark is an attractive maroon color, fissured and shredding into long scales. The dark green needles have a purple cast and are intensely fragrant. This species provides the wood used in most pencils, a familiar smell to most of us. The trees need well-drained soil in full sun to partial shade; they grow fairly fast but remain tightly columnar. Bruising the foliage to smell the pungent aroma is one of the great delights of the winter garden.

Elaeagnus pungens, the thorny elaeagnus, is an evergreen shrub reaching a height of 9 to 12 feet, with a 6- to 10-foot spread. The oblong, 2- to 3-inch-long leaves are a bright glossy green above and silvery beneath. Insignificant flowers appear in late October, only 1/2 inch long but extremely fragrant, smelling of gardenias. Like most elaeagnuses, these plants are fast growing and make a great background hedge for any kind of garden. The April fruits are very popular with birds. Provide full sun with a good, well-drained soil of medium fertility. *Elaeagnus* comes from the Greek for "olive" and "chaste tree."

Laurus nobilis, the sweet bay or poet's laurel, is the true laurel of the ancients, the one used to make crowns for heroes, athletes, and poets (hence the term poet laureate), and the dried leaves are used as herbal seasonings. "Of all growing things," wrote Gertrude Jekyll in *Flower Decoration in the House*, "there is nothing much more beautiful in detail than a little branch of Bay, the leaves are so well set on the stems and their waved edges give a satisfying impression of graceful strength" (*Country Living*. London: 1907). The flowers of the bay are inconspicuous. If the garden is too cold, the plants are fine in pots. Laurel does well along the Coastal Plain and in the piedmont of the Carolinas, as long as it receives full sun and good drainage, along with plenty of moisture. Unfortunately, it isn't hardy in Zone 6. 'Aurea' has golden-green leaves, and 'Undulata' has wavy leaf margins.

Lavandula angustifolia, the English lavender, is an evergreen plant, even in Asheville. This marvelous sun lover is a shrub that when young, bears white tomentose leaves that turn green with age. The usually purple flowers bloom in summer. Mrs. Wilder pointed out that in a 1633 description of a garden of health, "forty-five ills of flesh or spirit are named as curable by various decoctions of Lavender, and just to smell it was said to comfort and cleare the eyes." We grow it in the winter garden not only for color of the evergreen leaves, but also for the chance on warm winter mornings to pick a few leaves and crush them between the fingers to get that marvelous smell. It should be noted that English lavender also gives off a slight scent of turpentine, but not enough to spoil the fragrant mood.

Myrtus communis, the wax-myrtle, is an evergreen shrub growing to a height of 12 feet, with a 10-foot spread. The sweet-scented flowers open in early spring but are inconspicuous until they turn into small globular berries, which are covered with a whitish resin and last through the winter. But it's the 3-inch leathery leaves that are the reason for this plant in the winter garden. "Its small evergreen leaves," wrote Mrs. Wilder, "pointed and shining, respond to your gentlest caress with such a gift of fragrance as makes it a blessing in your garden." Plant in sun or shade in good garden soil with medium drainage, and provide moisture during dry periods. Though wax-myrtle does well along the Carolina coast, it does not take to salt spray. It's also not hardy in the mountains.

Osmanthus americanus, the devilwood or wild olive, is a small evergreen tree or shrub found from southeastern North Carolina, including the lower Cape Fear River, to Florida and on to the west. The leaves are smooth and shiny, about 4 inches long, and the tree can reach a height of 15 to 20 feet, with a 15-foot spread. It's called devilwood because the wood is devilishly hard to split. *Osmanthus* comes from the Greek for "fragrance" and "flower." And fragrance is the highlight here. In early spring, inconspicuous, creamy white, marvelous-smelling flowers appear, followed by dark purple-blue fruits that ripen in the fall. Leonard E. Foote and Samuel B. Jones, Jr., in *Native Shrubs and Woody Vines of the Southeast* (Portland, OR: Timber Press, 1989), wrote, "The loose and open habit of the wild olive makes this a wanted shrub whether used in a naturalized landscape or in a more formal setting as a foundation plant." Readily available in nurseries, *Osmanthus americanus* deserves a place in southern gardens.

Osmanthus (Siphonosmanthus) delavayi, the Delavay tea olive, is an evergreen shrub between 4 and 6 feet high, with a 5-foot spread. The form is upright and twiggy, and the branches are covered with 1-inch toothed leaves of a glossy deep green. The tubular flowers are white, about ¹/₂ inch long, and extremely fragrant, blooming in early spring. It's termed an excellent substitute for the common boxwood in the lower piedmont and the Coastal Plain. With its handsome foliage and fragrant flowers, it's another shrub for every southern garden in Zones 7 to 9. *Osmanthus* comes from the Greek for "tube," and the species and common name are in honor of Pierre Jean Marie Delavay (1834–95), a French missionary and botanist.

Osmanthus fragrans, the tea olive, is grown more for the fragrance than the flowers. This shrub or, along the Coastal Plain, small tree, reaches a height of 10 to 12 feet, with a 10- to 14-foot spread. The evergreen leaves are a deep green and give an attractive appearance to the shrubs. From October through January, they bear very small but extremely sweet-smelling flowers. In China, the tea olive has been in cultivation for centuries and was often planted in the courtyards of temples so that monks could gather the sweet-scented blossoms for offerings to the gods. One or two flowers are said to fill a whole greenhouse with fragrance, and when dried, the flowers were often used to perfume tea. Provide sun or partial shade in any good garden soil with medium drainage and medium fertility. Unfortunately, in western North Carolina, it is often killed to the ground in bad winters.

Populus × jackii 'Gileadensis', the balm of Gilead, is a large tree found along roadsides and in old and abandoned fields. It is a hybrid between the northeastern species *Populus balsamifera* and *P. deltoides*, the eastern cottonwood, and is of unknown origin. The very large red buds of this tree are varnished with an abundance of a sticky, fragrant resin. It's grown in gardens and farms for the sap produced by the buds and, as a quick-growing tree, is useful as a screen. It is tolerant of most conditions but does best in a light, sandy soil in full sun. Strangely enough, only sterile female trees are known, so the only way the tree can be reproduced is by digging up suckers or taking cuttings. But one way or another, the true balm of Gilead now grows along the Pigeon River in Haywood County, on into the Smokies, up through the Appalachians, and into New York's Catskill Mountains.

Rosmarinus officinalis, the common rosemary of herbal fame, has a deserved reputation as being one of the most fragrant of plants. It's an evergreen shrub from the Mediterranean region, having square stems, simple leaves, and pale blue, sometimes pink, and rarely white flowers like tiny snapdragons. As devotees of potpourri say, a sprig of rosemary is great in a fingerbowl, dried in a nosegay, or used to season roast meats. Years ago, branches of rosemary were put under the bed to prevent nightmares and hung on closeted clothes to keep the moths away, and when boiled in water, the resulting solution was said to guard against all manner of evils that attacked the body. The plant is hardy in Zones 7 to 9. The flowers appear off and on from late fall, through winter, and into early spring, but it's the aromatic leaves and stems that are important to the winter garden. If you live in Zone 6, rosemary is one plant that will do exceptionally well in pots. Rosemary wants full sun, a soil of low fertility, and perfect drainage. 'Albus' has white flowers; 'Arp' grows about 3 feet tall and is reputed to be hardy to –10°F (but not in a stiff wind); 'Prostratus' is a trailing ground cover for Zones 8 and 9; and 'Tuscan Blue' is taller and more upright than the noncultivar, with rigid stems and bearing blue-violet flowers.

Santolina virens, the green santolina, is an evergreen shrub from the Mediterranean that forms very dense mounds of emerald green, feathery foliage, about 18 inches high, and with a 2- to 3-foot spread. Yellow, buttonlike flowers appear in the summer. This is a great plant in the rock garden, for edging pathways, or in herbal beds. Unfortunately, it's only marginally hardy in Zone 6, so in gardens where cold is a problem, choose a good microclimate and protect it from bitter winter winds. Provide full sun, poor soil, and perfect drainage. *Santolina* comes from the Latin *Sanctum linum*, "holy flax."

Skimmia japonica, the Japanese skimmia, is a native moundlike shrub of the Himalayas, China, and Japan. It grows about 4 inches high, with a 3-foot spread, and bears simple leaves between 3 and 5 inches long. Skimmia has long been a winter favorite for the scarlet fruit that appears in the fall and lasts into winter, and many gardeners forget that the white flowers of late winter are beautifully fragrant; the plant is worthy of growing for that fact alone. The flowers on the male plants are larger and more fragrant. These shrubs are unisexual, so be sure to plant a male near the female to guarantee fruits. Provide partial or full shade in good garden soil with good drainage in Zones 7 and 8. 'Formanii' is a form with larger clusters of red fruit, and 'Rubella' is a male clone with red flower buds through the winter that are very fragrant in spring.

Thuja occidentalis 'Lombart's Wintergreen', the wintergreen arborvitae, is apparently a rare tree in cultivation. This is unfortunate, because it's one of the most distinctive of the arborvitaes especially because in the winter, when the dark green, flattened sprays of needle leaves produce a wonderful fragrance of pine and fir; in the summer, it's just an ordinary nonsmell. The trees grow well in Charlotte, reaching a height of 12 feet in eighteen years. Does that qualify it for a dwarf conifer? Probably not, but at least it's a slow-growing one. It forms a dense, tight, conical crown in light shade and has withstood droughts, cold, and poor soil. This is one of the few conifers with needles made for fondling.

8

EVERGREEN FOLIAGE

In winter the glitter of green leaves is like sunlight on water. I suppose it is the low angle of the sun, and the quality of the light, that brings out the beauty of evergreens, 'it seeming from them to be summer all winter.' The glossier the leaves, the more cheerful the garden; the wider the leaves, the greener they seem.

—Elizabeth Lawrence, *Gardens in Winter*

JOSEPH ADDISON (1672–1719) WAS AN ENGLISH POET, essayist, and statesman who wrote essays on landscape gardening in the *Spectator*. Like the "Salesman Bogs" stories of the old *Saturday Evening Post*, Addison created a character, one Sir Roger de Coverly, to whom he could address his comments about life and about gardening. In the 477th issue of the *Spectator*, dated September 6, 1712, Addision wrote about evergreen plants, chiefly because his alter ego, Sir Roger, had voiced an objection to filling an English garden with them.

"I have often wondered," Addison wrote, "that those who are like myself, and love to live in gardens, have never thought of contriving a winter garden, which should consist of such trees only as never cast their leaves. We have very often little snatches of sunshine and fair weather in the most uncomfortable parts of the year, and have frequently several days in November and January that are as agreeable as any in the finest months. At such times, therefore, I think there could not be a greater pleasure than to walk in such a winter garden as I have proposed [and] I have so far indulged myself in this thought, that I have set apart a whole acre of ground for the executing of it."

So we present the following evergreen plants for the gardener's consideration, beginning with trees and shrubs, followed by herbaceous plants, including vines, grasses, and ferns.

Trees and Shrubs

Abelia × *grandiflora*, the glossy abelia, is a very popular landscape shrub, especially in upmarket malls. Height is from 4 to 6 feet, with a 4- or 5-foot spread. The simple leaves are oval, about 1½ inches long, of a purple-green in the summer and changing to a bronzy purple in the wintertime. The whitish pink, tubular flowers bloom in the summer, often continuing on and off until well into the fall. Smaller and more refined selections include the more compact 'Sherwood' and the elegant 'Edward Goucher'. Provide full sun or partial shade in a good garden soil with added humus. The genus is named for Clarke Abel (1780-1826), physician and writer.

Arctostaphylos uva-ursi, the bearberry or kinnikinnick, is a prostrate, spreading shrub never more than a foot high. Branches, which root at the joints, are usually between 12 and 24 inches long, but over a long period of time they can reach many feet. Leathery, evergreen, spatulate leaves are about an inch long and turn bronze in the winter. The small, urn-shaped flowers are pink or white, followed by red fruit. Bearberry is great for the rock garden, especially when the plants can trail over the edge of a rock wall. In the South, provide partial shade, planting in a light, sandy soil or a scree mix of small gravel and soil. These plants do not do well south of Zone 6. *Arctostaphylos* comes from the Greek *arktos*, "bear," and *staphyle*, "berry."

Aucuba japonica, the Japanese laurel, is a native of Japan usually grown for its stunning evergreen leaves, although it also blooms in early spring and bears the red berries in winter (both sexes are required for fruit). A well-grown shrub can reach 10 feet in height, and leggy plants can be cut to the ground in spring, allowing new shoots to appear at the base. There are a number of cultivars, each with leaves showing different patterns of dots or splashes of color on a green base. 'Crotonifolia' has leaves finely spotted with white and gold; 'Nana' grows about 2 feet tall; and 'Variegata' (also called the gold-dust tree) is spotted and blotched with yellow. These shrubs are very useful in that they show their best color in the shade and actually burn and bleach in the southern sun; they are also damaged by cold winter winds. Soil should have good drainage and high fertility, and these plants do well in modified clay. The genus is the Latinized form of the Japanese name.

Berberis darwinii, Darwin's barberry, is a 5- to 6-foot shrub that, in addition to blue berries and bright golden flowers, bears 1/2-inch-long evergreen leaves with two or three coarse teeth on either side. *Berberis julianae*, the wintergreen barberry, reaches a height of 4 to 6 feet, with a 3- to 5-foot spread. The foliage grows in rosettes, with 3-inch leaves of a glossy medium green, some leaves becoming stained with red in the winter. *Berberis verruculosa*, the warty barberry, grows about 4 feet high, with a 4-foot spread. The leaves are a dark, shiny green above and white beneath, turning bronze in the winter. It is the most refined and compact member of the barberries, although it is not suitable for Zones 8 and 9.

Buxus harlandii, Harland's boxwood, reaches a height of 2 to 4 feet, with a spread of 3 feet. The evergreen leaves are a bright green, a little over an inch long, and notched at the tip. These small shrubs lack the drama to be good specimen plants but are very effective as edging plants or as a low hedge. Provide sun to partial shade and a good garden soil with adequate drainage. They are not hardy in Zone 6. *Buxus microphylla* var. *koreana*, the Korean boxwood, is an attractive small shrub about 4 feet high at maturity, with a 5- to 6-foot spread. The foliage is a glossy yellowish green, turning a bronzed green in the winter. This is the hardiest of all the boxwoods and makes it to Zone 4. 'Tide Hill' maintains a dark-green foliage during the winter and stays about a foot high. 'Winter-

green' is much the same. *Buxus microphylla* var. *japonica*, the Japanese box, is especially adapted to regions of hot, wet summers and also shows resistance to both nematodes and root rot. There are many smaller selections that make wonderful border edges, rock garden specimens, and miniature green mounds. 'Kingsville Dwarf' is very low growing; 'Morris Midget' takes on a formal rounded shape; and 'Variegata' has attractive yellow and green leaves on a plant that remains dwarf. *Buxus sempervirens* 'Arborescens' is the common or, as it's sometimes called, American boxwood. It's usually a shrub, sometimes a small tree, and occasionally a tree to a 30-foot height. This is the time-honored plant for a hedge or long border, responding to trimming and of great value in formal gardens. The foliage is a lustrous dark green. There are a number of cultivars, all beautiful in the winter, but 'Suffruticosa', the dwarf or edging boxwood, is one of the best with its dark-green, dense foliage and maintaining a height of 2 to 3 feet, with a 3- to 4-foot spread. Provide partial shade in a good garden soil with adequate drainage, as boxes resent wet feet. In warmer parts of the South, the shallow root system benefits from a good mulching. *Buxus* is the classical Latin name for the box.

Cephalotaxus harringtonia, the plum yew, originally comes from China, Japan, and Formosa. It has sharp-pointed needles and is somewhat similar to the yew (*Taxus*). Plum yews are very adaptable, tolerating shade, wet soils, and hot, humid weather. Unlike most conifers, plum yews produce fleshy, plumlike seeds. These seeds, however, are rarely seen in gardens. Kim Tripp writes in *The Year in Trees* (Portland, OR: Timber Press, 1995): "[An] advantage of *Cephalotaxus harringtonia* over *Taxus* species is that deer do not like the foliage of Japanese plum yew [while they] can completely defoliate a well-grown common yew in one feeding." There are several cultivar forms of the plum yew. 'Fastigiata' is upright, with erect branches bearing leaves whorled around the stem, producing a distinctive structure; 'Duke Gardens' originated at the Duke University Gardens in Durham, North Carolina, and is a low-growing spreading cultivar; and 'Prostrate' is an award-winning 3-foot-high, spreading form that can, if given time and space, ramble through the garden.

Choisya ternata, the Mexican orange, is a native of the American Southwest. These are evergreen shrubs growing between 6 and 8 feet tall, bearing three-part, 2-inch leaves of a bright, shiny green and smelling of citrus or eucalyptus leaves when crushed. The flowers

(Left) *Aucuba japonica* 'Picturata'

Choisya ternata 'Sundance', Mexican orange

appear from April to July. Provide full sun and a well-drained garden soil of average fertility. While many references claim the Mexican orange is hardy only to a few degrees below freezing, a friend of Louise Beebe Wilder's grew a shrub in Philadelphia to great effect, and plants are quite hardy in Charlotte. 'Sundance' is a fast-growing selection, with bright yellow foliage when grown in full sun, and very easy to root. The genus is named for J. L. Choris, a traveling artist who in the early 1800s followed the Russian explorer Otto von Kotzebue around the world.

Cleyera japonica is especially known for surviving city conditions. This Japanese shrub has a potential height of 8 to 10 feet, with a 5-foot spread. The 2- to 6-inch evergreen leaves are a glossy green to reddish bronze. Plants make excellent shrub borders and are especially valuable as screening. Fragrant flowers appear in spring, followed by red berries in the fall. Provide partial shade and a good garden soil with very good drainage. This is not, however, the plant commonly called "cleyera" in garden centers; that plant is usually the similar-looking *Ternstroemia gymnanthera*, a fine and adaptable species, even if overused by the landscape industry. *Ternstroemia* grows fast and often is overpruned by the homeowner when trying to rediscover his or her windows and porch. *Cleyera* was named for Andrew Cleyer.

Croton alabamensis, the Alabama croton, is an attractive semievergreen shrub that reaches a height of 10 feet. The elliptical leaves are about 5 inches long, with silvery scales beneath; the leaf stems and twigs are also silvery scaled. Found growing only in restricted sites in northern Alabama, dense colonies of these shrubs are called privet brakes. The species has shown great hardiness, surviving to −6°F in Charlotte, although somewhat killed back. The leaves turn a unique color of orange in the fall and persist well into the winter. This feature, combined with the overall silvery coating, makes for marvelous winter detail. Light yellow flowers appear in late spring. Provide full sun or

(Right) *Croton alabamensis*

partial shade and well-drained soil that is not too acid. *Croton* comes from the Greek word for "ticks," because the seeds resemble these creatures.

Daphne × burkwoodii 'Carol Mackie', the Burkwood daphne, is probably a better selection for northern gardens, where it forms dense mounds of beautiful foliage. It is a marginal shrub in the South, however, and if attempted, should be provided with some shade. Nevertheless, it should be tried, as the narrow variegated leaves do add an interesting pattern in the winter, and the promise of interesting flowers keeps one hoping for success. As with other daphnes, it should have good drainage.

Daphniphyllum macropodum is an evergreen shrub or small tree that hails from Japan. Rounded in form, it usually reaches a height of 10 to 12 feet, with stout, glaucous shoots, often reddish when young. The oblong leaves are from 3 to 8 inches long and often have a red stalk. They give the appearance of a large, shiny rhododendron leaf, and the plant form is also

(Right) *Elaeagnus ebbingii* 'Gilt Edge'

similar. Because this is one of the largest evergreen leaves that we can grow, the plant is well worth a try. The flowers are insignificant. Provide partial shade and a good, moist soil with added humus. This plant is not hardy above Zone 8. 'Variegatum' has a broad creamy margin on the leaves. The genus name means "leaves like a daphne."

Elaeagnus pungens, the thorny elaeagnus, is an evergreen shrub that reaches a height of 8 to 12 feet, with a spread of 6 to 10 feet. The 2- to 3-inch-long oblong leaves are a glossy bright green above and silvery beneath. 'Maculata' has glossy leaves with yellow centers, and 'Simonii' has larger leaves that are often variegated with yellow or pinkish white. 'Gilt Edge' is a hybrid cultivar that has even more leaf area devoted to bright yellow variegation than 'Maculata'; it is a brilliant showstopper in the winter sun. It grows much less vigorously than the noncultivar, and significantly less

Daphniphyllum macropodum

Euonymus japonicus 'Ovatus Aureus'

than the other cultivars, and is easily pruned when a long, arching branch grows into the nearby space. Overall, it is a brighter and more refined garden plant than other variegated cultivars.

Euonymus japonicus 'Aureomarginatus', an upright compact shrub that grows to 3 feet, with plenty of creamy white, variegated leaves, has been the best euonymus in the Harwood Garden at UNC-Charlotte. It has never developed the dreaded euonymus scale, which so many others seem to attract, and remains a shining light in the mixed-shrub border all year, especially so in winter. It rarely needs pruning and has shown virtually no damage from cold, wind, or heat.

Euonymus japonicus 'Microphyllus', the dwarf Japanese euonymus, is a small shrub about 3 feet high with a 2-foot spread. The glossy green leaves are up to an inch long. Provide sun or partial shade and a well-drained soil with added humus. It is easier to propagate and therefore less expensive than boxwood for a garden edging.

Euphorbia amygdaloides var. *robbiae*, Miss Robb's spurge, is a perennial evergreen ground cover with rosettes of dark green leaves. It reaches a height of 15 inches and slowly spreads to a 3-foot diameter. Provide full sun or partial shade in any reasonable garden soil.

Eurya japonica, a relative of the camellia, can become a small tree in time or remain a large shrub, reaching a height of 6 feet. Elliptical leaves over 2 inches long and about 1 inch wide are most attractive, and these leafy branches are used in Shinto ceremonies in Japan. Small, pinkish white flowers appear in early spring, but they have a very strong odor disliked by most people, so the plant is grown for its evergreen foliage. The cultivar to look for is the 2-foot dwarf 'Winter Wine', whose leaves darken from a rich green in summer to a shining burgundy in winter. Plant in partial shade in a good, moist garden soil, providing extra water until the plant is established.

Ilex spp., the hollies, are covered in chapter 4 for their winter berries. But even without the berries, these are stunning shrubs and trees for the winter garden. Except for *I. verticillata*, the winterberry or deciduous holly, the shiny, spined evergreen leaves of the hollies are always stunning in the landscape. For special winter beauty, we recommend the following: Burford's holly, *I. cornuta* 'Burfordii', a cultivar with lustrous, dark green foliage with a waxy sheen, reaching a height of 10 to 15 feet, with a 6- to 8-foot spread; *I. latifolia*, the leatherleaf holly, an excellent landscape plant reaching a height of 12 to 20 feet, with a 10-foot spread (plants can become small trees with maturity), and lustrous, dark green foliage up to 8 inches; *I.*

pedunculosa, the longstalk holly, reaching 15 feet in both height and width, and bearing spineless leaves up to 3 inches long, of a glossy medium to dark green; *I. pernyi*, the Perny holly, which grows about 12 feet tall, with a 6-foot spread, forming a pyramidal outline of drooping twigs, and bearing light green, shiny leaves with irregular spines about an inch long; and finally, two forms of *I. vomitoria*, the Yaupon holly, the species up to 15 foot high, with a 12-foot spread, bearing gray-green leaves about an inch long, and 'Pendula', a few feet shorter at maturity but of a most beautiful weeping form that is an asset to any garden. Provide sun or partial shade for all of these shrubs, along with good garden soil of a medium fertility.

Kalmia latifolia, the mountain laurel, covers the mountains from the Catskills to the Appalachians to the Great Smokies with bountiful flowers from May to June. But even without the glorious flowers, this beautiful native shrub would deserve a spot in the winter garden because of the evergreen leaves and the striking overall appearance of older specimens. Either a shrub or a small tree reaching a 10-foot height, the mountain laurel has dark brown bark bearing vertical striations that look almost as if a giant cat went wild with its claws. The elliptical leaves are a deep, shiny green above and a bit paler underneath. 'Myrtifolia' is a dwarf form growing less than 6 feet high, 'Obtusata' is a dwarf form with leathery oval leaves, and 'Willowcrest' bears blush pink flowers but, more important, has narrow willowlike leaves. There are many other cultivars having various color changes in the normal pink flowers. Plant laurels in the sun only if the ground is moist or

Ilex verticillata 'Chrysocarpa'

153

by a stream or lake; otherwise, provide overhead shade. These plants want acid soil with good drainage. They are susceptible to leaf spot, but that's a minor defect. They will do well as far south as Zone 8. The genus is named for Peter Kalm (1715–79), a botanist and plant explorer.

Leucothoe spp., the fetterbushes or dog-hobbles, include two evergreen shrubs of great beauty and utility. The first is *L. axillaris*, the coastal leucothoe, a shrub reaching a height of 3 to 4 feet, with a 4-foot spread, producing arching branches of glossy-green evergreen leaves up to 5 inches long that turn purple-green in the winter. Small, bell-shaped flowers appear on racemes in leaf axils. The drooping leucothoe, *L. fontanesiana*, is a larger shrub, reaching a height of up to 6 feet. The 5-inch leaves of a rich, lustrous dark green turn bronze-purple in the winter. 'Girard's Rainbow' is a lovely form first seen in Girard's Nursery in Ohio, with new growth showing white, pink, and copper tones; 'Nana' is the dwarf form. Provide partial

shade and a good acid garden soil with medium fertility and additional humus. Remove three-year-old canes after blooming to stimulate new growth and make the shrubs bushier. These are beautiful woodland plants.

Leucothoe populifolia, now known as *Agarista populifolia*, is a large and wonderful southeastern native that grows to a height of 12 feet tall, with robust, arching stems and 4-inch shiny, light green leaves formed in a flat plane along the stems. It makes an interesting architectural statement with its arching-weeping branches. Half-inch white flowers appear in early summer. This plant is very hardy and can take sun or shade and, unhappily, is vastly underrated. Used carefully, and given room to grow, you will enjoy it every day of the year. The first genus is named for a love of Apollo's, and the second is named for the beautiful daughter of Cliothenes.

Lithocarpus glaber (*Quercus glaber*), the Japanese oak, differs from the general run of oaks by having the male flowers appear in erect spines rather than

Ilex pedunculosa, long-stalked holly

154

Ilex pernyi

Magnolia grandiflora 'Hasse' is a striking cultivar of the southern magnolia that has a very narrow columnar habit. The dark, lustrous evergreen leaves are somewhat smaller than the species, as are the numerous fragrant flowers. Heat and cold tolerant, this slow-growing cultivar is a noble plant for any small garden.

pendulous as in the true oaks. They are evergreen trees to a height of 30 feet, sometimes staying in shrub form. The lancelike leaves reach a length of 5 inches, sometimes toothed at the tips, and are woolly gray beneath when young. They are effective as single specimens. Provide full sun and good garden soil with medium drainage. They are not hardy in Zones 6 and 7.

Magnolia grandiflora, the southern magnolia, is an evergreen tree reaching a height of 40 to 60 feet, with a 30-foot spread. The large, lustrous dark green leaves reach a length of 8 inches. White flowers appear on and off from May to June, followed by splitting fruit in late summer. 'Little Gem' stays about 25 feet high;

'Majestic Beauty' has very large, dark green leaves. Use this tree as a specimen, making sure to allow plenty of room for growth. Choose one of the more refined named selections, because the wild species is apt to give you an undesirable giant. Provide sun or partial shade and good garden soil with good drainage. This

155

Pieris japonica 'pygmaea'

plant is not hardy in Zone 6. The genus is named for Pierre Magnol.

Mahonia spp., the Oregon grapes, are popular evergreen shrubs with two species, *M. aquifolium*, the mountain grape, and *M. bealei*, the leatherleaf mahonia, perfect for the winter garden. The first is a 5-foot shrub with glossy dark green foliage that turns reddish purple to bronze in the winter. The second, a larger shrub reaching a height of 5 to 6 feet, with a 3- to 4-foot spread, has bronze-green foliage that turns a reddish green in the fall. The yellow flowers appear in March, blooming in clusters about 6 inches long. The summer fruit is blue. A selected hybrid between *M. lomarifolia* and *M. bealei*, called 'Arthur Menzies', has outstanding foliage and flowers. Provide partial or full shade for these dependable shrubs, planting in soil of medium fertility with high organic content and good drainage. Heavy pruning of the side branches on old or neglected plants will lead to a rush of new growth.

Nandina domestica, the heavenly bamboo, is really a member of the barberry family. These usually evergreen shrubs are from 4 to 6 feet tall, with a 3-foot spread. Many upright canes bear compound leaves of individual leaflets about 1½ inches long. The green foliage turns greenish maroon or red in the wintertime. White spring flowers eventually produce red or white berries. 'Compacta' has lacy foliage that turns red in the fall; 'Harbor Dwarf' stays about 3 feet high; 'San Gabriel' bears delicate lacy foliage; 'Fire Power' and 'Gulf Stream' produce brilliant red-orange foliage, the latter cultivar being more compact and upright. Provide sun or partial shade and a good garden soil of medium fertility, with added humus. Not reliably hardy in Zone 6, losing their leaves in bad winters. Prune old plants to correct the leggy look of age. The genus is the Japanese name for the plants.

Osmanthus spp., the tea olives, represent a genus of evergreen shrubs often cited for their fragrant flowers, and they are also included in chapter 7, but their evergreen leaves make four species attractive in the winter garden. *Osmanthus fragrans*, the fragrant tea olive; *O. heterophyllus*, the holly osmanthus; *O. het-*

erophyllus 'Rotundifolius', the round-leaved tea olive; and *O. americanus*, the devilwood.

Paxistima canbyi, the mountain lover or cliff green, is a short little bush rarely over a foot high, with a 1-foot spread, hailing from limestone areas in the mountains of Virginia and West Virginia. The hollylike leaves are small and very dense, medium green in the warmer months and bearing bronze-colored tints in colder weather. The flowers are insignificant. *Paxistima myrsinites*, the Oregon boxwood, is a taller species, growing up to 2 feet high. This plant makes a marvelous edging or addition to a small knot garden. Provide partial shade and well-drained garden soil with some added humus. New plants are easy to obtain by covering the end of a branch with a thin layer of dirt weighted down with a small stone. *Paxistima* comes from the Greek *pachus*, "thick," and *stigma*.

Pieris japonica, the Japanese andromeda, has a long history as a garden plant. This evergreen shrub reaches a height of 4 to 6 feet, with a 4- to 6-foot spread. The foliage appears in heavy whorls at the branch tips and consists of 3-inch-long leathery leaves of a rich, shiny green, with the new growth being a rich bronze. The flowers appear in early April, blooming in pendulous clusters. It's a lovely shrub, and the presence of the conspicuous flower buds along with the leaves adds greatly to the winter charm. 'Bisbee Dwarf' is a more compact plant with glossy dark green leaves; 'Dorothy Wycoff' has a compact growth habit with dark pink to red flowers; 'Mountain Fire' produces new foliage that is bright red; 'Temple Bells' has the largest blossoms, 1/2-inch creamy white flowers held above the light green leaves; and 'Variegata' has white margins on the leaves. Provide partial shade and a good acid garden soil with medium drainage and added humus. The andromeda dislikes being moved, so start with a containerized plant. The genus is named for a Greek muse.

Pinus spp., the pines, are represented here by one species, *P. bungeana*, the lacebark pine, and three special cultivars, *P. densiflora* 'Oculus-draconis', *P. thun-*

Pieris japonica 'Temple Bells'

157

Pinus wallichiana 'Zebrina', Himalayan dragon-eye pine

bergiana 'Oculus-draconis', and *P. wallichiana* 'Zebrina'. It's obvious that the evergreen pines are wonderful additions to the winter garden, but these choices are especially beautiful. The lacebark pine, unlike most conifers, is usually multitrunked, and those trunks often reach heights of 40 to 50 feet, with a 40-foot spread. This tree is included in chapter 3 for its beautiful bark, but it is also grown for the year-round 4-inch needles. Plant the lacebark pine in full sun and a well-drained acid garden soil blessed with good fertility. *Pinus densiflora* 'Oculus-draconis' and *P. thunbergiana*

'Oculus-draconis' are known for their variegated needles that are especially brilliant on new growth. The former tree has performed especially well in several plantings in Charlotte that employed fairly clayey soil. *Pinus wallichiana* 'Zebrina' is more graceful, with longer, weeping, creamy white variegated needles. One of the fifteen-year-old specimens in the Susie Harwood garden at UNC-Charlotte is at home in light shade and is actually growing on the horizontal, spreading like a prostrate form and making the mop heads of recurved needles the more accessible to viewing. These tree cultivars are all outstanding in the winter because of the greatly increased intensity of the variegations. Give them full sun and a good garden soil of medium fertility.

Pittosporum tobira, the Japanese pittosporum, is an evergreen shrub reaching a height of 8 to 10 feet, with a 6- to 9-foot spread. The blunt leaves are thick and leathery, about 4 inches long, and the overall growth of pittosporum makes it a valuable specimen plant, an excellent hedge or screening plant, and especially good in planters. 'Nana' is the dwarf form, reaching 2 feet in height, and 'Variegata' has white and green leaves. Provide sun along the Coastal Plain and some shade in the piedmont, along with a good garden soil of medium fertility. It is hardy only in Zones 8 and 9. *Pittosporum* comes from the Greek for "pitch" and "seed," referring to the resinous seed coats.

Podocarpus macrophyllus var. *maki*, the slender-leaf podocarpus, makes a most attractive specimen shrub or hedge candidate. The pyramidal form reaches a height of 8 to 10 feet, with a 3- to 5-foot spread. The lustrous medium green, 3-inch leaves are each 1/3 inch wide, with a distinct midrib. Podocarpus will respond to pruning and is a good subject for topiary. This shrub does well in the heat of the Coastal Plain but often suffers winter damage in the piedmont. It is not hardy in Zone 6. Provide sun or partial shade and a good garden soil with medium drainage. *Podocarpus* comes from the Greek for "foot" and "fruit," referring to the prominent bluish purple stalk of the fleshy seed.

Prunus laurocerasus 'Otto Luyken' is known in the trade as the Otto laurel. It's a short evergreen shrub reaching a 4-foot height, with a 5- to 7-foot spread. The 4-inch leaves are a glossy dark green and point to the sky as they advance up the spreading branches. It's an excellent shrub for a foundation planting because it has a compact form and rarely needs pruning. We finally pruned a few branches from our specimen in the Harwood Garden at UNC-Charlotte after fifteen years because it was getting too wide, but not too tall. Provide sun or partial shade and a good garden soil with medium drainage and added humus. The genus is from the Latin name of the plum.

Quercus acuta, the Japanese evergreen oak, is termed a small tree. Reaching a height of 20 to 30 feet, with a 20-foot spread, this evergreen oak is effective both as a specimen tree surrounded by open space and as a screen, especially because it tolerates urban conditions. The leathery foliage of a dark, glossy olive green is between 3 and 5 inches long. Provide sun or partial shade and an acid garden soil of medium fertility with good drainage. *Quercus glauca*, the ring-cupped oak, resembles *Q. acuta* in size, bearing 3- to 5-inch evergreen leaves of a glossy olive green with a grayish cast on the undersides. It's another excellent specimen tree and is also useful as a screen. Provide sun and a good garden soil of high fertility. It is not hardy in Zone 6.

Raphiolepis indica, the Indian hawthorn, was originally imported from China and despite its qualities is rarely grown. A rounded shrub, it reaches 4 or 5 feet in height, with a 5-foot spread. The dark green leaves are thick and leathery, up to 2½ inches long, and turn purplish in the winter. White or pink flowers appear in late spring. 'Ballerina' stays about 2 feet tall, and 'Jack Evans' stays compact with a broad and spreading growth habit. The Indian hawthorn is a perfect plant in the herb garden or for a low hedge and also tolerates the root restrictions of a pot. Provide full sun and an average garden soil with excellent drainage. *Raphiolepis umbellata*, the yeddo-hawthorn, is a larger plant, reaching a height of 6 feet, with a 6-foot spread. The leathery, dark green leaves are almost round and about 3 inches long. White flowers appear in May. 'Majestic Beauty' is resistant to leaf spot, a virus disease that attacks many broadleaf evergreens. This plant does well in sun or partial shade and any good garden soil with average drainage. As this shrub grows, it has a tendency to become leggy, and you might eventually need to put smaller plants in front of it for camouflage. Distinctive selections of both species have the potential to become very useful garden subjects for the Southeast, especially as foundation plants. *Raphiolepis* comes from the Greek for "needle scale," referring to bracts in the flowers.

Rhododendron spp., the rhododendrons and azaleas, represent some eight hundred species of evergreen and deciduous shrubs (and a few trees), that we covered from the standpoint of winter flowers in chapter 6. Although many garden authorities have written against the overuse of these plants because of a same-

ness to their foliage, they remain very important additions to the winter garden. The evergreens that we call rhododendrons, with their large, thick leaves and conspicuous stem-tip flower buds, usually capture the public eye. The genus also includes a number of evergreen azaleas, however, with much smaller, thinner leaves and less conspicuous flower buds. These are mostly hybrids of Japanese species and provide the abundance of colorful-flowering foundation plants widely used in the South.

There are relatively few evergreen species of rhododendrons that do well in southeastern gardens. Three of these stalwarts are noted for their unusual

Rhododendron linearifolium, spider azalea

159

Rhododendron serpyllifolium, thyme-leaf azalea

and distinctive foliage. *Rhododendron linearifolium*, the spider azalea, is a semievergreen shrub growing to 4 feet tall with 3-inch leaves that are less than $\frac{1}{2}$ inch wide. The leaves turn rich colors in early winter and usually persist all winter to early spring. Even temperatures as low as 6°F have never caused our specimens to drop their leaves. It is one of the most asked-about plants in the UNC-Charlotte gardens. Its spring flowers are not terribly showy, being pink with very narrow petals. *Rhododendron oldhamii*, sometimes called the copper azalea, has 1-inch ovate leaves that are covered with $\frac{1}{4}$-inch stiffened hairs, giving the whole plant a very hirsute appearance that demands to be touched— like stroking a very large cat. Plant it near a path and it will reward you, although the bright orange-red flowers with metallic purple highlights may seem garish. Grow

this plant for its winter leaves. *Rhododendron serpyllifolium*, the thyme-leaved rhododendron, is a mounding shrub to 3 feet high and 4 feet wide. It has very tiny leaves about $\frac{1}{4}$ inch long that give the plant a fine texture. Ours is quite evergreen, though it may lose its leaves farther north in Zone 6. The $\frac{1}{2}$-inch pink spring flowers are charming. Visitors will never guess this is a true rhododendron.

As a general rule, most evergreen azaleas lose some of their leaves in winter, and those left on the plant will turn various shades of bronze, purple, or yellow. These color changes can be interesting and should be considered in making additions to your garden. Visit a well-stocked nursery in late December, after a few hard freezes, and carefully examine the azalea selection, looking for plants that have good form, have retained a majority of their leaves, and exhibit winter colors to your taste. This way you see them in their winter form, analogous to picking them out in bloom for flower color in the spring.

As for the evergreen true rhododenrons, there are no species that we would recommend, though people like to try to grow the wild mountain ones, especially the rose bay (*Rhododendron maximum*), the purple rhododendron (*R. catawbiense*), and the charming Carolina rhododendon (*R. minus*), which is certainly the most adaptable and rewarding in the garden. We would, however, caution that none of these perform as well nor look as beautiful as they do in their mountain homes.

For the warmer zones of the South, we recommend a hybrid rhododendron, the best by far being 'Roseum Elegans', the standard lavender-flowered plant seen all across the eastern United States. It will become a beautiful shrub to 8 feet, with large, dull green leaves, and conspicuous pointed flower buds on each branch terminal. They can take a good bit of sun if you keep them moist and well mulched in the South. One additional recommendation is the hybrid known as 'P.J.M.' (named after the nurseryman-developer Peter J. Meaitt of Massachusetts). This is a cross between our native *R. minus* and the Asian winter-blooming *R. dauricum*. The resulting hybrid, actually a group of similar hybrids, has become a very common plant seen in every yard in New England. One outstanding feature of this compact small-leaved shrub is that the foliage turns a bronze-purple color in winter, reverting to green in summer. Bright lavender-pink flowers appear in late winter, sometimes sporadically in the fall. It's one of the hardiest and adaptable hybrids ever created, growing in shade or sun. Watch out for lacewing bugs on any sun-grown evergreen in the South; we spray for them in June if necessary. For all rhododendrons and azaleas, at least afternoon shade is best, as well as evenly moist, well-drained soil. The roots are very shallow and can dry out in hot weather. Pruning is rarely required.

Rhododendron, 'P.J.M.'

Rhododendron yakusimanum is another species worthy of cultivation. A dwarf evergreen rhododendron from Japan, in time it will reach a height of 3 feet. The leaves can be 1 to 2 inches wide and 3 to 4 inches long, generally half as large as a typical large-leaved rhododendron. Another plus for this species is the velvety indumentum on the undersides of the leaves. This thick, tan hairy layer is quite soft and pleasant to the touch. The flowers, though shyly produced, are usually pure white. Plant in well-drained soil that is mulched and kept moist. This species is well adapted to Zone 8 and below and is quite hardy up north.

Rosmarinus officinalis, the common rosemary, remains one of the all-time favorite herbs, consisting of an evergreen shrub that is upright, shrubby, or even cascading, depending on the variety grown. The beautiful dark green, aromatic leaves are long and thin, usually up to an inch long. In the Southeast, rosemary is best as a containerized plant so that it can be moved to the shade during the hot summer months, especially in the piedmont. The cultivars 'Arp' and 'Hilltop' are especially tolerant of heat and cold, the first being hardy to –10°F, but they are not hardy in Zone 6. The other rosemaries are limited to Zones 8 and 9. Provide full sun to partial shade and well-drained garden soil of average fertility. The genus is the ancient Latin name for this plant.

Sabal palmetto, the palmetto, produces a straight trunk crowned with lustrous, green palm leaves that resemble giant fans up to 6 feet long and 4 to 7 feet wide. Mature trees (really herbaceous plants) reach a height of 30 feet. They excel as street trees, specimens, or surrounding the home landscape. They do well in full sun or partial shade and any good garden soil of average fertility but require a great deal of moisture. Palmettos are best transplanted in June and July. They are hardy only in Zones 8 and 9. *Sabal* is said to be the native name in South American.

Santolina chamaecyparissus, the lavender cotton, forms a low-growing hedge about 2 feet tall, with a 4-foot spread. The silvery gray aromatic leaves are about an inch long, and the stems resemble small feathers. These plants are especially useful as small hedges or in knot gardens. 'Nana' forms a foot-high compact mound of foliage. Provide full sun and average to poor soil, but with excellent drainage. Cut back the top branches of the crown every two or three years to renew luxuriant growth. The stems will root where they touch the ground. *Santolina* comes from the Latin for "holy flax."

(Left) *Rhododendron yakusimanum*

Taxus baccata, the English yew, has long been a favorite for winter gardens because its soft green needles and round scarlet berries (really drupes) have both decorative and classic qualities. They also tolerate heavy shearing and can easily be rejuvenated at almost any time. Unpruned, the English yew can reach a height of 15 feet and becomes a rounded tree with spreading branches. 'Standishii' bears golden-yellow-striped foliage, with the color more intense in warmer parts of the country and on the sunny side of the garden; 'Repandens' is slow growing with a flattened top and will often spread to 10 feet. The English yew is not reliably hardy in Zone 6. *T. cuspidata*, the Japanese yew, can reach a height of 20 feet if unpruned and will become an upright tree, but like other yews, it can easily be pruned. 'Densa' has a flat top and can grow to 4 feet in height, with a spread up to 20 feet. *Taxus × media* is the hybrid between the English and Japanese yews. The original hybrid can grow to a height of 20 feet but usually stays about 12 feet tall with a 10-foot spread. The inch-long foliage is needlelike, a shiny dark green above and light green beneath; new growth is a soft yellow-green. There are a number of cultivars, including 'Hicksii', exhibiting a columnar habit; 'Sentinalis', 8 feet tall and very, very narrow; and 'Wardii', reaching a height of 7 feet, with a 20-foot spread. Provide sun or partial shade and a good garden soil with excellent drainage. The intermediate yew does not do well south of Zone 8. *Taxus* is the classic Latin name for the yew.

Ternstroemia gymnanthera, the Japanese ternstroemia or, as it's mistakenly called, the cleyera (the true cleyera is discussed earlier in this chapter), remains an undiscovered garden treasure. It's an evergreen shrub from Japan, reaching a height of 15 feet, with a 7-to 8-foot spread. The leathery oval leaves are olive green and arranged in clusters, taking on a wine and moss green color in the winter. Small, creamy white flowers form deep red, cherrylike fruits in the fall. 'Variegata' has leaves marbled with silver and white, developing a pink tinge in winter; 'Burnished Gold' has new foliage opening to a bronzed gold, overlaid with burgundy. Provide as much shade as possible, as this tree resents the hot summer sun of the South, and average garden soil, short of plain clay. It is not hardy in Zone 6 and will suffer leaf and twig kill in severe winters. It is named for Christopher Ternstroem, an 18th-century Swedish naturalist and traveler in China.

Thuja orientalis, the oriental arborvitae, is a lovely evergreen shrub reaching a 10-foot height, with a 10-foot spread, broadly conical in form. The tiny, aro-

Trachycarpus fortunei, Chinese windmill palm

and dwarf conifers in general, we have chosen to highlight one very unusual cultivar of this species: 'Lombart's Wintergreen'. Its growth is conical and trees bear flattened sprays of foliage, a beautiful green on both sides. However, in winter the scalelike needles stay a handsome dark green, developing a very strong spicy-pungent cedar aroma that is unique among these conifers. The aroma is similar to, but distinctly different from, that of the incense cedar. Although the wintergreen arborvitae is rare in cultivation, gardeners should seek it out. The handsome fifteen-year-old specimen at UNC-Charlotte is about 15 feet high and half as wide, surviving all the hot, dry, wet, cold, windy conditions, plus poor soil. *Thuja* is the Greek name for juniper.

Trachycarpus fortunei, the windmill palm, is a subtropical palm that is very attractive as a landscape specimen. It reaches a height of 20 to 35 feet, with a 15-foot spread, and is topped with medium to dull green, fan-shaped leaves that are 2 to 3 feet wide. The straight trunk is covered with a black, hairlike fiber. Plant in partial shade and a good garden soil with good drainage, average fertility, and added humus, and provide some wind protection. Give the tree additional moisture when it is young, and transplant in spring or summer. The only pruning necessary is to remove dead leaves. Our young specimen at UNC-Charlotte survived −6°F with no damage, but the leaves can be burned by very cold winds. *Trachycarpus* comes from the Greek for "rough" or "harsh," referring to the fruit.

Herbaceous Plants

Acorus gramineus, the grassy-leaved or Japanese sweetflag and its many cultivars, is a perennial herb that has long been used in winter gardens located in warmer climates. Swordlike, dark green leaves usually grow up to 10 inches high. Their fragile beauty can be used to highlight pond edgings, spotted along the open border in a woods, set in pots as decorations at the edges of rock gardens, or planted as small specimens in bogs or actual water gardens. 'Albovariegatus' bears leaves with alternate, longitudinal stripes of gold and green; 'Ogon' produces variegated leaves with alternate, longitudinal stripes of green and gold; 'Pusillus' has bright green, sword-shaped leaves and never tops 6 inches; and 'Variegatus' has longitudinally striped leaves of alternate green and white stripes, arranged like folding fans. Provide shade during the hottest hours of the day and a fertile, moist or wet soil. In pots, use a mix of equal parts of soil, sand, and peat

matic, overlapped leaves are dark green, yellow-green when young, and form flattened, fanlike branchlets held on the vertical. They are excellent as hedging, as specimens, and in containers. 'Berckmanii' stays about 6 feet tall and shows a compact, globe-shaped growth habit with golden-tipped branches. Provide sun and a good garden soil with good drainage.

Thuja occidentalis, or arborvitae, is another handsome conifer with many cultivars, some needle-leaved, some with scalelike leaves, and some with both. While a whole treatise could be written on *Thuja* in specific,

164

moss, but it must always be moist. *Acorus* is the ancient name for this plant.

Agave parryi, one of the century plants, hails from southern Arizona and is always a stunning sight that borders on the exotic. The very tough, thick leaves are beige-green, with a glaucous blue-green exiting from a tight rosette that may reach a diameter of 1 to 2 feet in time. With these leaves and their accompaning spines, the century plant makes an impressive specimen in the sunny, well-drained rock garden. Expect to begin with a small plant about 4 to 6 inches across.

Ajuga reptans, the bugleweed, forms an all-spreading ground cover that is bemoaned by lawn people but liked by gardeners. The 3- to 5-inch-high plants spread by stolons to form dense mats of foliage. Individual leaves are dark green, 3 to 4 inches long and an inch wide. Short, pyramidal spikes of blue flowers appear in mid-April. 'Atropurpurea' has bronze-tinted foliage; 'Burgundy Glow' bears new leaves of burgundy red, with mature leaves turning creamy white and dark pink; and

'Variegata' has gray-green leaves with creamy markings. Provide partial shade and a good, well-drained garden soil, spacing plants about 6 inches apart. The genus is Latin for "yoke," referring to a flower feature.

Alstroemeria psittacina (*A. pulchella*) is a tuberous-rooted herbaceous perennial from Brazil, described by Elizabeth Lawrence as delighting her with "whorls of thin, pale-green leaves, [proving] to be hardy in Charlotte . . . though the foliage is ruined by very cold weather." The alternate lancelike leaves are 3 inches long and grow on 2- to 3-foot stems. The lovely summer-blooming flowers are a rich red-brown. The leaves disappear by summer's end. Provide full sun or partial shade and a good, well-drained garden soil with added humus. They are not hardy in Zone 6. The genus was named in honor of Baron Clas Alstroemer, a friend of Linnaeus's.

Antennaria neodioica (*A. tomentosa*), the pussytoes, and *A. plantaginifolia*, the plantain-leaved pussytoes, have little rosettes of leaves that remain

Agave parryi, century plant

Asarum (Hexastylis) shuttleworthii 'Callaway', wild ginger

throughout the winter, ready to send up flowers in very early spring. Pussytoes have 1-inch leaves that are white-woolly, single-veined, and spoon-shaped; the plantain-leaved pussytoes have longer basal leaves, up to 3 inches. These densely growing plants will often dominate a field of shorter grasses and are quite attractive in the rock garden. Small white flowers that resemble cat's toes bloom in spring. Provide a spot among or near deciduous trees to provide partial shade in the hot summer, planting in average well-drained garden soil. The genus is so named because of small scales in the male flowers that resemble butterfly antennae.

Arum italicum, the Italian arum, belongs to the family that contains the jack-in-the-pulpit. It's a perennial tuber that produces 1-foot-high arrowhead-shaped leaves with a pronounced yellow-green midrib and veining. The leaves first appear in late October and remain through the winter. Unusual spring flowers, like

(Left) *Arum italicum* 'Pictum'

large ghostly kites, are followed by orange-red berries in early fall on 1-foot stems. The flowers and leaves are gone by late summer, leaving stalks topped with clusters of bright orange-red berries, easily mistaken for jack's. By September's end, the berries are gone and the process begins again. Italian arum makes a beautiful border plant and a great backdrop for early-spring flowers. It is particularly fine when viewed against a stone wall or naturalized at the end of a wild garden. The leaves are especially valuable for winter floral arrangements. 'Pictum' has a more pronounced marbling. Provide partial shade and ordinary moist garden soil with some added humus. *Arum* is the classical name for this genus, first penned by the Greek philosopher Theophrastus, who wrote extensively about plants.

Asarum spp., the wild gingers, are known for their beautiful heart-shaped, aromatic, evergreen leaves that are used to carpet both the woodland garden and the rock garden. *A. europaeum*, the European wild ginger, grows about 5 inches tall and has 2- to 3-inch glossy

167

Brassica, flowering kale

green leaves. *A. shuttleworthii* (*Hexastylis shuttlewor-thii*), the mottled wild ginger, was called by Elizabeth Lawrence "the most striking species, with large leaves—to more than three inches across and four inches long—which vary in form from arrowheads to almost perfect circles, and in color from plain green to very fancy patterns." Dull purple, three-petaled flowers bloom at ground level in late spring. Both species make excellent ground covers and are often planted underneath rhododendrons, azaleas, and mountain laurels. Provide partial shade and good rich, moist garden soil with added humus. *Asarum* is the Latinized form of an ancient plant name.

Aspidistra elatior, the cast-iron plant of British houseplant fame, forms upright clumps of evergreen foliage that spread slowly by rhizomes. The dark green leaves are up to 20 inches long and 2 to 3 inches wide, spreading for 2 to 3 feet. Inconspicuous star-shaped flowers appear at ground level and are pollinated by slugs. 'Variegata' bears leaves with alternate green and white striping. Provide shade and any average garden soil. These plants also do well in pots. Occasionally remove scarred and battered leaves. Aspidistras are not hardy above Zone 7. The genus comes from the Greek and refers to the flower structure.

Aurinia saxatilis (*Alyssum saxatile*) grows wild in the mountains of Central Europe. It is a hardy herbaceous perennial, woody at the base. The soft and woolly leaves are a gray-green and are rarely longer than an inch, and they remain on the plants through the winter. Bright yellow flowers appear in April, and the plants easily seed about. They are especially suit-

168

able for walls, rock gardens, and pots. Provide full sun and any thin but well-drained garden soil. Named for a gold-point lace originating in France.

Bergenia spp., the Siberian tea and heartleaf bergenia, would be welcome in the winter garden even without the early-spring flowers. The thick, leathery leaves remain evergreen in most of the Southeast and turn a reddish bronze in areas that experience colder weather. The heartleaf bergenia (*B. cordifolia*) has oval leaves up to 10 inches wide; the leaves of the Siberian tea (*B. crassifolia*) are similar in size but rounder in shape. For the best foliage, provide partial shade in good, moist garden soil with added humus or organic matter.

Brassica oleracea, the ornamental cabbages and kales, are annual members of the cabbage family that produce beautifully colored leaves during cold weather. Start seeds four weeks before the last frost or sow directly outdoors in early spring. Provide average garden soil and full sun. The colors begin to gleam in the fall,

with the shorter days and cooler nights. Space plants 12 to 14 inches apart, according to your garden designs. *Brassica* is an ancient Roman name for the cabbages.

Calluna spp. and *Erica* spp., the heathers and the heaths, are both mentioned in chapter six for their delightful winter flowers. But it should be noted that both of these subshrubs also are excellent for providing needlelike foliage that just gets more colorful during the colder months of the year. There are far too many cultivars available to mention here; consult Plant Sources for various suppliers. Provide full winter sun, and plant in an acid, well-drained garden soil. In the mountains, protect these plants from heavy winds. Cut back branches immediately after flowering.

Corydalis cheilanthifolia, the fernleaf corydalis, is a perennial from China that bears erect, fernlike, evergreen leaves that are 8 inches long and a bluish gray. Plants may form large mounds to 1 foot tall by 2 feet wide; individuals are more delicate in appearance. This corydalis may act as a biennial or become a weak

Corydalis cheilanthifolia, grown for evergreen delicate foliage, to 2 feet in diameter and mounding

perennial, and plants should seed themselves around the garden. Provide moist soil and light shade.

Cyclamen hederifolium (*C. neapolitanum*) belongs to the Persian violet family, holiday blossoms of florists' fame. They would be excellent for the winter garden even if they did not produce charming and beautiful flowers late in the fall, for which they have also been included in chapter 5. Ivylike leathery leaves of a deep glossy green, often marbled with various patterns of muted silver, appear in October and last well into the following spring before going dormant for the summer. Eventually a new tuber forms that grows in size, year after year, rather than dividing like bulbous plants. A shaded colony of cyclamen is a prize to be cherished for a lifetime. *Cyclamen coum*, still charming but a less graceful plant, will take very cold temperatures (below 0°F with snow cover) but is less adaptable to chill and damp than *C. hederifolium*. Provide partial shade and good, moist garden soil with excellent drainage and added humus.

Dichondra carolinensis (*D. micanthra*), the lawn leaf, is a creeping tropical vine that grows about 3 inches tall and has medium green rounded leaves about 1/2 inch wide. Flowers are insignificant. It's considered an evergreen ground cover by the trade and is often used as a substitute for grass, although it will not stand up to traffic. Provide sun or partial shade and an average garden soil of medium fertility, but also fertilize annually. Once established, dichondra can be mowed three or four times a year. It is not hardy in Zones 6 and 7. *Dichondra* comes from the Greek *dis*, "double," and *chondros*, "grain," referring to the fruit.

Digitalis purpurea, the old-fashioned garden foxglove, is usually termed a summer perennial, but when planted in the fall, the evergreen leaves make a great addition to the otherwise bare perennial border. Leaves may be up to a foot long, though they are usually smaller in the winter. Harsh winter cold and winds may kill back some of the outer leaves, but usually the plant survives. There are new selections, like 'Straw-

Heuchera 'Pewter Veil'

170

Liriope muscari 'Variegata', lilyturf

berry', that are more compact and refined in manner than the old varieties. Provide good, moist soil and light shade, although plants will survive full sun.

Equisetum spp., the horsetails or the common scouring rushes, produce multitudes of simple green stems, each consisting of many sections (about 3 inches long in the species) resembling green pop-its (plastic beads that pop together) that are joined by whorls of reduced leaves. They are very architectural in appearance and are most effective when grown in attractive pots. *Equisetum hyemale* is the most common species, growing 3 to 4 feet tall. Its cultivar 'Robustus' can reach up to 6 feet or more. *E. scirpoides*, the dwarf horsetail, rarely grows above 6 inches and covers the ground like loose Brillo. Provide full sun or partial shade and any garden soil; these plants especially like damp or wet sites, and common horsetail will grow in water. Be warned: These are very invasive plants and must—repeat must—be contained! Grow them in deep pots sunk into the ground, or surround the growing area with a metal or plastic shield at least 18 inches deep. Watch for runners. *Equisetum* comes from the Latin *equus*, "horse," and *seta*, "bristle."

Euphorbia amygdaloides var. *robbiae*, Miss Robb's spurge, forms a tight green mound of deep green leaves about fifteen inches high and up to thirty inches in diameter.

Fragaria chiloensis × *ananassa*, the strawberry, provides dainty rosettes of dark green, toothed leaves up to 6 inches across, with runners that end in plantlets that will root all around the parent plant. It is similar to ajuga but not as dense. White flowers of spring are about 3/4 inch across. 'Panda' has pink flowers, and you might even get a ripe berry or two. Provide good garden soil and full sun, and let them run.

Heuchera americana, the alumroot, native American coralroot, or rock geranium, is another plant that would be grown regardless of the flowers it produces or the endless garden cultivars the genus has been responsible for. The attractive heart-shaped, lobed leaves are from 3 to 4 inches wide and sit on 2- to 3-foot stems. When young, the leaves are mottled with various shades of pewter and maroon, all suffused on a dark green background. When they are older, green becomes the dominant color. The unimpressive drooping flowers appear in May. These plants look especially fine when growing from crevices in rock walls or in and around rock gardens. 'Palace Purple' is a cultivar developed from the western wildflower *H. micrantha* and has dark bronze-red leaves throughout the year. Provide full sun or partial shade and a good garden soil with excellent drainage. *Heuchera* is named for Johann Heinrich Heucher (1677–1747).

Liriope spp., the lilyturfs, represent five species of plants that belong to the lily family and are native to

171

Pachysandra terminalis 'Variegata'

China, Japan, and the Philippines. They are tufted, sod-forming, evergreen perennials that produce terminal spikes of flowers in summer, followed by berrylike fruits in the fall. *Liriope muscari* forms clumps of dark green, grasslike leaves up to 2 feet high that recurve toward the ground. Its cultivar 'Variegata' has yellow stripes, and various other cultivars are being introduced by the trade. Creeping lilyturf, *L. spicata*, has a suckering habit and spreads willy-nilly rather than clumping. Both make excellent ground covers or edgings. For the plants to look their best, partial shade must be provided; if pushed and given plenty of water, however, they will tolerate full sun. Use average garden soil slightly on the moist side. Cut back old growth to 1 inch in March before the new growth begins. Plants are named for the Greek nymph Liriope.

Ophiopogon spp., mondo grass, are sod-forming perennial herbs with evergreen grasslike leaves. Like the lilyturfs, they also belong to the lily family. *Ophiopogon jaburan vittata*, the snakebeard, produces dark green leaves with white stripes, up to 18 inches long, that recurve to the ground. 'Aureus' has yellow-striped leaves. *O. japonicus*, mondo grass, has dark green foliage up to a foot long that also recurves to the ground. 'Gyokuruu' is grasslike, growing about 2 inches high; 'Nana' stays about 4 inches tall; 'Shiroshima Ryu' has dark green and white striped leaves; and 'Variegatus' also has white and green striping. Both bear summer flowers, followed by fall fruits. *O. plansicapus*, black mondo grass, has bluish black leaves at maturity, and the cultivar 'Ebony Knight' has even darker leaves. They are all excellent as ground covers or edgings and make fine container plants. Unlike lilyturf, these plants are hardy only to Zone 7. Provide partial shade, although these plants can adapt to full sun, and average garden soil slightly on the moist side. Cut back old growth to 1 inch in March before the new growth begins. *Ophiopogon* comes from the Greek *ophis*, "snake," and *pogon*, "beard."

Pachysandra terminalis, the Japanese spurge, and *P. procumbens*, the Alleghany spurge, represent the two cultivated species in a genus of perennial herbs or subshrubs. The Japanese species bears 4-inch evergreen leaves to a height of about 1 foot, acting as a useful evergreen ground cover; whitish flowers appear on a terminal spike in spring. 'Cut Leaf' has deep green leaves with serrated edges; 'Green Carpet' grows very close to the ground; 'Green Sheen' has leaves of a glossy green; and 'Variegata' has leaves bordered with white. New cultivars are continually being introduced. Unfortunately, Japanese pachysandra has become a garden cliché, but southern gardeners can also grow the more beautiful American native, the Alleghany spurge. This plant is also an effective evergreen ground cover; in the winter, the leaves become marbled with muted silver tones, producing a far more beautiful plant. And the spring flowers that appear in tall spikes easily outshine those of their Japanese relatives. Pinching the tops in spring leads to bushier plants. Neither species plant is comfortable south of Zone 7. Provide shade and a good, moist garden soil. *Pachysandra* comes from the Greek "*pachys*," thick, and "*andros*," man, referring to the thick stamens in the flowers.

Stachys byzantina (*S. lanata*), the lamb's-ears or woolly betony, is an erect perennial to 10 or 12 inches with stems bearing densely white-tomentose leaves up to 4 inches long. Whorls of small pink or purple flowers appear on 18-inch stems in summer. 'Silver Carpet' is nonflowering and makes a denser, more compact ground cover. Lamb's-ears are especially attractive in an herb garden, massed in a perennial bed, or as an edging. Leaves can be seriously damaged in a bad winter. Cut back winter-damaged leaves in early spring. Provide full sun and average well-drained garden soil. *Stachys* is an ancient Greek name for this plant.

Verbascum thapsus, the common mullein, is a biennial plant that is often found growing on steep banks and at the edges of ditches on backcountry roads. The first year, plants are limited to rosettes of woolly leaves, each leaf often a foot long and not unlike a piece of flannel. Tall stalks covered with 1-inch yellow flowers bloom in the summer of the second year.

But during the first year, a line of mulleins still is an attractive addition to the winter garden. Provide full sun and average garden soil. They will survive poor, dry soil with ease. *Verbascum* is the ancient Latin name for this plant.

Vinca spp., the myrtles or creeping periwinkles, are evergreen crawlers originally from Europe that are excellent for naturalizing as ground covers, especially on banks or under trees. *Vinca major*, the big periwinkle, bears glossy, light green leaves up to 3 inches long to a 1-foot height. The light blue, five-petaled flowers begin to appear in late March, but most appear from mid-April on, continuing on and off throughout the summer. 'Variegata' has cream-colored markings on the leaves. They are not hardy in Zone 6. *Vinca minor*, the common periwinkle, remains one of the favorite old-time evergreen ground covers brought over from Europe with the colonists and now found in every old cemetery. It's a perennial evergreen subshrub with shiny 2-inch leaves that spread about on long stems that will root at every node. Five-petaled violet flowers bloom in spring and fall. Common periwinkle is a great plant for clothing steep banks, carpeting problem areas, and covering rocks. Provide partial shade and good garden soil with added humus. *Vinca* (or *pervinca*) is the ancient Latin name for these plants.

Yucca spp., the yuccas, are marvelous plants for the winter landscape. They form stout clumps, often over 3 feet wide, of stiff, dark green, sword-shaped leaves, often with needle-sharp tips. Bell-shaped flowers on stems to 12 feet appear in midsummer, and the pods last into the winter and make great decorative additions to the plants. The most popular yucca is *Y. filamentosa*, the Adam's-needle, named for the sharp point and the fine white hairs that line the leaf edges. 'Bright Edge' has variegated foliage, with the leaves edged in yellow-gold, and 'Variegata' has leaves with various-sized stripes of creamy white. *Yucca aloifolia*, the Spanish bayonet, eventually reaches a height of 8 feet, topped with a rosette of the stiff leaves. 'Marginata' has leaves edged with yellow; 'Tricolor' has white and yellow bands up and down the leaf; and 'Variegata' bears white-striped foliage. It is not hardy in Zones 6 and 7. The mound-lily yucca, *Y. gloriosa*, grows with or without a trunk, reaching a height of 4 to 6 feet, with a 3- to 4-foot spread. The dark green leaves are often 30 inches long and 2 inches wide, with a sharp point. 'Nobilis' has better form and dark green leaves. For all three species, provide full sun and a good garden soil with low fertility but excellent drainage. Once established, these are excellent plants where water is at a premium. *Yucca* comes from the Latinized version of the Spanish vernacular name for the plant.

Vines

Akebia quinata, the five-leaved akebia, twines around arbors or trellises, reaching an ultimate length of 30 to 40 feet. The medium green leaves consist of five leaflets, each about 2 inches long, spread out like fingers on a human palm. The leaves turn purplish in the winter and may fall from the vines in severe winters. Provide sun or partial shade and good soil with medium drainage. The growth is rapid, and this vine is especially attractive rambling over an arbor. *Akebia* is the old Japanese name for this vine.

Bignonia capreolata (*Anisostichus capreolatus*), the crossvine, climbs between 50 and 60 feet by tendrils that can be trained to cling to masonry walls. Smooth, dark green leaves consist of two long, pointed leaflets up to 6 inches long that turn purplish in the winter. Orange-red, trumpetlike flowers appear in mid-April, followed by pods in the summertime. 'Atrosanguinea' has leaves longer and narrower than the noncultivar. Provide full sun in any good garden soil. Named in honor of the Abbé Bignon (1662–1743), librarian to Louis XIV.

Clematis armandii flowers in late winter and thus is also listed in chapter 6, but it would be worth growing even if it didn't. It climbs with twisting stems, growing about 20 feet long. The leaves are a medium to glossy green, about 5 inches long, with three leaflets. The flowers appear on last year's growth, so if you must prune, wait until midsummer. Not hardy in Zone 6, as a bad winter can kill the roots unless effectively mulched. Provide full sun for the vine, but as with all clematises, the roots must be shaded and cool.

Euonymus fortunei, the wintercreeper, is a vinelike shrub climbing with aerial roots that cling to solid surfaces. The height is from 4 to 6 feet, with a 4-foot

Euonymus fortunei 'Silver Queen'

Gelsemium rankinii is almost identical to Carolina Jessamine, *Gelsemium sempervirens*, differing only in that it has slightly more rounded leaf bases and odorless flowers. The former is a much rarer plant of the Gulf Coast region and North Carolina, but it still makes an exceptional evergreen climbing plant that may actually bloom a little earlier.

spread. The 2-inch leaves are dark green with whitish veins, turning reddish in the fall, and grow from green stems. Provide sun or partial shade in any good garden soil that includes additional humus. The wintercreeper will tolerate salt spray. 'Coloratus' has 1- to 2-inch leaves that turn reddish purple in winter; 'Cushion' makes a dwarf mound of deep green foliage; 'Emerald 'n Green' in early spring is a mass of bright yellow, almost chartreuse, the leaves centered with green splotches that lose some of their brightness as summer advances, until the winter foliage is a burnished bronze with pale yellow accents; 'Kewensis' is a prostrate spreader with $1/4$-inch leaves that will climb with support; 'Minimus' has $1/2$-inch leaves; 'Silver Queen' grows as a compact shrub to a height of 4 feet; and 'Variegata' bears gray-green leaves with white or pinkish margins.

Fatshedera lizei, the bush-ivy, is a bigeneric hybrid between English ivy (*Hedera helix*) and the Formosa rice tree (*Fatsia japonica*). Eventual height is about 10 feet. The ivylike foliage is a dark, lustrous green, reaching a width of 10 inches in older plants.

The pale green flowers appear in 1-inch spherical heads and are followed by blue berries. 'Variegata' has leaves bordered with white. Provide shade in a well-drained, good garden soil. This vine makes a good espalier and does well in planters. It is not hardy in Zone 6. *Fatshedera* is a combination of the genus names *Fatsia* and *Hedera*.

Ficus pumila, the climbing fig, is a vine belonging to the fig family. It climbs with aerial rootlets that hold the leaves flat against most surfaces. Juvenile leaves are about an inch long, and mature leaves reach a width of 2 inches. Small, inedible figs appear on older plants. This vine looks beautiful on a stone or masonry wall, but keep it away from wood. 'Minima' is a dwarf variety, and 'Variegata' has leaves of green and white. Provide partial shade and any good garden soil with good drainage. The climbing fig is hardy only in Zones 8 and 9. *Ficus* is the classic name for the fig.

Gelsemium sempervirens, the Carolina jessamine, will climb just about anything, reaching a height (or length) of 20 feet. The 2-inch-long, pointed leaves are a shiny dark green that turn a wine red in the wintertime. Carolina jessamine has flowers that appear from February to April and is also included in chapter 6. The vine should be sheared after flowering. This vine grows well in sun or shade but has more flowers in the sun. It's tolerant of poor soil and has no pest problems. Jessamine grows well on fences and will climb small trees without doing any harm. The genus is the Latin version of jessamine.

Hedera canariensis, the Algerian ivy, uses aerial roots for climbing and bears thick, leathery leaves of a glossy dark green up to 6 inches long. Inconspicuous greenish flowers are followed by blue-black berries. 'Canary Cream' has white margins on the leaves; 'Shamrock' has smaller leaves; and 'Variegata' bears leaves of dark green, with gray and cream markings. Provide partial shade in any good, moist garden soil. Hardy only in Zones 8 and 9. *Hedera* is the ancient Latin name for ivy.

Hedera colchica, the colchis ivy, originates in the ancient area of Colchis, on the northeast shore of the Black Sea. The vine clings by aerial roots. The dark green foliage is distinctly heart-shaped, up to 6 inches long, and fragrant when crushed. Small greenish flowers are followed by blue-black berries. 'Dentata-Variegata' has very large green leaves with gray and yellow markings. Provide shade and good, moist garden soil. This vine is a rapid spreader, so care must be used in a small garden. The colchis ivy is not hardy in Zone 6.

Hedera helix, the English ivy, climbs on solid surfaces using aerial roots that cling to stone or masonry. Because of the roots, ivy can grow on tree trunks without causing damage, but homeowners should be warned that ivy can damage wood siding. The leaves are usually lobed and come in many colors and shapes; the flowers are greenish and inconspicuous, followed by tiny black berries, but appear only on adult specimens. A shaded garden of tall trees planted with one of the variegated forms of ivy, allowed to grow up to flagstone walkways, around a stone bench or two, and about a small garden sculpture, is a treasured place to sit and think on a warm winter's day. Of the myriad cultivars of ivy, look for 'Anne Marie', with variegated medium gray-green leaves with yellow margins; 'Buttercup', with bright gold, shiny leaves about 2 inches wide that turn green in the shade; 'Mandas Crested', with light green, 3-inch, fluted leaves with an inward curl and light green veins, the leaves turning a copper color in winter; and '238th Street', a very hardy cultivar with gray-green, heart-shaped leaves and white veining. Provide partial shade and ordinary moist garden soil, with added humus. The species name *helix* refers to the spiral climb of the vine.

Jasminum officinale, the common jasmine, is a shrublike vine that reaches a height of 15 feet and is evergreen in the warmer parts of the Southeast. The leaves are featherlike, with each pointed leaflet up to 2 inches long and a fresh green. 'Aureo-variegatum' has variegated leaves. Provide sun or partial shade and good garden soil. *Jasminum* is the official Arabic name for jasmine.

Kadsura japonica, the scarlet kadsura, is a twining vine with thick, glossy green leaves that have red petioles. The vine can reach a length of 12 feet, with an indeterminate spread. This is a nonaggressive vine, more like a climbing bush, and makes an excellent ground cover. 'Variegata' has leaves with off-white markings. Provide partial shade and good garden soil with plenty of moisture.

Lonicera sempervirens, the trumpet honeysuckle, is a strong-growing vine that can reach a height of 50 feet. The undersides of the gray-green leaves have a slight bloom and are evergreen in most of the Southeast. Provide sun or partial shade and good garden soil. Prune to keep within bounds.

Rosa banksiae, the Lady Banks' rose, is a spreading shrub that reaches a height of 10 to 20 feet. Typical roselike leaves are a deep green and remain evergreen except in severe weather. The small yellow flowers

Hedera helix 'Glacier', variegated ivy

appear from April to May. Provide full sun or partial shade and any good garden soil. This rose is not hardy in Zone 6. *Rosa* is the old Latin name for the rose.

Smilax lanceolata, the smilax, is a marvelous vine with only a few prickles, spreading with tendrils, and is not to be confused with the common—and thorny—catbrier (*S. rotundifolia*). The vine can reach 30 feet long, with an indeterminate spread. The shiny, bright green leaves can be up to 6 inches long, and this vine is very attractive in the garden. Provide sun or partial shade and good garden soil. Prune in December. *Smilax* is the ancient Greek name for this genus.

Trachelospermum asiaticum, the yellow star jasmine, climbs by twining, reaching a length of about 12 feet with a 15-foot spread. The pointed leaves are 2 inches long and a dark, glossy green. This vine is not hardy in Zone 6 and can sometimes be damaged in Zone 7. 'Variegatum' has variegated foliage, and the variety *oblanceolatum* has smaller leaves and is a bit hardier. Provide partial shade and good garden soil with high fertility.

Trachelospermum jasminoides, the star jasmine or Confederate jasmine, also climbs by twining, bearing dark, glossy green, leathery leaves and reaching a height of 10 to 12 feet, with an indeterminate spread. The common name refers to the Confederate States of Malaysia, not the U.S. South. This vine is hardy only in Zones 8 and 9. 'Japonicum' has white-veined leaves that turn bronze in the fall; 'Madison' is hardy in Zone 7; and 'Variegatum' has white and green leaves and is hardier than the species. Provide partial shade and good garden soil with better than average drainage. *Trachelospermum* means "necked seed" and refers to that structure.

Ornamental grasses

We've mentioned the ornamental grasses before, in chapter 4. This time around, the plants listed are really sedges but are usually grouped with the ornamental grasses by the trade. Unless winters are particularly bad (like the already infamous winter of 1995–96), these sedges will stay evergreen throughout the colder months of the year. Then, in early spring, the gardener comes through and cuts them back so their exuberance can continue for another season.

Carex spp., the sedges, constitute a genus of triangular-stemmed, grasslike plants that differ from the grass family in their internal structure and the flowers. A number of these plants produce attractive mounds of evergreen foliage, and many are early-flowering, making them useful in the winter garden. Most prefer partial shade and a good, moist soil. Most sedges do well in pots. *Carex baccans*, the crimson seed sedge, comes from India and, as such, is reliably hardy only in Zones 8 and 9. This is a clumping sedge with dark green leaves 2 to 3 feet long. *Carex buchananii*, the leather leaf sedge, is a New Zealand import bearing coppery, reddish brown leaves that can reach a length of 3 feet when well grown. Especially attractive is the habit the leaf tips have of curling like delicate corkscrews. This plant prefers a cool root run, preferably near a running stream. When so sited, it's a beautiful thing to see.

(Right) *Cymophyllus fraseri*, Fraser's sedge

Carex comans, the hair sedge, is another New Zealand import with light green, almost cylindrical, hairlike leaves that form dense tufts of luxuriant growth. There are many cultivars with interesting color variations on today's market, but 'Frosty Curls', with leaf tips that are almost white, and 'Marginata', with short, dark green leaves edged with white, are two of the best. *Carex flagelifera*, the weeping brown New Zealand sedge, has fine-textured leaves that form a fountain about 2 feet high.

Carex morrowii, the Japanese sedge, is an old garden workhorse with a number of attractive variegated cultivars. 'Goldband' has foot-long lustrous green leaves edged with golden yellow bands, and 'Variegata' bears 2-foot leaves with a distinct silver edge. Both plants need a good, rich soil in partial shade. *Carex nigra*, the black-flowering sedge, is grown not for its flowers but for its 6- to 9-inch blue-gray foliage that is

Carex morrowii

178

Sasa veitchii, Kuma bamboo grass

a native of the shady woods of the eastern United States. The bright green, broad, flat leaves have longitudinal veining and resemble seersucker. The early-spring flowers are very attractive. These sedges require plenty of moisture, a good, fertile soil, and plenty of shade. Sunlight will burn the edges of the leaves.

Cymophyllus fraseri (*Carex fraseri*), or Fraser's sedge, forms clumps of attractive evergreen, straplike basal leaves that over time can become very lush and very large. The white, moplike flowers of very early spring are additional reasons to grow this woodland plant.

Bamboos
Unless specified, the following evergreen bamboos are runners. Once a bamboo settles in, it begins to spread its roots in all directions and can easily get out of control. This means that to keep peace with your neighbors, you must contain the roots or plant them where you can keep them mowed. At UNC-Charlotte, we use steel pipe from 3 to 4 feet in diameter sunk 3 to 4 feet in the ground to contain several species, especially *Sasa veitchii*. When the leaves fall, let them remain at the base of the culms, or stems, because the silica they contain slowly goes back to the soil, where the roots absorb it. Without silica, bamboos eventually go into a decline.

Bambusa glaucescens (*B. multiplex*), the hedge bamboo, reaches a height of 10 to 12 feet, with a 4- to 6-foot spread. The 6-inch leaves are a yellow-green with silver undersides. There are a number of cultivars, the most popular of which is 'Alphonse Karr', commonly called the golden-striped bamboo because of its yellow culms conspicuously striped with longitudinal dashes of green. 'Silverstripe Fernleaf' has white-striped leaves and is a clumping bamboo rather than a spreading bamboo. It is not hardy in the mountains, so its use is limited to Zones 7 to 9.

Phyllostachys aureosulcata, the yellow grove bamboo, stays green throughout the winter unless it's buffeted by extremely cold winds. But even then a stand of these dense, chartreuse canes is very effective. The height can reach 20 to 30 feet, and unless checked, the spread can go on until the roots meet an impenetrable barrier. Provide sun or shade and any good garden soil with added humus or organic matter.

Phyllostachys nigra, the black or Henon bamboo, can reach a height of 15 to 25 feet but usually in a garden setting remains a bit shorter. The new erect culms begin as green but with age become speckled, a purple to brownish black upon maturity. The 4-inch foliage is

powdery white beneath and curls around at the tips. The winter foliage is a combination of light tan and emerging green. *Carex pendula*, the great pendulous wood sedge, hails from England and Europe. The dark evergreen leaves emerge from a dense clump and can reach a length of 3 to 4 feet. Although the drooping flower spikes emerge in summer, they persist on the plants well into winter. This is one of the most effective landscape sedges for the winter garden and is easily grown from seed. With age, plants can become very large. *Carex plantaginea*, the plantain-leaved sedge, is a light green. This bamboo does well in pots, where it stops at 9 feet. The black culms with green leaves make this a very effective plant in the winter garden.

Sasa veitchii, kuma bamboo grass, is one of the most beautiful winter-garden bamboos in present cultivation. After the new growth appears in spring, up until late in the fall, this bamboo has pleasant-looking green leaves reminiscent of many bamboos. It appears to be a good choice for filling an area that has, up to now, resisted a gardener's attempts at landscape design. With the arrival of the first frost, about an inch of the tissue along the leaf edges dies and turns a light tan, a color that appears to be off-white from a distance. It's as though the leaves were iced on the edges. This persists through the winter until the following spring brings a new crop of leaves. A stand of this bamboo is a winter delight.

Ferns

A number of ferns have evergreen blades in most of the Southeast. The following species are especially attractive in the winter garden. Unless otherwise noted, provide partial shade and a good, moist, and humusy garden soil.

Asplenium platyneuron, the ebony or brown-stem spleenwort, is a common fern found growing in rock walls and along banks, producing foot-high, ladderlike leaves along dark brown or black stems.

Cheilanthes tomentosa, the woolly lip fern, is an unusual fern that prefers to be high and dry rather than low and damp. Like the time-honored resurrection plant, this fern becomes dust-bunny brown in dry weather, then changes to a cute tufted fern when conditions are favorable. Between 8 and 10 inches high, the blades are densely woolly, especially on the undersides. *Cheilanthes lanosa*, the hairy lip fern, is similar, but the blades are bluish green when fresh and a rusty dead appearance when dry. Look for both on dry, rocky ledges, but grow them from spores provided by the American Fern Society Spore Exchange (see Plant Sources).

Cyrtomium falcatum, the holly fern, has dark green blades, the individual leaflets being very leaflike in shape. This fern is especially fond of growing on old stone walls in Florida. Originally from Asia and Africa, it's an introduced plant that spread after surplus garden plants were disposed of.

Dryopteris marginalis, the marginal woodfern, has leathery, dark green leaves that grow from an exposed rootstock that resembles a tiny palm tree. The woodfern is easily spotted, especially against a light dusting of snow.

Phyllitis scolopendrium, the Hart's-tongue fern, has bright green, leathery leaves that grow in circular tufts, the shape of the leaf resembling a deer's tongue. They prefer to be near an area with adequate limestone, such as the edge of a mortared wall. This is an especially attractive fern.

Polypodium vulgare, the common polypody, is a well-known fern growing about a foot high that rambles over rocks and rocky ledges, forming great mats that are especially thick when found near water.

Polystichum acrostichoides, the Christmas fern, is probably the best known of the evergreen ferns. Found throughout the Southeast, it is thought to have spread from the North to the South during the last Ice Age, some ten thousand years ago. Florists often collect the fronds for winter decorations. In especially bad winters, the ferns become prostrate on the ground, but the leaves remain fresh and green. Like the woodfern, the Christmas fern is one of the best additions to a winter garden, especially when planted along pathways and under a canopy of trees. Don't stint when planning your fern additions because they look especially beautiful when planted in groups.

Mosses and Moss-like plants

In the dead of winter, few gardens are more beautiful than a moss garden. A healthy and well-cared-for collection of mosses will glow with tints of gold and bronze under the February sun. And in the heat of summer, such a garden can be a cool and comfortable oasis of green. If you live in an area with a reasonable year-round supply of moisture, you can establish a moss garden.

According to Dr. Peter Gentling of Asheville, an expert on Japanese garden design with a special knowledge of using mosses in the landscape, there are three types of mosses: tall, flat, and humpy. The tall mosses are really *Lycopodium*, or club mosses, plants that resemble little pine trees. They like full sun; rich, acid soil; and moisture most of the year. In hot, dry summers, club mosses become dormant and turn brown. The flat mosses, or sheet mosses, are found on rock surfaces and flat stretches of ground under the shade of a grove of trees or in the woods. Humpy mosses are found in the same places as sheet mosses but look like pincushions.

Mosses can be established in a number of ways. Collecting them from the wild may be illegal; check

Mosses and club moss

with conservation authorities before doing so. But they can also be ordered from speciality nurseries (see Plant Sources), and they often can be collected from waste places in your own and your neighbors' yards.

To plant moss, says Dr. Gentling, lay it flat on soil that is rich in humus and has been roughened so that the moss will seat. Press it into this soil, then dust fine sand over the surface and use a fine spray of water to settle it in. If possible, it's best to do this on a rainy day.

When this job is finished, scatter a thin layer of pine straw over the top, but never smother the moss or deprive it of air and light. A daily misting or gentle watering will speed the establishment of the new moss.

Other ways of establishing moss take a little longer, but if conditions are favorable, it will grow quickly from spores, particularly in late winter and in autumn. When gathering moss, look for fruiting bodies—tiny capsules of various shapes and sizes, each at the top of a thin, graceful, threadlike stem. Lay this

moss on a sheet of newspaper, then when it's dry, crumble it into small pieces. Mix this powder with some clean sharp or builder's sand, then broadcast it on the garden, pressing it in and watering. Don't cover it with plastic, but a thin layer of peat moss will often help. Although this is a slower method and is very dependent on watering, it eventually leads to a beautiful carpet of green.

Dr. Gentling says that moss is quite adaptable to pH, or acidity; it is less dependent on pH level than other plants. It will grow to perfection on chalk or damp limestone cliffs, along with maidenhair fern, both happy with the alkaline conditions. You can see it grow beautifully in deep acidic woods, in peat bogs, and on exposed granite crags where dampness and light are found together.

He cautions gardeners that mosses will go dormant when dry or when temperatures are extreme, but they

(Right) Japanese moss garden

182

Rock pockets with mosses, grayish lichens, and *Sempervivum* rosettes make a charming Lilliputian combination for shallow soils and crevices. Resurrection fern (*Polypodium polypodioides*), in the background, is a common southern fern found on rocks and tree branches. Impossible to transplant, it could be brought in on a piece of bark.

quickly awaken, growing rapidly when the conditions are good. An expanse of luxurious green mosses never has to be cut, and they'll withstand winter sun if there's enough moisture.

Moss-like Plants
Lycopodium complanatum var. *flabelliforme* is a variety of the running pine that is usually found in warmer areas of the country. Each individual plant looks like a miniature Norfolk Island pine (*Araucaria heterophylla*). We hesitate to mention this woodland beauty because it is continually raped and pillaged by florists and other collectors, who rip it out of the forest floor to make entwined wreaths at Christmastime. The plant prefers moist, shaded woodland but is also often found growing under pines edging a cultivated field. It is very difficult to transplant but grows widely in moist, acid soils across the South. *Lycopodium obscurum*, the tree club moss, is a primitive plant that looks like a tiny, fully branched pine tree, usually standing about 6 inches high above the forest floor. The little evergreen leaves are a shiny green.

PLANT SOURCES

American Fern Society
Botany Department
Smithsonian Institution
Washington, DC 20560

Appalachian Gardens
P.O. Box 82
Waynesboro, PA 17268
Trees and shrubs
Catalog $2

Kurt Bluemel, Inc.
2740 Greene Lane
Baldwin, MD 21013
One of the largest suppliers of ornamental grasses,
sedges, and the like

Camellia Forest Nursery
125 Carolina Forest Rd.
Chapel Hill, NC 27516
Trees and shrubs

Daffodil Mart
7463 Heath Trail
Gloucester, VA 23061
Bulbs
Catalog $1

Fairweather Gardens
Box 333
Greenwich, NJ 08323
Trees and shrubs
Catalog $3

Forest Farm
990 Tetherow Rd.
Williams, OR 97544
Trees, shrubs, and herbaceous plants
Catalog $3

Gossler Farms Nursery
1200 Weaver Rd.
Springfield, OR 97478
Good selection of woody winter plants
Catalog $2

Greer Gardens
1280 Goodpasture Island Rd.
Eugene, OR 97401
Good variety of woody winter plants
Catalog $3

Heronswood Nursery Ltd.
7530 288th NE
Kingston, VA 98346
Good variety of woody and herbaceous winter plants
Catalog $4

Niche Gardens
1111 Dawson Rd.
Chapel Hill, NC 27516
Limited selection of native winter plants
Catalog $3

Owen Farms
Rt. 3, Box 158A
Ripley, TN 38063
Limited selection of woody plants

Plant Delights Nursery, Inc.
9241 Sauls Rd.
Raleigh, NC 27603
Grasses and herbaceous plants
Catalog $2

Roslyn Nursery
211 Burrs Lane
Dix Hill, NY 11746
Good selection of woody plants
Catalog $3

Wavering Place Nursery
Rt. 2, Box 269
Eastover, SC 29044
Limited selection of woody plants

Wayside Gardens
Hodges, SC 29695
Wide variety

We-Du Nurseries
Rt. 5, Box 724
Marion, NC 28752
Wildflowers of the United States and Japan

Windrose
1093 Mill Rd.
Pen Argyl, PA 18072
Wide variety

Woodlanders
1128 Colleton Ave.
Aiken, SC 29801
Wide variety
Catalog $2

REFERENCES

Allen, Oliver E. *Winter Gardens*. Alexandria, Virginia: Time-Life Books, 1979.

Bloom, Adrian. *Winter Garden Glory: How to Get the Best from Your Garden from Autumn Through to Spring*. London: HarperCollins, 1994.

Darnell, A. W. *Winter Blossoms from the Outdoor Garden*. Ashford, Kent: L. Reeve & Co., Ltd., 1926.

Dirr, Michael. *Manual of Woody Landscape Plants*. Champaign, Illinois: Stipes Publishing Company, 1990.

Glasener, Erica, Editor. *The Winter Garden*. Brooklyn: Brooklyn Botanical Garden, 1991.

Graff, M. M. *Flowers in the Winter Garden*. Garden City, New York: Doubleday & Company, Inc., 1966.

Hinkley, Daniel. *Winter Ornamentals for the Maritime Northwest Gardener*. Seattle: Sasquatch Books, 1993.

Lawrence, Elizabeth. *Gardens in Winter*. Baton Rouge: Claitor's Publishing Division, 1961.

Lay, Charles Downing. *A Garden Book for Autumn and Winter*. New York: Duffield & Company, 1924.

Loewer, Peter. *Gardens by Design: Step-by-Step Plans for 12 Imaginative Gardens*. Emmaus, Pennsylvania: Rodale Press, 1986.

Pearson, Robert. *The Winter Garden*. London: Cassell Educational Limited, A Wisley Handbook, 1989.

Schuler, Stanley. *The Winter Garden*. New York: The Macmillan Company, 1972.

Thomas, Graham Stuart. *Colour in the Winter Garden*. Portland: Timber Press, 1994.

Tripp, Kim E. and J. C. Raulston. *The Year in Trees*. Portland: Timber Press, 1995.

Verey, Rosemary. *The Garden in Winter*. The New York Graphic Society. Boston: Little, Brown and Company, 1988.

Wilder, Louise Beebe. *Hardy Bulbs*. New York: Dover Publications, Inc., 1974.

INDEX